THE POLITICAL ECONOMY OF THE
ARMS RACE

Also by R. T. Maddock

THE GROWTH OF THE BRITISH ECONOMY, 1918–1968
(*with G. A. Philips*)
*THE POLITICAL ECONOMY OF SOVIET DEFENCE SPENDING

Also published by Palgrave Macmillan

The Political Economy of the Arms Race

R. T. Maddock
Senior Lecturer, Department of International Politics
The University College of Wales, Aberystwyth

MACMILLAN

First published 1990

Published by
THE MACMILLAN PRESS LTD
Houndmills, Basingstoke, Hampshire RG21 2XS
and London
Companies and representatives
throughout the world

British Library Cataloguing in Publication Data
Maddock, R.T. (Rowland Thomas), *1937–*
The political economy of the arms race.
1. Defence. Economic aspects
I. Title
355
ISBN 978-1-349-09844-6   ISBN 978-1-349-09842-2 (eBook)
DOI 10.1007/978-1-349-09842-2

I Margaret,
unwaith eto

Contents

List of Figures

List of Tables

1 The International Dimension

In the anarchic international system military spending is normal and routine and does not in itself define an arms race. Arms races are conceptually narrower, a state of conflict over the distribution of power between nations whose relationship is highly and mutually salient which escalates into 'a repeated, competitive and reciprocal adjustment of war-making capacities'.[1] They differ from routine armaments dynamics in the morphology and in the intensity of reciprocal interaction characterised by an abnormal rapid increase in armaments over a period of time. Arms race expenditures are therefore those in excess of normal spending on defence. Despite being intuitively appealing, there is in reality no measure of normal. *Ad hoc* measures of 'rapid' or 'abnormal' yield widely varying estimates of the historical number and morphology of arms races.[2] A particular rate of mutually stimulating growth sustained over sufficiently long periods of time might transform to normal what at the outset might have been considered abnormal, or a routine arms dynamic to an arms race. The concept of abnormal is relational; compared with what? the historical national norms? past or current international norms? growth in GNP and hence in the defence burden? There is no need for these or for other criteria which can easily be devised to be mutually consistent. A comparison of the absolute sums of money spent each year by the USA and the USSR, or of long term growth rates suggests comparable behaviour. Yet the USA by virtue of its larger economy, currently spends less than seven per cent of its GNP on defence activities compared with 15 to 17 per cent for the Soviet Union. In terms of relative burden whereas the Soviet Union is racing, the United States is engaged in nothing more strenuous than a brisk stroll.

Even if the armaments behaviour of two or more countries are mutually stimulating the morphology of interaction differs between states and over time. There are no historical 'laws' of arms races which apply at all times to all countries. Nevertheless some generalisations can be made. If as conventionally assumed, military spending does not add to social welfare[3] but is rather a means to an end, it is reasonable to hypothesise that societies seek to minimise the opportunity cost of civilian goods foregone, and allocate resources only to the degree they perceive a threat which can only or best be countered by military means. The psychological basis of an interactive process of action–reaction between competing states is insecurity in the presence of ignorance and latent aggression,[4] the anthropomorphic extension to states of the individualistic process described thus,

> 'When I consider the adversary may shoot out of sheer prefer-ence, it makes me nervous; this nervousness enhances the likeli-hood that I may shoot him even though I prefer not to. He sees my nervousness and gets nervous himself; that scares me more, and I am even more likely to shoot. He sees this increment in my nervousness and matches it with one of his own, scaring me further . . ..'[5]

Countries do not know with any degree of conviction the intentions of adversary states, and as a clearly inadequate surrogate, substitute instead their knowledge of adversary capabilities, on the simplistic grounds that the larger the capability or the quicker it is being increased the greater the threat to security and sovereignty. (For countries which derive positive utility from defence expenditures, the inducements and hence the explanations for spending money on armaments are different). The conception of arms races as a linear progression of action and reaction is given some credence by the views of those who have been closely involved in making and manag-ing the defence policies of nations. That between the USA and the USSR has been described precisely in such terms by ex-Secretary of Defence Robert McNamara.[6]

Although action–reaction establishes an analytic framework it does not in itself predict the morphology of actual races. Both action and reaction take various forms,[7] and parsimonious formal models use-fully bridge the gap between abstract theorising and otherwise uncon-nected heuristic description. Since arms races are part and usually a consequence of prior political disputation between a pair or a group of nations, motivation for racing is exogenously given. Stylised de-scriptions often assume a revisionist state challenging an established power by a rate of armaments expansion perceived to be threatening.[8] Unless the *status quo* state is prepared to accommodate the new it too must increase its arms expenditures or production and the race is joined. Most simply the race is described as a sequential interactive progression, the intensity of which is assumed to be a function of the rate of military expansion in the adversary countries.

Arms expenditures which are wholly mutually interdependent quickly reach runaway proportions and there must exist some domestic constraints which prevent the armaments sector claiming ever increasing ratios of national wealth. As military production/expenditures increase so does the social opportunity cost (probably non-linearly) as consequently do domestic political pressures to constrain further expansion. In short some expenditures are incurred even in the absence of specific threat, some are directly consequential on the size of a perceived specific threat, but a domestic preference for civilian over military goods holds in check unbridled expansion. Formally

$$\frac{dx}{dt} = ky - ax + g$$

$$\frac{dy}{dt} = lx - by + h$$

when
x, y = armaments expenditure in countries 1 and 2 respectively.
k, l = the defence reactions in either country, that is, the level of response in one country to military expenditure in the other.
a, b = the fatigue coefficients, that is, the domestic economic constraint on military expansion.
g, h = the general armaments dynamic sometimes described as the grievance term, expenditures incurred irrespective of a specific threat.

The equations show that defence expenditures or production in one country are a function of those in the other, the intensity of the response being determined by the coefficients

$$y = \frac{ax - g}{k}$$

$$x = \frac{by - h}{l}$$

As described in Figure 1.1 the arms race is ultimately stable in the sense that there exists for either country levels of expenditure or production which will not provoke further expansion by the other, and are therefore mutually accommodating. The arrows show the

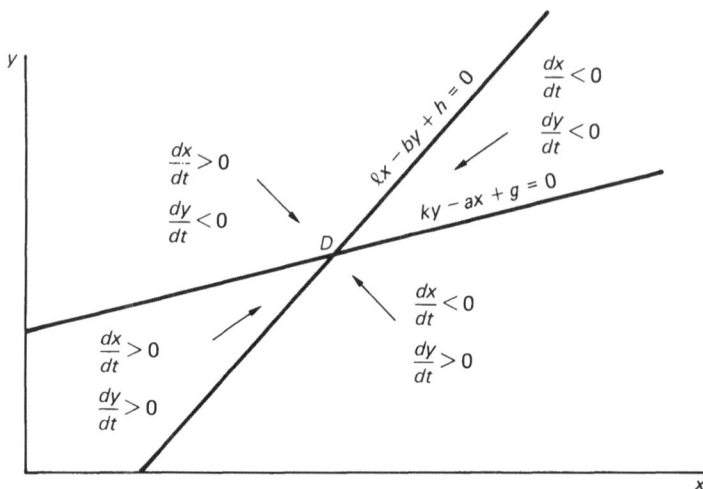

Figure 1.1   Stable arms race with equilibrium point

direction of change for both countries as they move to desired
positions for given levels of production or expenditure by the other.
The race will eventually stabilise at point D. Any movement away
from D will stimulate countervailing forces to push the two countries
back to equilibrium. Some expenditures are incurred irrespective of
those obtaining in the adversary country, which though they do not
influence the morphology of the arms race, help to determine where
the equilibrium point will be located. The morphology of the race,
that is, the slopes of the two reaction curves, will be determined by
the combined influence of the defence function and the domestic
constraint function, that is, by the product of k,l and of a,b respectively. The greater the product of k,l compared with a,b the greater
will be the intensity of the arms race. If k,l exceeds a,b the arms race
will formally cease to be one of equilibrium and the pretensions of
the two adversaries cannot be reconciled.

In the area banded by the two reaction curves in Figure 1.2 the
arms race attains explosive proportions. At the point a_1 country 2
expects country 1 to produce x_1 armaments in response to its own
production of y_1. Country 1, in fact produces X_2. At X_2 however
country 2 produces Y_2. There is no point of mutual accommodation.
Because explosive arms races are more likely to end in war they are
to that degree more dangerous.

In a modification of the basic model each country is assumed to

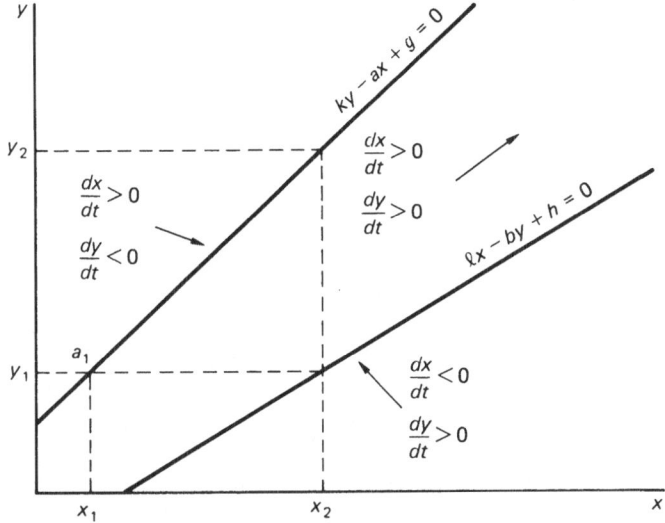

Figure 1.2   Unstable arms race with no equilibrium

respond not to the level of expenditures or production in the other, but to the difference between the two countries.

$$\frac{dx}{dt} = k\,(y-x) - ax + g$$

$$\frac{dy}{dt} = l\,(x-y) - by + h$$

Given some simple mathematical transformations and appropriate data the models can be employed to verify the armaments behaviour of pairs or groups countries which are presumed, from exogenous evidence, to be racing one another. In contrast to assertions by McNamara and others that action–reaction typifies the armaments policies of the USA and the USSR, most investigations conclude that military expenditures in one country have little impact on those of the other.[9] Although empirical investigations have for obvious reasons concentrated on the USA and the USSR, evidence of the armaments behaviour of other dyads and alliances which are conventionally described as racing, for example, India and Pakistan also fail to provide unconditional support to the action–reaction thesis.[10] Such empirical evidence has led some to conclude that although the USA and the USSR compete there is no closed cycle of tightly coupled interactions.[11] Whereas Soviet expenditures show a reasonably steady long term trend the American pattern has been characterised by a high degree of variance, and often negative real growth. The notion of generalised interactive arms race it is argued is but a chimera.[12] The term has taken on emotive overtones and should be avoided by the fastidious scholar.[13]

Nevertheless the action–reaction dynamic and by implication the existence of a mutually stimulating Soviet–American arms race should not be rejected out of hand. The failure to measure a significant degree of mutual stimulation may be due to incomplete data or to inadequate statistical tests, for recent investigations employing powerful modern techniques do show evidence of cointegration between the armaments behaviour of the USA and USSR,[14] or to a mis-specification of the response in one country to the other's stimulus, which in reality must be more complex than described in the model. Even if after endogenising for one or all of the above, an action–reaction dynamic is not statistically revealed, it cannot thereby be concluded that the two nations are not racing, for the morphology of a race may take some configuration other than action–reaction. The robustness of tests of interactive behaviour are considerably influenced by the type of data which are employed[15] and by the source from which they are obtained.[16] Soviet military economic data in particular are seriously flawed.[17] Western estimates differ widely and must be treated with caution.

Theory lacks the richness to provide an unambiguous measure of military activity[18] and both real and monetary data have been variously employed. Military variables such as missile numbers or megatonnage have the advantage of being directly and immediately comparable, and, it is argued, since arms races occur only between specific dyads and weapons systems, for example, battleships between Germany and the United Kingdom[19] or ICBMs are most appropriate. Polymological variables offer detailed and accurate morphologies of particular races located within overall defence expenditures which by definition are not wholly related to arms race dynamics. Some polymological races are, in consequence of embodied technology, inherently equilibrating, irrespective of the underlying political tension between adversaries. Robert McNamara argued that American security required a fixed number of ICBMs beyond which further numbers were of little strategic value, and the same was true of the Soviet Union[20]. Inevitably therefore an American–Soviet arms race measured by ICBMs would end in equilibrium once the limit was reached, and the duration of the race determined by some combination of technological and economic forces, clearly not the case in fact. As equilibrium levels are reached in one weapons system, the race can be switched to new systems and hence sustained indefinitely, but to regularly change the idiom of the race is limiting and undesirable. Furthermore single weapon models conceal nations' capabilities to trade-off one system against another. Reacting countries can imitate or offset a challenge. The wider the range of weapons and the higher the level of technological development the greater the degree of freedom in responding to adversarial challenge.

Action	Reaction
offensive	offensive
offensive	defensive
defensive	offensive
defensive	defensive

More likely, since weapons are seldom exclusive, some combination of offence/defence will be deployed. The offensive/defensive choice influences the morphology of the arms race in that offensive deployment usually makes the security dilemma more virulent and sustains the arms race momentum while a mainly defensive alignment is less threatening and, makes a mutually acceptable equilibrium more likely.[21] To glean more than purely statistical information the polymological variables must be systematically related to the strategic precepts which are the source of their intellectual rationale,[22] their contribution to the ultimate output, security. Although it is possible to define an arms race in terms of self-contained offensive/defensive systems, for example, submarines and anti-submarine systems, for the USA and the USSR the race is too broad to be comprehended by a simple, single metric.[23]

Value data on the other hand are by definition comprehensive, and reduce multifaceted variables otherwise difficult to compare to a single measure. They are not however unambiguous. Their very comprehensiveness conceals specific arms races making it impossible to distinguish between those expenditures undertaken for normal security and those specific to a race against a particular adversary. Value data contain no military information, and since a high proportion of military expenditures are normally spent on overheads, the strategic elements in arms races are essentially concealed. Value data are also compromised by a variety of conceptual and empirical problems. They too, to transcend the purely statistical, should be related to the choice theoretic assumption of economic theory.[24] They provide incomplete measures of military force potential[25] which presumably is what countries seek to maximise.

Weapons stocks are better indicators of force potential than annual current expenditures which measure only the increase in force potential each year. Although current production and to a lesser degree expenditures are reasonably well-known for most countries, depreciation rates are notoriously difficult to calculate.[26] Weapons wear out, are destroyed in war, are replaced by superior models and are sometimes mothballed to be used in emergencies for spare parts.

Furthermore given different doctrinal emphasis on technology, countries pursue different inventory policies. Even between the two superpowers with a similar inventory of weapons, the Soviet Union as the technological follower tends to keep its weapons longer than does the USA.[27] Nations may respond not to perceived differences between the supply of new military equipment but to the total accumulated stocks.[28] A ratio goal, that is, the desired level of weapons for given quantities held by the adversary, depends on the perception of threat posed by the other country and/or other indicators of international tensions. In periods of high tension the desired ratio of own to adversary stocks increases.

Formally

$$\frac{dx}{dt} = k\ (y-x) + g\text{APT}$$

$$\frac{dy}{dt} = l\ (x-y) + h\text{RPT}$$

Where

APT = perceived tension of country 1 with
        respect to country 2;
RPT = perceived tension of country 2 with
        respect to country 1.

The additions to stock is determined by the difference between actual and desired levels. The stock adjustment model reveals a statistically significant though not simple and sequential relationship between the USA and the USSR. For most of the post-war period the Soviet Union as the follower country has been adjusting its total weapons inventory to that of the USA, to make up a perceived gap.[29] Although the determination of which country is the leader and which the follower is exogenous to the model, it is consistent with *ad hoc* descriptions of the arms race in which the leadership role is assigned to the USA.[30] The model fails however to explain the motivation or the morphology of the leader, but predicts an eventual regime change, that as the Soviet Union closes the gap, the USA will become more directly responsive to Soviet capabilities.[31]

Once national and hence different goals and means are posited the race ceases to be mechanistic and inevitable. In the Soviet Union, bureaucratic decision-making, a preference for evolutionary techno-logical change and a war-fighting strategy, lead to expectations of a different response to military challenge than in the USA, though in view of the greater similarity of the military compared with the civilian sectors in the two societies brought about by the intense degree of international competition, the difference should not be exaggerated.

Technological change which so dominates the race between the USA and the USSR makes the action–reaction dynamic complex and difficult to identify. Rapidly changing technology makes a reasoned assessment of what are the security implications of a stimulus and hence of the appropriate response difficult. Given the degree to which nations conceal new technologies, intelligence information by one country on the activities and performance of others is limited and uncertain. The American intelligence community admits to being least confident of its estimates of Soviet expenditures on military R and D,[32] which differ widely from those calculated by civilian experts using different methodologies.[33] Western military experts are con-stantly surprised at the level of technology embodied in Soviet weapons,[34] and estimates of the rate of catch up in the Soviet Union differ, often markedly.[35]

Given the inevitable uncertainty about adversarial intention and capability, there exists an entirely rational pressure in terms of the balance of benefits to overestimate the intensity and the likelihood of threat and to prepare accordingly. This prudential rationale tends to be reinforced by a psychological propensity to overcompensate for a given level of threat[36] which induces countries to deploy weapons out of all proportion to the scale of the original stimulus.[37]

Research, development and deployment cycles vary according to the complexity of the weapon, to the degree of improvement sought, the planned time horizons and on the amount of resources devoted to their completion. Complex systems may take up to 15 years for a new theoretical concept to be embodied in a deployed weapon. At any one time in technologically advanced societies, research and development laboratories are working on projects the fruits of which will be embodied in new weapons some time in the distant future. Strategic planners seek above all to avoid being taken by surprise by unanticipated developments, and given the time element inevitable in weapons development are obliged to anticipate rather than respond to change elsewhere.[38] Scientists in any country are only partially acquainted with classified research work being done elsewhere, and in compensation tend to project onto other countries their own assumptions and preferences. It is an intellectual short cut to assume that current research and development being undertaken domestically is replicated in the adversary country, especially as the weapons economies of competing countries are often more similar than their civilian counterparts. One explanation for the belief in the USA in 1960 of the missile gap was that because the so-called 'bomber gap' of a few years earlier had turned out to be illusory, it was assumed by American scientists and strategic planners that since the USA was in the process of expanding its missile stocks so must the USSR.[39] Subsequent evidence shows this projection of American experience on to the Soviet Union not to have been justified. The combination of ignorance and fear induce a nation's weapons laboratories and strategic think tanks to race against others in their own domain.[40] Where, as in the USA the weapons culture provides a self-sustaining endogenous boost to technological momentum,[41] progress in one country becomes only slightly connected with that elsewhere and in a fundamental sense is autonomous.[42] As the technological leader, American weapons development is historically replete with examples of technological improvements which had little intellectual or strategic linkage with what was known or subsequently understood to be occuring concurrently in the Soviet Union. Deployment and therefore expenditure may result not from current strategic concerns, but may simply reflect a particular stage in the weapons cycle, the consequence of decisions taken and money spent in past periods[43].

Implicit in much arms race analysis is the assumption that adversaries start from the same position, race at roughly similar rates and in consequence have similar objectives. This is unlikely to be the case if, as often assumed, arms races are consequences of disputes between revisionist and *status quo* powers. For most of the post-war period the Soviet Union has been the follower country, and although it did not seek to match American military technological progress everywhere, it could not allow itself to fall too far behind and become hostage to

American superiority. Imitating state of the art technology elsewhere is therefore widely characteristic of its developmental style. Its response to the armaments challenge; to reduce and eventually eliminate the gap, differed from the USA. The *status quo* power can accommodate the revisionist demand, match it action for action or more than match it to reveal a determination to hold on to its superiority and to raise the cost of the challenge. The response depends on domestic economic and political circumstances and on what is assumed to be the eventual goal of the revisionist power, for instance parity or compellence.[44]

Lewis Richardson justified his mechanistic action–reaction models on the grounds that in determining their security issues countries 'follow tradition, which are fixtures and their instincts which are mechanical'.[45] This assumption has been rejected by behavioural scientists who argue that explanations of arms races must be choice theoretic.[46] Since military expenditures create opportunity costs for society, arms race behaviour can be understood only in terms of societal objectives. At a very minimum it can be posited that societies or more correctly their representatives seek some composite value of welfare and security which minimises cost, maximises deterrence and war-winning capability should deterrence fail.[47] Counterforce strategies to fight and win wars are more expensive than those designed to deter[48] and propel the arms race more energetically, for neither side can afford to allow the other to gain a meaningful advantage.

In Figure 1.3 each country produces some armaments irrespective of its adversary (a_1 and b_2 respectively). As production increases beyond a_1 and b_1 in each country progressively more resources have to be allocated for given allocations by the adversary to attain counterforce, as compared with deterrence objectives. Thus for instance, to meet production level a_2 in country 1 and country 2 will have to produce b_2 to meet its deterrence targets and, b_3 its counterforce or deprivation target. If both nations are deterrers, the arms race is equilibrating, equilibrium being achieved at point D. If one country pursues a policy of counterforce and the other one of deterrence, stability can still be attained, but at a higher global stock of weapons, either points E or F, and with gross disparities between the stocks of the two nations. If both nations pursue counterforce strategies the race is explosive and theoretically endless in that there exist no endogenous forces to bring it to a mutually acceptable conclusion. (Logically at certain joint levels of production, indicated by E and F, the implications of deterrence and deprivation are mutually inconsis-

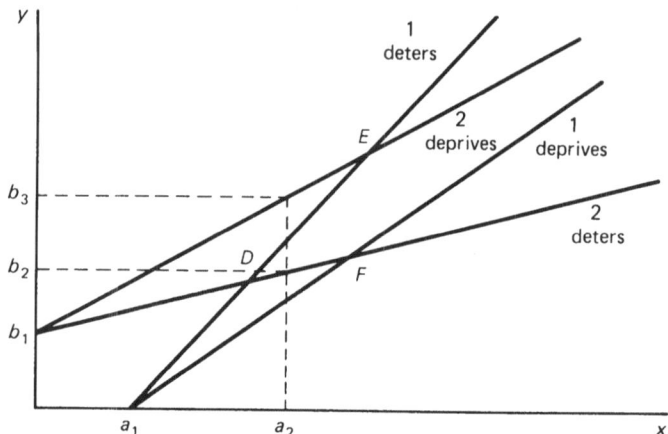

Figure 1.3   Arms races with counterforce and deterrence strategies

tent. At *F* for instance country 2 has enough weapons to deter 1, but country 1 enough to initiate a first strike attack on 2, and similarly for point *E*.)

Formal and comprehensive models of arms races are limited in their assumptions and therefore in the conclusions which can be inferred from them. Although mathematically it can be shown that given certain assumptions, arms races are equilibrating, it is not entirely clear what equilibrium means. In races characterised by rapid technological progress, in which weapons are continuously being modernised and replaced, the notion that weapons production will eventually cease to expand is inappropriate. In the presence of technological progress deterrence policies may bring about a tendency towards mutual accommodation, but one which is constantly being readjusted to incorporate new information and capabilities. Given the tendency for technology to be, by and large, equally available,[49] the race may be institutionalised in a manner which does not destroy the confidence of either side in the other's intentions and capabilities.

Even in explosive arms races, nations do not allocate continually increasingly proportions of their budgets to arms production. After the desired level or ratio of armaments has been identified, economic factors determine the pace at which the nation moves to the target level or output. Economic constraints rein-in expansionist forces and historically have been most potent in inhibiting the arms race dynamic.[50]

Arms races clearly are not amenable to general and universal laws of history,[51] but reflect local circumstances of time and place. Nevertheless formal analysis does provide qualitatively useful information on their morphology. In the largest sense action–reaction has been fundamental in animating that between the USA and the USSR[52] though its precise morphology has been dominated by domestic factors in either country.[53]

Expenditures currently in excess of $200bn. per annum each by the USA and the USSR, though burdensome, may yet be justified if benefits exceed costs. If governments are assumed to behave purposively, they will not deliberately allocate resources such that costs exceed benefits, and global defence expenditure should provide at least an equivalent degree of benefit. In fact however governments are not always rational. They may lack the economic information to effectively compare costs and benefits, they may be captive to a small elite which distorts allocations to satisfy local rather than national objectives and in any case there exists no objective measure of security.

Military expenditures create a security dilemma which may effectively reduce as increase security and welfare. The very act of competitively expanding the armaments stock can increase international tension and uncertainty and exacerbate, though not necessarily create, 'autistic' behaviour in competing countries.[54] Racing makes it more difficult to keep in check adversarial foreign policy images propounded by those sections of society which benefit economically, socially, politically or ideologically from arms production.[55] Nations which have spent large sums of money in designing, producing and deploying armaments may be induced to use them. Mutual Assured Destruction theory is after all of quite recent origin and may already be in the process of being thrown over for a more aggressive weapons-using strategy. The greater the variety and quantity of weapons the greater is the difficulty in controlling all eventualities, and hence the higher is the probability of error or poor judgement escalating to war.

War is not exclusively the consequence of competitive arms behaviour, but if the race results in imbalance which one side believes to be temporary, it may induce a pre-emptive strike before the lagging country catches up. In races dominated by technology the fact or the fear of a technological breakthrough by one side may so destabilise a crisis as to increase the likelihood of escalation. In the presence of new and exotic technology the possibility of misreading adversary intention is magnified and if the technology is not fail-safe there may be an incentive to strike first to protect vulnerable systems from an adversarial attack.[56] Technological change also reduces the incentive to co-operation between adversarial states by increasing the reward to unilateral defection more than to mutual co-operation, and may indeed be the most detrimental barrier to co-operation.[57]

Nevertheless given all the conceivable reasons for having had a major war in the past four decades[58] there has not in fact been one. Since 1945 weapons of deterrence have, apparently, kept the peace in Europe; (arms races in non-nuclear states however have been frequent, have sometimes ended in war, have sometimes been managed and have sometimes petered out). Military spending of itself does not provoke war.[59]

Indeed failure to match an aggressive accumulation of arms by a revisionist power challenging for enhanced status in an anarchic world may increase rather than decrease the likelihood of war, for it is in the nature of international society that a redistribution of economic power inevitable in the uneven ebb and flow of expansion and decline be reflected in political and eventually military challenge. Offsetting military responses by *status quo* power(s) may effectively steer challenge and potential conflict into managed, routinised channels and away from war,[60] and technological progress can create stabilising as well as destabilising weapons.[61] Historians point to the failure of France and the United Kingdom to confront Hitler's re-armaments programme early enough as an encouragement to his irridentist claims which eventually and inevitably led to the Second World War.[62] In alliances which do not immediately lead to war, the likelihood of escalation is low[63] suggesting that races can be institutionalised and managed. Furthermore the very uncertainty of races characterised by a high rate of technological progress – especially since countries tend to embody new technology in weapons at much the same time – may reduce the likelihood of escalation.[64]

The debate on arms race expenditures and escalation raises two issues, one methodological and one empirical. What, if anything, is the endogenous dynamic of arms races which leads to war or no war? and what has been the historical experience?

Itriligator and Brito examine how in terms of the theoretical calculus of gain and loss different alignments of armaments might determine whether nations choose to escalate conflicts to war or not. In the model, countries are assumed to choose between counterforce or countervalue (deterrence) strategies. A country initiating a first strike fires its missiles at the weapons stock of the other to reduce its

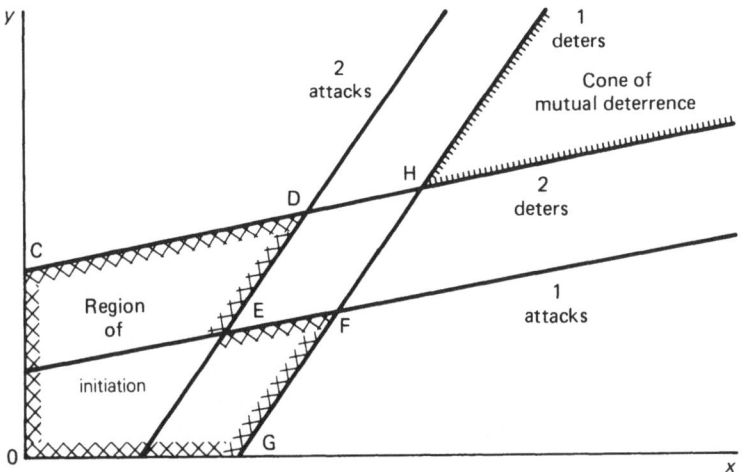

Figure 1.4   Arms races and escalation to war

war-fighting capability. In stage two, which may escalate in a matter of minutes or hours, both countries fire their remaining missiles at countervalue targets. An offensive policy by either country requires correspondingly higher weapon stocks than one of deterrence for given quantities of weapons held by the other. The crucial conditions when it would be rational for one country to initiate a first strike and thus escalate to war are when it can anticipate a successful attack upon, but is unable to deter, its adversary; and it can expect to suffer less than a maximum acceptable level of casualties[65]. Under such circumstances it will have a powerful motive to initiate a pre-emptive strike. The same is true for the other country.

Given these assumptions countries have an incentive to initiate an attack if the combined stock of weapons lies within the area *CDEFG*. Beyond *CD* country 2 has sufficient weapons to deter 1 from attacking, and likewise for country 1 beyond *FG*. In the cone beyond *H* neither side has sufficient weapons to guarantee success from a first strike, both have a sufficiently large stock of weapons to deter the other country. *CDEFG* is the region of initiation where either country has an incentive to strike first and is particulary dangerous, and beyond *H* is the region of deterrence where neither side has an incentive to initiate a war. Given the assumptions of the model if arms races proceed beyond a certain stage they do not escalate into war. Paradoxically, unstable – in the sense of ever expanding – arms races lead to stable peace. A certain ratio of armaments may be necessary but not sufficient for the initiation of war.

Different objective functions naturally lead to different outcomes. The assumption that countries might be prepared to initiate a war if casualties are anticipated to be less than a minimum acceptable level has been criticised as inadequate because it contains no criterion of win or lose.[66] If a success criterion is endogenised, for example, that at the end of the war the initiating country must also possess a larger stock of weapons, the incentive to escalate differs from the initial model, though again, perhaps unexpectedly, there is no guarantee that a small weapons stock reduces the likelihood of escalation. For that to occur the supply of weapons must be part of an exogenously determined relationship between the two countries. Different assumptions such as non-linearity, while adding to the complexity of the morphology, do not change the overall conclusions that logically arms races do not necessarily contain within themselves the seeds of war.

Models offer only stylised facts in that they necessarily exclude the geo-political dimension which would explain why other than in purely statistical terms nations might want to go to war, and the real economic and social calculus of going compared with not going to war.

Historically, evidence on the correlation between arms racing and war is inconclusive, measurement being made difficult by the lack of *a priori* guidelines on what constitutes an arms race. Definitions which identify the stylised morphology of arms races must be supplemented by empirically based judgements on the minimum pace of military expansion. One metric is a straightforward rate of global expansion beyond a pre-determined minimum, which has been arbitrarily defined as from eight per cent per annum[67] to ten per cent per annum[68]. Where the race is measured as the product of military expansions in the dyads or alliances, one conceptual problem is whether growth rates on both sides need be approximately equal, pertinent for the American–Soviet race where the trajectory of growth has differed so much.

Different measures of racing yield different numbers of races which it is appropriate to measure. One based on deviations from mean growth rates identifies a far smaller number of races than one based on absolute growth[69]. The number of historically measurable races depends also on how they are coded. For those between dyads the number of races as well as their morphology will differ from races between allies. Allies sometimes arm against a single common foe, for instance, Arab countries against Israel, and sometimes against another alliance, such as NATO and the Warsaw Pact. Races between allies are often inter-independent, creating problems of autocorrelation which distort the significance of the statistical tests. To measure as separate those races in which two or more allies exercise a common grievance against an identified foe, may statistically exaggerate the true relationship between races and escalation, for if one dyad in an alliance escalates to war, so almost by definition must the others.

One early investigation showed a high correlation between arms races and escalation. Serious disputes between countries which were accompanied by competitive arms behaviour almost always ended in war, while disputes which were not accompanied by an interdependent arms build-up seldom escalated to war.[70]

	Arms races	No arms races
War	23	3
No war	5	68

The hypothesis that arms races lead to war correctly predicted 91 out of 99 instances investigated. Even after adjusting in response to criticism for the fact that some dyads were not independent of one another[71] the success rate was a high 74 out of 80 instances. As Wallace carefully points out, the evidence does not prove that arms races lead inexorably to war but provides little support for those who argue that to preserve peace nations must prepare for war. His findings have not gone unchallenged however. The empirical evidence is heavily influenced by the participants in the two World Wars which account for up to 80 per cent of the explanatory power of the initial study. If these are re-coded to a single race only 25 per cent of disputes which were preceded by a mutual arms race escalated to war, and 77 per cent of major wars were not preceded by arms races.[72] This adjustment however eliminates too many cases from the sample to support the contrary hypothesis that arms races are unrelated to war escalation.[73]

Since historically wars are often assumed to be the consequence of attempts by revisionist powers to redraw the balance of power in the international community, the relative pace at which the nations race may be as important to the outcome as the global rate of expansion. War has been hypothesised to be more likely if the revisionist state is expanding more quickly that its *status quo* adversary. Statistically this appears not to be the case. The likelihood of races escalating to war is not significantly influenced by which country is expanding most quickly.[74]

The failure to logically distinguish serious disputes from arms races as independent sources of escalation distorts the empirical evidence.[75] Four hypotheses are possible:

(*i*) arms races increase the probability of escalation to war;
(*ii*) arms races increase the likelihood of serious disputes;
(*iii*) serious disputes increase the probability of war;
(*iv*) the simultaneous occurence of arms races and serious disputes increase the likelihood of war.

Empirically the most potent explanator of escalation was the prior incidence of serious dispute,[76] more so even than the joint existence of serious dispute and competitive arms race behaviour. Arms races tend however to promote serious disputes and may therefore indirectly as well as directly create the conditions of war. Given the evidence currently available the most judicious conclusion is perhaps the negative one that the *para bellum* argument is not statistically sustained.

Armaments are designed to deter, but also in the event of failure to enable countries to fight wars effectively. Thus even if arms races do not reduce the probability of war they might still be considered rational if they influence its outcomes such that wars following an arms race were less destructive of life and property. Four possible relationships have been hypothesised:[77]

(*i*) arms races make wars shorter and less severe;
(*ii*) arms races make wars longer and more severe;
(*iii*) arms races make wars shorter but more severe;
(*iv*) arms races make wars longer but less severe.

Despite the inevitable problems with data, wars preceded by competitive racing by and large tend to be longer and more severe.[78] Arms races have not historically provided the insurance to the arming states which is sometimes claimed as their justification.

Although the evidence cannot be conclusive, there is little statistical support for the hypotheses that arms races reduce either the likelihood or the costs of war. What then sustains them? For participants in a specific race statistical historical evidence may be of only limited relevance. Although arms races in general do not reduce the likelihood of or the cost associated with war they sometimes do, and there may be a psychological need in racing countries to assume, for perhaps precautionary reasons, that the race in which they are engaged is one of the exceptions.

Furthermore the conventional justification of arms races in terms of security benefits conceals other and perhaps truer reasons for racing. Even in the age of overkill, armaments serve political purposes when relative numbers and firepower count in the search for power, status and influence. Numbers are measures of political power and potent messages of intent. After a certain level of mutual deterrence has been achieved, which in the East–West arms race has long been passed, the perception of who is ahead is important.[79] Perception of imbalance provides a dynamic, psychological justification for spending money, developing new weapons, and so on, independent of real military need. Although the rationale differs, perception theory adds weight to the view that action–reaction is the dynamo which sustains the arms race. If success is having as much or more than the other side any action by the adversary to increase its armaments must be matched even if the stimulus does not pose a military threat. Many of the weapons which have boosted the Soviet–American arms races can be rationalised only in terms of the perception of power and status they give to the two countries. Given also the psychological tendency to overcompensate, the competitive dynamic is powerfully sustained. This need not of itself be irrational if it diverts the latent aggression and hostility which exists between two states into less harmful activities.

Arms races and in particular that between the USA and the USSR, may have a role equivalent to that of posturing in the animal kingdom, where animals sustain their self-esteem by puffing and strutting without actually fighting.[80] If ideological and geo-political animosities are embedded in the very structure of the international system, races which allow the countries to channel their animosities may be acceptable second best solutions. Military strength is however not easily translated into effective political power. For both the USA and the USSR failure to use military power to achieve political objectives has been as frequent as success, and their overall record has not been impressive.[81] It should not thereby be concluded that force has no utility, for in its absence the ratio of failure to success might have been even more unfavourable.

The expenditures of such huge sums of money on armaments can perhaps be justified in that, regrettable though it may be, arms races are preferable to the alternative. It would be ironic and tragic if the

Figure 1.5   The prisoner's dilemma

Country 1

		Co-operate		Defect	
		2	1	2	1
Country 2	Co-operate	200	200	50	250
		2	1	2	1
	Defect	250	50	100	100

ultimate rationale for racing is the very irrationality of the anarchic system, that nations, by the very nature of individualistic decision-making, are caught in a social trap,[82] in that alternative social arrangements would lead to both parties and the international community as a whole being better off. The security dilemma is an example of such a social trap, where both adversaries could benefit if both disarm, but each is individually even better off if it arms and the adversary disarms. In that case 'an arms race may be understood as an outcome of a prisoner's dilemma game'[83] the logic of which can best be explained as a game between two countries which have two policy choices, to co-operate, that is, not to engage in a competitive arms race, or defect, that is, to arm competitively. Because it is assumed that weapons yield no or at best less utility than civilian goods, an equivalent ratio of mutual security at lower absolute levels of weapons, provides higher domestic and international welfare. For the international society co-operative behaviour is hypothesised to be superior to defection. The outcomes are shown in Figure 1.5 where higher ordinal numbers indicate higher levels of pay-offs to countries U and R respectively.

The logic of choice is as follows:

If 2 co-operates:
   If 1 co-operates the pay off to 1 is 200;
   If 1 defects the pay off to 1 is 250.

If 2 defects:
   If 1 co-operates the pay off to 2 is 50;
   If 1 defects the pay off to 1 is 100

Whatever 2's strategy country 1 is led inexorably to a strategy of defection. The same is true for country 2. The international society chooses the suboptimal collective pay-off represented by the bottom right-hand box, which is inferior for each country and to the society as a whole than mutual co-operation represented by the potentially available top left-hand box. Unless each country believes the other will co-operate it will not, and anarchy encourages behaviour that leaves both sides worse off. Although nations know that they seek a common goal, because they are caught in the social trap they are unable to reach it.

Arms races extend over many years and involve numerous decisions, so that a single-period prisoner's dilemma is less useful than an iterated model where at each point of time nations not only endogenise evidence of adversarial behaviour from past periods, but also extrapolate into the future. Although in iterated models the pay-off to unilateral co-operation is higher[84] it is still insufficient to compensate for the perceived benefit of unilateral defection,[85] especially if accompanied by rapid technological progress.

The logic of prisoner's dilemma is appropriate only if countries prefer spending money on civilian goods. If they have a preference for weapons, the prisoner's dilemma ceases to be relevant. It is sometimes argued in the West that this is indeed the case in the Soviet Union.[86] Soviet status in the international community is derived almost exclusively from its possession of military power,[87] the only area of international affairs in which it competes effectively with the West. The Soviet Union has lost its ideological *élan* and poor economic performance makes it a less attractive model for newly developing countries than might at one time have been the case. The superior economic performance of the military sector due to unique institutional factors suggest to some that the Soviet Union would be most reluctant to see the end of a controlled and institutionalised race.[88]

In the USA on the other hand the capture of the legislative process by a comparatively small sector of society which directly benefits from military expenditures, or a weapons culture which promotes an exaggerated and uniquely military response to the Soviet challenge, also gives a powerfully autonomous dynamic to the arms race.[89]

Although on the broadest scale action–reaction plays a fundamental role in determining the course of the East–West arms race, it is not mechanistic, its precise morphology also being animated by political, ideological, psychological and economic determinants in each country.

2 The American Defence Economy

Despite a view which dates the beginning of the Soviet–American arms race to 1918,[1] before the Second World War the USA allocated just one per cent or so of its national product to defence. The low quotient was consistent with a widely held conservative fiscal view that excessive military spending would unbalance the budget, and with a traditional strategy of maintaining a small peacetime professional army and rapid mobilisation of men and industry in wartime.[2] After the war traditional forces reasserted themselves, and demobilisation was rapid. Between 1945 and 1947 military spending (in constant 1972 $s) decreased from $255bn. to $30bn., the armed forces fell from 3 100 000 to 391 000. Department of Defense military and civilian employment fell from 14.8m. to 2.4m. and total military-related employment from 25.8m. to 3.2m.[3] The dominant conservative fiscal forces in Congress relegated military spending towards the end of the queue in the competition for federal resources. President Truman sought to establish a fixed 33 per cent ceiling irrespective of strategic requirements, arrived at only after essential domestic programmes had been funded. President Eisenhower likewise sought to limit defence spending to an equally arbitrary ten per cent of GNP despite pleas from the Joint Chiefs of Staff that the sums were inadequate.[4]

By 1987 military spending was $282bn. Procurement alone amounted to over $100bn. making the Pentagon the largest single customer in the nation for equipment, most of which has no other market.[5] Up to ten per cent of the nation's workforce has been directly or indirectly employed in defence,[6] some six to seven million jobs in the public and private sector. Its dominating presence in many markets profoundly affects industrial structure, the degree of monopoly and hence industrial efficiency.[7] Although the Department of Health exceeds the Defense Department in the level of federal disbursements most are in the form of transfer payments, and the Pentagon accounts for over 70 per cent of federal procurement. Because it dominates the R and D process it has a critical influence on technological progress in the business sector, on the type and the pace with which new products are made available to civilian business and consumer markets.[8] The Pentagon is in short the largest single feature in the economic political landscape.[9] The parade of bald statistics does not of itself answer the single most important issue; whether $282 bn. is too little, too much or is just about right to optimally meet America's security, growth and welfare objectives. Too little could jeopardise security, too much is wasteful. Economic theory, even in the presence of perfect competition cannot determine whether military expenditure is too high or too low, for there exists no objective measure of the final good, security.[10] Since no military strategy is entirely riskless the trade-off between security and cost is necessarily judgemental. At one pole is the view that the cut-off point between expenditures which are justified and those which are not is essentially arbitrary.[11] Governments should therefore calculate from full employment output what is required to meet domestic programmes and 'only then' estimate the resources available for defence.[12] Economists argue that waging war is no different in principle from any other resource transformation process and should be just as eligible for the improvements in efficiency that have accrued elsewhere from technical substitutions.[13]

Some critics argue that conventional economic efficiency is essentially irrelevant to military activities.[14] National security is not in the final analysis economically motivated, an excessive concern with which may undermine the very objectives which military spending is designed to attain. Waste in the sense of duplicate, and hence during peacetime redundant, facilities might in wartime be crucial to the effective conduct of the armed forces. Heterogenous weapons which reduce the potential benefits of scale and standardisation might nonetheless be effective in increasing the resource cost to the enemy. Inefficient firms with surge capacity might justify peacetime support when strict economic accounting might require their elimination. This is especially so since defence contractors seek short term profits[15] and are often reluctant to remain in the defence contracting business if these fall below what they might reasonably expect to obtain elsewhere. Narrow budgetary concerns in short are not necessarily conducive to efficiency in the proper sense of minimising the resources to achieve given goals. If those goals require peacetime surplus and duplication, so be it. Surplus and duplication which are not necessary for the achievement of goals cannot be justified however. The exact degree of excess is an empirical issue, and although the cut-off point cannot be precisely resolved, it is in principle clear enough. President Eisenhower understood this when he graphically, if perhaps simplistically, identified the cost of one heavy bomber as a modern brick school in more than 30 cities, . . . two electric power plants each serving a town of 60 000 population, . . . two finely equipped hospitals, and 50 miles of concrete highway.[16] Expenditures which are widely judged to be excessive or which sustain fraud or waste are unlikely to be politically conducive to good management. Excessive expenditures may also so provoke a reaction in adversary countries as to be eventually self-defeating, or induce allies to free ride. The nature of the dilemma is illustrated by the fact that since 1958 the government has on more than 6000 occasions bailed out defence contractors in trouble.[17] On the one hand saving contractors from bankruptcy may effectively sustain surge capacity, multiple sourcing or reduce imports. If however firms know they will be rescued, the market ceases to perform its essential function of reward and penalty. Governments must balance the calculus of long term efficiency and risk against short term inefficiency and security.

Despite the large and growing sums spent annually on defence the proportion of the nation's resources devoted to this end in peacetime has – until the recent boost to expenditures under President Reagan – declined from the high ratios of the early Cold War period. In 1955 expenditure was ten per cent of GNP. By 1979 the ratio had fallen to five per cent and has since then climbed to 6.8 per cent. Compared with the 15 per cent to 17 per cent spent by the Soviet Union, the current American ratio of less than seven per cent is relatively modest. The different quotients in the two countries is largely explained by the far smaller Soviet economy, though as measured in dollars the Soviet ratio is nonetheless higher than would be anticipated from a strict comparison of national income.

Compared with its major allies however, the USA spends absolutely and relatively much more, but as the hegemonic leader and the only member of the anti-communist alliance with global interests and responsibilities this is to be expected. The higher American ratio is not in itself evidence that the USA is overspending, but may simply reflect the well-known fact that the smaller members of an alliance tend to free ride and therefore to contribute less than their proper share of the collective burden.[18]

Statistical comparisons between nations are in any case of only limited relevance, the proper criterion being whether security increases *pari passu* with expenditures. Although a conclusive answer is not possible, there is wide measure of agreement, and not only amongst those who are in principle opposed to defence spending that the USA spends too much for the level of security it obtains. One American estimate claims that the USA could obtain significantly better defence for 75 per cent of the present budget,[19] and though it spends ten times as much as the UK, it buys a force only six times as much.[20] It is in short not getting value for money,[21] a state of affairs quite separate from the security dilemma attendant on all military expenditures. This judgement, if correct, implies that the institutions and processes by which the USA decides each year how much to spend on defence are both inefficient and powerful.

Defence is the quintessential public good, possessing in extreme form the characteristics non-excludability and non-exclusiveness which in free markets limit total supply to that freely offered by the altruistic gifts of individual members of society[22] almost certainly below the optimal level. Thus for reasons of economic efficiency as well as more obviously for political and social control, defence is provided outside the market, even in societies otherwise organised on fiercely capitalist principles. In simple public sector models the state is depicted as a unitary actor with the objective and the means to maximise the individual preferences of all citizens which are expressed as a collective function. Electors who are well-informed transmit their preferences to appropriate legislative bodies which manage the nation's resources in a non-self-interested and unbiased manner. The state is an optimising agent. In fact governments do not and cannot know the preferences of the median voter, and as a surrogate replace some hypothetical national norm with their own more tangible preferences. Electors who individually have only an occasional and marginal influence on legislative outcomes are not induced to become well-informed about the budgetary implications of overall policy. They benefit most from the legislative process however by concentrating on the small number of issues which are of particular importance to them. One solution to legislative impotence is to join special interest groups with similar objectives, to which democratic governments are in fact highly responsive.

Where feasible the special interest consumer or producer groups form alliances with those specialist government departments and bureaucracies without which modern states cannot function. Although these are in principle merely agents of the state, bureaucratic momentum inevitably creates organisational interests which coexist parallel to and semi-independently of the national interest. The state is not therefore, as hypothesised, a unitary actor[23] but is rather the arena where different interests and bureaucracies, in a complex *mélange* of alliances and competing groups, seek their share of the nation's resources. The final allocations are consequent on the outcome of these alliances and competitions, which depending as they do on political and bureaucratic bargaining skills and influence, are unlikely to be optimal. In the USA where checks and balances are deliberately fostered the outcome is a highly structured division of labour and routine practices. To minimise the known, damaging consequences of competition, the bargainers agree to a satisficing compromise which is optimal for none but acceptable to most. Output will almost certainly exceed the competitive level. Bureaucratic rewards, salaries, perquisites, patronage and so on are by and large positive monotonic functions of the total budget,[24] and maximising the departmental budget becomes the major objective, an easily understood and highly visible success indicator. Under certain assumptions it can be demonstrated that the level of output of organisations in the political marketplace may be twice that produced under perfect competition[25] (though in the presence of externalities and other market failures there is no necessity for the competitive output to be optimal). Even though the strict conditions seldom obtain in reality, American bureaucrats – conditioned by a competitive business environment – are, compared with their British counterparts, impelled to seek higher budgets[26] and therefore a larger role for the department in which they work. If in addition bureaucrats have the possibility of transferring to the private sector of the industry, evidence of maximising skills increase their recruitment potential. The lack of temporal coincidence between costs and benefits also induces bureaucrats to seek levels of output higher than strictly warranted. Benefits are often instantaneous and highly visible whereas costs are postponed and diffused to later generations by which time the bureaucrat will have moved on.[27]

Although models of organisational behaviour are necessarily stylised, the theoretical analysis which projects a level of output in excess of optimal is confirmed by casual empiricism which concludes that, in the case of defence, American society is paying an inordinate share of the federal budget to satisfy the needs of an inflexible bureaucracy.[28] The Department of Defense is a maximising bureau to such a degree that it is claimed to be in business above all to spend money,[29] almost irrespective of what is bought with the money.

Congress as the sponsoring agency allocates resources between competing claimants. Although it has its own specific expertise, the weight of information relevant to efficient resource exceeds its collective competence such that on any specific issue special interest groups and professional bureaucracies are almost certainly better informed. Specialist information is a key bargaining asset which bureaucracies use to maximise their claims on the nation's resources.[30] Bureau have some degree of control over how much and in what manner pertinent information is released and have an interest in publishing only that which shows it off in a good light and withholding that which might bear adversely on its activities. The Department of Defense is induced to maximise and even exaggerate the likelihood and the intensity of the Soviet threat and the degree to which it can only or most effectively be contained by military as opposed to political means.[31] It also emphasises the beneficial economic consequences of defence spending in creating employment and income, and in increasing the rate of technological progress by maximising the spill-in effects from military R and D.[32] In this respect the Pentagon behaves much as any other government department. In other ways however it is so different as to effect a qualitative change in its relationship with the disbursing agency.

It is as already described the largest single feature in the economic political landscape and in the American legislative system political influence is positively related to mass.[33] No coalition of civilian agencies come near to matching the Department of Defense in the scale of its activities, which in total may be larger than the central government can control.[34] It is not only larger than its great rival, the Department of State, but as a consequence of its function is more aggressively managed with easily monitored success indicators.

The Department's large legislative liaison programme enables it to lobby effectively for its favoured programmes. Congress may often not give its approval for a particular tranche of expenditures in any one year, but it is difficult to cancel outright a programme which the Department or one of the services really wants.The Joint Chiefs of Staff, uniquely, have the right to appeal to the President if a request is turned down, and even if the appeal is unsuccessful, the Department or the service can come back with same or slightly modified request when the political or the budgetary climate is more propitious.[35] Such was the case with B-1 plane which after being cancelled by President Carter was later resurrected by President Reagan. Department of Defense budgets are highly autonomous. Whereas the civilian budgets are co-ordinated by the Office of Management and Budget, the Department of Defense constructs its own which is reconciled only late in the budget process.

The Pentagon claims a virtual monopoly of military information which in the nature of adversarial bilateral bargaining it is induced to conceal from the disbursing agency.[36] Its control of often technical, classified and emotive information is one of its most effective bargaining skills. Since there are no objective measures of output, analysts substitute surrogate, usually inadequate, measures of adversarial capabilities or intentions. Nor once they have been estimated is there a unique military response. There exists in short a great zone of uncertainty which the specialist agency can often exploit to its own advantage. The Department of Defense has been described as the single most powerful determinant of American attitudes towards the state of tension with the USSR.[37] Since uncertainty about Soviet behaviour is perhaps 'the single most powerful stimulant of the arms race'[38] its room for manoeuvre is clearly very great. It is the control over specialist information which gives to the CIA its special role in the defence community, which from its *raison d'etre* to provide unbiased information has transformed itself into an agency with its own organisational goals and programme.

By its effective use of propaganda and the national interest, the Department of Defense forecloses some options and makes others difficult for Congress to support.[39] Congressmen are reluctant to be seen to jeopardise the nation's defences and can often rationalise their support for programmes of doubtful legitimacy on the grounds that in the long run it is more economical to forego short term improvements in welfare than to have to pick up a larger bill later on. Because it controls more information and has the expertise and incentive to use it effectively, the Pentagon can often hoodwink Congress and sidetrack it to issues which are essentially marginal or where it can be easily defeated by superior skills. The Pentagon's relationship with Congress has been likened to a game,[40] whereby various strategies, which while not mutually consistent, are employed in propitious circumstances. Instead of relating its budget requests to American strategic needs the Pentagon tends to compare American force and troop levels with those in the Soviet Union. Soviet strategy has historically required large numbers of weapons and it is always possible to find categories where the USA appears to lag behind. Since numbers are easily understood they are often more potent than militarily significant but complex qualitative criteria.[41] Moreover Congress is not well served by its control systems. The General Accounting Office is broadly concerned with narrowly economic rather than military issues, often pursuing individual and atypical instances of mismanagement rather than broad scale management reviews.[42]

Congressional authority to hold down military spending is further compromised by the tendency of many of its members to use it as a source of patronage.[43] After being elected, Congressmen seek above all to be re-elected and immediately set out to create the conditions which maximise their chances of re-election.[44] These are related to the success of the incumbent in increasing income or employment in the constituency. Military bases or production lines are highly visible and potent generators of local wealth and employment. Representatives of constituencies where bases or factories are located are induced to seek election to key appropriations committees such as the Armed Services Committee, which in consequence tend to be staffed by members who have a material interest in keeping defence spending high. Competition for military spending in the key committees is usually resolved by compromise, a process not conducive to competition and efficiency. In one instance, when $2.5bn. for what was described as Support for the Free World was voted through in less than one hour, requests for $1.9bn. for local military construction took three weeks.[45] The Pentagon, well aware of the political–economic impact of defence spending, deliberately spreads its expenditures as widely as possible throughout the economy to maximise the number of representatives who have a personal interest in keeping alive particular programmes. Such a strategy of disbursement not only increases the likelihood of otherwise marginal programmes surviving Congressional scrutiny but also reduces economies of specialisation and thereby adds to the total costs of programmes unnecessarily. Such Congressional practices are estimated to have increased the cost of the MX missile from $150m. in 1978 to $600m. in 1988, and the B-1 bomber from $1m. in 1970 to $220m. in 1984.[46]

Procedural matters also tend to increase the cost of competing with the USSR. Annual budgeting inhibits effective long term planning and in contrast to the USSR, American military expenditures exhibit a remarkably high degree of variance, which inhibits investment in plant and machinery, inducing small component suppliers without the cushion of guaranteed profits to leave the industry. A stable multi-year budgeting system could, it is estimated, save up to 20 per cent on the defence budget.[47] The political justification for annual budgeting which in principle is real and valid, is eroded in practice by Congressional failure to address the crucial issues of budgeting for security. Congress tends to investigate individual instances of fraud

and mismanagement which though real enough are not the fundamental reasons for economic inefficiency in the military sector. Profits
are sometimes excessive, but because they are contractually negotiated are not the real cause of price inflation, which is more usually
due to the lack of incentives to hold down costs.[48]

Nowhere within the legislative process is there a unified view of the
costs and benefits of competing programmes[49] or a coherent procedure for linking military R and D to a comprehensive military
strategy and foreign policy in terms of which procurement decisions
are justified. In short Congress has been unimpressive in holding in
check those impulses which tend to exaggerate the level of, and
growth in, military spending.[50]

The basic model of bilateral bargaining between the disbursing
agency and the bureau is an incomplete conceptualisation of the
military allocation process in that it ignores the rivalry which exists
between relatively independent services over roles, missions and
hence resources. Inter-service competition is no accident, for when
Congress created an independent Department of Defense in 1947
(then called the National Military Establishment), it was concerned
to limit the potential for the abuse of power by a monopoly department. Autonomous army, navy and air force departments would it
was supposed not only hold in check the overweening ambitions of
their rivals but, because they were competing for the same finite
resources, would be induced to challenge those elements in their
rivals' requests which were not sustainable. Disagreements between
the services – often violent and public – attest to the at that time
fierce competition for resources especially in the early post-
unification period.

Each service funds its own large and independent intelligence
programme, that of the air force employing up to ten times more
officers than the Pentagon's Defence Intelligence Agency. Naturally
each is induced to interpret the sometimes inchoate data to its own
benefit. In 1955 the air force, partly tricked by Soviet subterfuge,
concluded that the USSR had built 30 Bison bombers and was
capable of building up to 70 per month thereafter. The CIA and the
other services disagreed and later evidence showed the Soviet programme fell short of air force estimate by around 30 per cent. Service
intelligence also tends to exaggerate the performance characteristics
of Soviet weapons, and American officers are continually surprised at
the primitiveness of captured Soviet weapons.[51]

Each service has the right to communicate directly with Congress,[52]
spending more on Congressional lobbying than the Secretary of

Defense, and service links with Congress, especially the influential committees, tend to be closer than those of the Secretary.

Each service manages its own procurement to the degree that 90 per cent of the Pentagon's annual procurement is spent by one or other of the services.[53] In response to this simple but crucial economic fact, defence contractors cultivate the services as being the vital support for commercially profitable research, development and procurement. Inter-service rivalry such as that between the air force and the army over the Thor and Jupiter missiles provides the competition which the structure was designed to nurture. More often, however, as the services have become bureaucratised and fund large procurement programmes, competition has been replaced with satisficing organisation goals typical of oligopolies. One time competition has been replaced by continuity and accommodation. Like most large and successful organisations the services are unwilling to relinquish traditional roles, and despite great changes in technology and strategy the shares of the defence budget allocated to each service have remained surprisingly constant. Each service is induced to emphasise programmes which distinguish it from its rivals, most easily achieved through weapons systems. New weapons are not only tangible and powerful symbols of success and therefore of the importance of the service in the overall scheme of things, they are also the cement which binds together the services to the other elements in the defence complex. Historically the navy and the air force insist on transporting army troops, and the air force initially opposed the medium range missile programme which the army argued was artillery and therefore claimed as its own. Three areas of sustained inter-service dispute are between the navy and the air force over naval aviation, the army and the air force over combat support and the navy and the marines over the latter's participation in ground combat.[54] Inter-service rivalry is common to all armed forces, but because of the relatively modest powers of the Joint Chiefs of Staff and the critical importance of procurement, is more deeply entrenched in the American system.[55]

Since the precise impact of force structure on security cannot easily be calculated,[56] mutually accommodating compromise is an effective device to attract more resources from Congress. Compromise pushes spending beyond the competitive level and minimises the pressure to devise an overall structure based on a unified view of objectives.[57]

Accommodation occurs even at the Chief of Staff level where according to one ex-chairman the military chiefs perceive themselves as representing their services.[58] They are led to recommend policies which benefit all and (reluctantly) to accept policies which penalise all more or less equally. They are inhibited from making choices which would greatly benefit one service at the expense of another, and tacitly support the favoured position of other members in exchange for guaranteed support of their own.[59]

The regular distribution of resources between the services gives some sustenance to the bureaucratic model which predicts marginal changes in budgetary allocations from year to year. In terms of global allocation, however, the model is incomplete, for what has characterised American defence spending over the entire post-war period has been a high degree of variance, from + 60 per cent to − 30 per cent.[60] Samuel Huntington has identified three spending cycles of unequal length,[61] within which a small body of experts revise military doctrine, but which requires an external stimulus for the new ideas to be matched by higher military expenditures. The external trigger animates the public to support rapid expansion in defence spending, which is however sustainable for a few years only, after which concern for the economic consequences of an overstretched economy provokes a reversion to lower but more sustainable growth. The cycles reflect an essentially political solution to the conflicting claims of a society unable to reconcile its long term commitments and resources.[62]

The political accommodation of irreconcilable claims cannot be independent of the ideological environment which informs American foreign policy. The ideological basis of American policy has been expertly analysed elsewhere,[63] but it is no accident that the Department of Defense has been the single most powerful determinant of American attitudes towards the state of tension with the USSR. Simplistic views of the enemy have been nurtured which, it has been argued, have imprisoned American diplomacy in an ideological straitjacket almost as confining as that of the Soviet Union.[64] Opinion polls throughout the post-war period show a consistent American antagonism towards communism as a system of thought and organisation. Upward of 80 per cent of Americans believe private enterprise to be a pre-requisite for a democratic government and that communism would make life worse for the American people.[65] In 1953, 92 per cent of the population held an unfavourable opinion of the USSR. Although by 1972 this had fallen to 60 per cent or so, by 1980 the ratio had again increased to 87 per cent. Such variations reflect as much domestic manipulation of the political culture as change in Soviet foreign policy.[66] Apart from one brief period towards the end of the Vietnam war and after its conclusion, when the American people and the armed forces regarded each other with mutual hostility, the majority of the public have shown high, though fluctuating, support for military expenditures.

The bureaucratic and political determinants of defence spending have been sustained by a technological momentum which to a remarkable degree has been the most dominating characteristic of the post-war Soviet–American arms race.[67]

Before the Second World War military research and development seldom exceeded one per cent of military spending.[68] It was unstructured, mainly undertaken in military establishments, responding to external challenge as circumstances warranted. The catalyst for change was the war, which demonstrated the strategic significance of new science.[69] The spectacularly successful fissionable bomb and radar were but the most visible evidence of a wide ranging dynamic momentum which profoundly influenced how American leaders perceived their nation's security. Even before the end of the war, Vannever Bush argued that 'the whole practice of warfare is being revised by the laboratories'.[70] By 1947 military R and D expenditures were $500bn, and the army and the navy had created a Joint Research and Development Board. Nevertheless, consonant with postwar demobilisation the institutional structure which had been so spectacularly successful was dismantled.[71] Not until the early 1950s, in response to a series of inter-related external shocks, did the USA systematically reassemble its military research programme, which reached an early apogee during McNamara's era. In the two decades or so following Sputnik, expenditures increased hugely, and civilian and military research organisations proliferated. In the words of a later Secretary of Defense, 'given America's disadvantage in numbers, our technology is what will save us'.[72] By 1984 military R and D was $32bn., 71 per cent of federally funded R and D.[73] Since that early period the distinguishing feature of American defence has been the pursuit of the magic weapon,[74] 'a depressing and obsessive pursuit of technology at all costs'.[75] (Together the USA and the USSR account for 80 per cent to 90 per cent of all military related R and D).

Because of its heavy concentration, a disproportionate number of the nation's scientists and technologists work on military-related research projects. Whereas in manufacturing industry as a whole engineers, engineering technicians, computer, life and physical scientists and mathematicians account for less than six per cent of total employment, the ratio is 41 per cent in the missile, and 22 per cent in the communications industries. In the early 1970s 22 per cent of electrical engineers, 48 per cent to 55 per cent of aeronautical engineers, and 23 per cent to 38 per cent of physicists worked on military-related projects. The ratio is almost bound to have increased since then.[76] In some plants the ratio of scientific workers to operatives reaches extraordinary proportions as in the El Segundo communications satellite plant owned by Hughes Aircraft, where 95 per cent of the 8000 workforce are engaged in research, development or testing.[77]

Such a concentration of resources on a relatively narrow sector of the economy cannot but influence and be influenced by the parameters which regulate the rhythm of technological progress. Science came to be important to the degree that it had technological, especially military, application. Only thus could governments otherwise so opposed to intervention in the economic affairs of the nation justify the deep penetration of the scientific and technological community.[78] The technological outcome was influenced not only by the volume of funding and its organisation, but also by the committed technological orientation of the military services and the culture of optimism which generally prevailed in the scientific community. America's strategic stance became dependent on unquestioned and unassailable technological superiority, to be achieved almost irrespective of cost.[79] The powerful psychological argument that the lives of American servicemen could not be compromised by equipment which was less than the best available was difficult to counter, and Pentagon procedures and cast of mind tended to screen out solutions which did not require or were not consistent with the attainment of technological excellence.

Military demand was matched by effective supply, the scientific imperatives to which most scientists respond. The innate curiosity of good scientists, the intellectually interesting problems which had to be solved and the high status which the work was accorded[80] complemented the economic and organisational stimulus to technological momentum. Defence scientists *sui generis* believed that technological advance in the USSR could only be countered by superiority at home, which was directly related to the amount of money the nation was prepared to spend. If something was technologically possible it should be funded. Scientists also believed that when weapons or equipment reached the stage of military effectiveness they should automatically be deployed, otherwise scientific morale and *élan* might be jeopardised.[81] Edward Teller, one of the most influential post-war defence scientists, argued that 'it is prefer-able not to ask military people what they want, but rather to push scientific research to its limits. Military need will follow'.[82]

The decisive push to the technological spiral however was the penetration of the research, development and production cycle by sovereign, profit-seeking firms. In contrast to before the Second World War, 70 per cent of military R and D and virtually all production is done by private corporations. In the immediate post-war period the corporate sector alone had the capital to manufacture weapons on a large scale, but also to involve it so decisively in the R and D process gave a quantitative and qualitative boost to the constituency which had a direct interest, in this case material, in spending more money on R and D. It was this which in part led the USAF to contract out its R and D work to private industry in the 1940s.[83]

Profit-seeking firms pursue the goal of continuous production to minimise overheads in the form of specialist plant, equipment and manpower. They are therefore induced to continually seek out new production, most effectively by making obsolete current weapons systems, either through new-in-principle weapons or by so improving the performance of existing weapons as to create an irresistible pressure to replace old with new. Firms structure their behaviour and organisation to maximise their impact, for instance by concentrating research where the production potential is greatest. They are induced to 'buy in' to research contracts by bidding low, for it is usually the case that firms which do the research will also win the contract to manufacture the resulting weapon, and it is production which pro-vides profit. At the bid stage the firms are competing with one another. The contracting service is a monopsonist, and in a strong bargaining position. Once the contract is awarded however the distribution of power changes to a bilateral monopoly. Military research and development is by its very nature uncertain: from the service side because of precisely what role the new weapon is to play, and from the corporation side by what technological parameters are feasible and economic.[84] The very uncertainty increases the bargain-ing power of the corporation, which as a monopolist is induced to renegotiate contracts on more favourable and profitable terms.

Firms which are so dependent on a single market, do not leave the possibility of profits to chance. They fund their own planning and research groups, and liaise with the disbursing services in anticipation of actual demands.[85]

Governments too could not leave to chance and the haphazard profitability of the market an activity so crucial to the nation's security, and have consistently subsidised commercial endeavour to push forward the rate of technological progress. Total federal investment in government-owned, controlled and operated (GOCO) schemes amount to $15bn.[86] As well as paying for specialist machinery and equipment, the government pays firms on a cost-reimbursement basis, an almost irresistible incentive to cost inflation, and allows monthly progress payments of between 80–85 per cent which eases cash flow problems. It also gives interest-free loans and allows deferment of tax payments, both of which increase the profitability of military contracts.[87] Firms can keep patents which have no security implication. In many such ways the benefits of socially-financed military research and developments are internalised to and by the firms.

Given America's strategic dependence on advancing technology, speed is of utmost importance. After the shock of Sputnik, American defence planners determined they would not again be caught unawares, and defence planning has been characterised by a series of crash programmes which, though effective in achieving their goals have been, according to economic criteria, inefficient.[88] Given the long lead times typical of military R and D, the pressure to make 'go no-go' decisions as early as possible in the cycle often results in inefficient decision-making. The preference for time compression was manifest in concurrent 'total package' procurement, when decisions to proceed to succeeding stages were often made before the evidence on the preceding stage had been fully appraised.[89] Engineers argued that they did not require all the information before being able to assess whether and when to proceed to the next stage in the cycle. Errors were carried forward, and had to be rectified later – often at high cost.

The pressure to reduce the length of the R and D cycle reflected in part the inevitable uncertainty surrounding the direction and the pace of the adversary's R and D effort. Because of the lengths to which the Soviet Union goes to conceal military affairs, American defence planners face a yawning uncertainty about crucial aspects of the current Soviet effort, the results of which will be embodied in new weapons a decade or more later. American scientists and defence planners must therefore create intellectual devices which might allow them to anticipate, in the absence of concrete information, future Soviet progress. One such is to assume that Soviet scientists are working on projects similar to those under investigation in American laboratories. That being the case it is merely prudent to widen the research net to investigate possible countervailing systems, both to offset the – at this stage – hypothetical Soviet response and to advance further research in the USA. American research teams are naturally more knowledgeable about R and D work being carried out in other American laboratories, and are thereby induced to race one another. By a series of logical progressions, Soviet intentions come to be equated with American capabilities. The technological dynamic is endogenised to the degree that the effect of actual Soviet behaviour on the American cycle is minimised. In a fundamental sense technological progress becomes autonomous, a 'mad momentum'[90] and the search for the perfect technological weapons takes on a life of its own. Strategic or political criteria are replaced by technology as the prime determinant of the arms race.

Individually each element in the research, development and production cycle provides a powerful impetus to rapid technological progress. Collectively they form a community of interest whose impact far exceeds the sum of its parts. New weapons are at the apex of the military economic system, the cement which binds the otherwise disparate interest of the separate groups. Weapons provide a wider range of roles and missions for the military, status for the bureaucracies, intellectual stimulation for the scientists, and profit for the firms. R and D lies at the heart of what Gordon Adams calls the 'iron triangle'.[102] The consequence has been progress which can only be described as phenomenal. Despite the alarmist claims of some defence spokesmen about the erosion of American superiority, the embodied level of American technology consistently exceeds that of the USSR, and to that degree technological momentum has been primarily an American phenomenon.[91] The American lead has been effectively maintained to the present time. In a study conducted by the Department of Defense in 1984, the USA was estimated to be ahead in 15 of the 20 most important technologies, equal in five, and behind in none.[92] American lags, when they do occur, are often though not always a consequence of the USA choosing not to compete.[93]

At its best American technology is characterised by a pragmatic and flexible response to technical opportunities which routinely and effectively incorporate advanced civilian improvements into military systems.

Progress however is bought at the expense of an inexorable increase in costs and prices. On average, each generation of weapons costs up to ten times as much as its predecessor.[94] Since 1945 the cost of aeroplane avionics has increased from $3000 to $25m., and engines from $40 000 to $2m., so that by 1980 F-14 planes cost between $26m. and $35m. each. Long term technological improvement is by its very nature costly and high prices must be anticipated. The real issue however is whether higher costs are matched by correspondingly better performance and whether American security is always best served by seeking technological excellence at any cost.

New technology is beneficial in *(a)* producing new, or better quality goods and/or *(b)* lower prices. When applied to civilian goods it usually produces some combination of both outcomes. When applied to military goods, however, the effect has historically been unidirectional. New products have been created, quality improves, but prices do not fall. Similar goods, such as electronics or computer equipment, show divergent trends in civilian and military markets, and the inflation in equipment bought by the Pentagon outstrips that in civilian markets by an average of four to five per cent per annum.[95] A simple comparison is not wholly valid in that military equipment usually embodies special requirements and meets finer tolerances than are required for civilian goods. In the final analysis weapons must be able to function effectively in the unique and usually far more demanding circumstances of battle; rugged terrain, poor repair facilities, extremes of air temperatures and pressures.

High costs are also a function of the greater urgency with which the armed services seek to bring the cycle to successful conclusion. Compression of the time scale almost inevitably means inadequate assessment of often incomplete information, and validation of operational requirements and parameters. Although technological progress is generally believed to be largely demand determined, supply constraints are seldom simultaneously overcome.[96] In lagging sectors extra resources must be deployed to complete the chain as quickly as possible, itself expensive and often inefficient. When in the 1970s the degree of urgency abated and prototype-testing prior to full scale production was more common, the pace of cost escalation declined.[97]

Higher cost is positively associated not only with the pace of technological progress, but in specific programmes to the improvement of technological advance which is being sought and the degree to which the programme and its requirements depart from known engineering norms.[98] The cost of front line aircraft, where technological progress has been particularly rapid, has increased by a real factor of 100 since 1945. In tanks, on the other hand, where progress has been more modest and evolutionary, costs have increased by a factor of ten.[99]

Large development and production programmes, often extending ten to 15 years and involving many billions of dollars, are by their very nature difficult to manage effectively. New weapons, embodying advanced technology, seldom come in on budget and on time; the degree of excess normally being related to the complexity of the programme. The Trident submarine, originally costed at $1.2bn., has been ten years in the making and is at the time of writing 40 per cent over budget. The F-18 Hornet is currently priced at over six times the original estimate, and the M-1 Abrams tank, after taking 18 years to get to the production line, costs $2.5bn.[100] Although these are the latest and most spectacular examples, they merely reflect a long standing general trend. During the 1950s cost overruns on average doubled the final price of weapons over the original estimates.[101] In the 1970s improved programme control – including the Packard reforms which required hardware tests to be completed before moving on to the production stage – reduced the growth of cost overruns but not schedule slippage.[102] Further recent improvements in the contracting system while yielding impressive results have not fundamentally changed the generic tendency towards poor management control. The armed services in general are not overly concerned with the economic costs of poor management, in that penalties for failing to meet performance specifications are more severe than those for exceeding cost estimates. The structure of rewards and penalties reflects military preferences in an uncertain environment. A different structure would in all probability result in different outcomes.

The preference for the most advanced, and therefore expensive, technology, cannot be reconciled with large numbers of deployed weapons. In 1952 the USA produced 5200 tanks. By the early 1980s, production had declined to 720. In the same period, production of planes declined from 3000 to 230 p.a. (compared with 500 or so for the USSR) and the American inventory has fallen from 18 000 to 7000.[103] A report issued by the Joint Economic Committee highlights the inverse relationship between price and quantity. One tongue-in-cheek projection estimates that if current trends continue, by 2054 the USA will be able to produce just one aircraft, to be shared on rota basis between the three services.[104]

Each plane, ship and tank is inevitably more adept at performing a

Table 2.1   Cost overruns in procurement

	Percentage change in price 1980–81	Percentage change in units ordered
Planes		
F16	+20	–20
A464	+43	–50
Missiles		
Patriot	+154	–67
Hellfire	+322	–82
Tanks		
XM	+49	–21
FFG7	+79	–75

Source: Hearings before the Subcommittee on Economic Goals and Inter-governmental Policy of the Joint Economic Committee, Congress of the U.S. Part I, Washington, DC, 1982.

wider range of tasks than its predecessor, so that a one for one replacement is not necessary and a comparison on that basis not wholly valid. Nevertheless, many expert observers believe that the sacrifice of numbers in the relentless pursuit of more exacting technical triumphs has been taken beyond the stage of economic optimality.[105] Improvements which are technologically feasible are often incorporated irrespective of cost, better performance of between five and ten per cent sometimes being bought at extra cost of 20–25 per cent.[106]

Poor quality control, allied to exacting demands, produces weapons which are not only expensive and late but which are also unreliable. At any one given time in 1979 only 50 per cent of F-15 planes were operational, the remainder awaiting repair. For aircraft in general the sortie rate, that is, the number of flights per day, has declined, and as with other parameters the degree of unreliability is partly a function of complexity.

The simple F-5 was capable on average of two and a half sorties per day, compared with only one sortie per day for the F-15. Since the F-15 inventory is smaller, the difference in the fleet sortie rate is amplified.

F-5:   1000 × 2.5 = 2500 sorties
F-15:   250 × 1 = 250 sorties.

After an investment of $10 to $15 bn. the worldwide Military Command and Control System, tested in 1972, broke down 62 per cent of the time.[107] Higher costs not only reduce the numbers produced and deployed, but adversely affect other aspects of American security. To compensate for the lack of numbers, American submarines take up more threatening positions,[108] less glamorous activities such as training and preparation are neglected, and in February 1988, Mr James Ambrose, the Under-Secretary of the Army, claimed that a fall in personnel strength to a ten year low of 772 600 soldiers and a possible drop to pre-Korean levels was forced upon the army by the need to pay for high-tech equipment.[109]

Moreover, soldiers, airmen and sailors are finding it increasingly difficult to use modern weapons to their full capability because of their complexity. Advanced equipment design, however outstanding, is effective only if complementary inputs are equally adept. In testimony to a Congressional sub-committee, the President of the Naval Board of Inspection expressed grave concern about the ability of American sailors to carry out relatively simple tasks, while an army investigation found that more than 20 per cent of tank gunners in West Germany, and an even higher ratio of those stationed at home, did not understand the procedure for setting battlesights.[110] The educational levels of the professional military workforce routinely falls below that of the civilian population in general,[111] despite recent success in improving recruitment and in inducing skilled men to re-enlist. The importance of appropriate complementary inputs is demonstrated by studies which show that the differences in effectiveness between weapons are often swamped by differences in the quality of the men using them.[112] Technical superiority in short is no guarantee of military success[113] and there are numerous occasions where a larger quantity of weapons of modest performance are more useful, strategically and politically, than a smaller number incorporating the most advanced performance characteristics. Nevertheless so long as the different elements in the military industrial sector have an interest in pursuing rapid technological progress, the generic inefficiencies will remain.

Outstanding scientists are motivated by scientific curiosity and a belief that their efforts are vital to the security of the nation. They draw prestige from the embodiment of their research in new weapons. Science representatives typically tend to argue that weapons incorporating new or improved performance characteristics should be deployed as they become ready, on the grounds that failure to do so would lower scientific morale.

Defence contractors have an economic interest in continuous technological improvements. Research, which is subsidised and therefore cheap, increases the rate at which existing systems are made obsolete and have to be replaced. Given that profit rates are, in principle, contractually controlled, large profits can be made by a regular renewal of production embodied in the follow-on.[114] High turnovers mean high profits, and the structure of military contracts usually mean that higher costs increase rather than decrease profits.

The Pentagon and the military services benefit from a wider range of roles and missions. The services naturally want the best for their personnel, and the Pentagon, because of its bureaucratic dynamic, is motivated by a culture of procurement, according to which it prefers weapons because, and not in spite of, high costs.[115] Weapons, as they proceed through the R and D and production cycles, almost invariably become more complex, seldom simpler. The F-16 Hornet was initially designed as a simple and cheap lightweight alternative to the F-14 fighter. Pentagon chiefs so altered its parameters, making it more sophisticated, complex and heavy, that its price increased by 75 per cent, thus destroying its original rationale.[116] Nor is the F-16 an isolated case of gold plating.

Congressmen also have an incentive to promote technological progress in that more production means more jobs and higher incomes for constituents, and therefore a higher probability of re-election.

Complexity is due partly to poor management control, to premature commitment to production and to compromise over performance parameters. It is also due to a cultural, political and economic preference for complexity which is reflected in the pattern of research spending. Although both product and process innovation occur, the emphasis is heavily concentrated on the former. Around 60 per cent of R and D expenditures is for full scale development work, building and improving prototypes, etc.,[117] which almost necessarily result in a high rate of product innovation, and a strong incentive to incorporate improved or new-in-principle weapons into the inventory. Process innovation is relatively neglected. The stock of machine tools, for instance is on the whole old and comparatively inefficient. More significantly high product innovation pushes change rapidly, but in conservative directions.[118] Given that firms seek to minimise risks they prefer familiarity, where they can expect successful outcomes. The services accede to conservative preference which, despite periodic disagreements over roles and missions, sustains traditional roles.

Because of high living standards, American servicemen are culturally induced to demand more and better nice-to-have facilities, a demand which defence contractors indulge. The elimination of nice-to-have gold plating could, it is argued, increase the combat capability of American forces. Soviet superiority over Western forces to the degree it exists is arguably due not to higher spending but to excessive gold plating in the West.

Technological exuberance may even be so effective, despite the systematic tendency towards excess, if it solves clearly identified problems of defence and security. The dynamic source of technological progress, whether it is primarily demand or supply determined is thus important. Although the distinction is seldom in fact as clear as stylistically described, there is a strong opinion that in capitalist societies technological change in general is demand determined. The military technological dynamic differs however in that its essential rationale is not commercial. It cannot therefore be assumed that what may correctly describe the commercial sector is also true of the military. Research scientists usually aver that military technological progress is demand determined, that it is the military which decides what technology programmes should be funded.[119] According to this hypothesis, most projects are initiated in response to the stated needs of a military service, which identifies a gap in the nation's defences which can and should be translated into weapons. In fact the actual process is more complex. Even if a security gap is identified, there may be no necessity for it to be sealed by purely military means, with high priority or with new weapons. If new weapons have been identified as the best response they can incorporate evolutionary or revolutionary design. Clearly the range of supply responses to an observed demand is substantial.

Indeed, the very nature of technological competition makes it irrational for the USA, which bases its strategy on technological superiority, to wait until an operational gap is perceived – for given the long time horizons typical of much R and D and the uncertainty which surrounds the Soviet effort, by the time the embodied weapon is ready to be deployed, the gap may have disappeared or may have shifted elsewhere. In any case, a powerful commercial sector dependent on technological progress for profit is unlikely to play so passive a role as hypothesised. The major contractors fund large research teams not only to carry out contract research and development, but also to identify and anticipate areas of development likely to be of interest to the military. They regularly consult with the Pentagon and the services and often in highly sophisticated research programmes with uncertain outcomes draw up the basic request proposals. Defence planners who have left the Pentagon, and military contractors themselves, describe a complex process, where 'the defence contractors are profoundly influential in the organisation and development of new programme ideas.'[120] The close association between contractors and the services blurs the conventional adversarial interests of buyers and sellers,[121] a pre-requisite for efficient market outcomes. Although not exclusively so, in a number of historic instances technology preceded strategic doctrine.[122] Sir Solly Zuckerman, one time chief scientific adviser to the British government and an acute observer of defence practices, concludes that 'at base the momentum of the arms race is undoubtedly fuelled by technicians in government laboratories and the industries which produce the armaments'.[123] According to a Pratt and Whitney representative 'the day is past when military requirement is set by the military'.[124] As military technology becomes more complex and expands into the soft sciences, the simplistic sequential linking of a perceived security gap and a straightforward technological response is even less tenable. The simultaneous exploitation of different scientific and technological advances to create a building block style of advance in many instances replaces the more traditional linear pattern of scientific and technological progression. Science and technology are applied in unanticipated and imaginative ways. Perhaps the best known serendipitous exploitation of apparently unrelated technology, some of which had been in the public domain long before its eventual exploitation, is the unique combination of electronic microminiaturisation of missile guidance systems, coupling of inertial with terminal guidance, Terrain Contour matching, and an efficient small turbofan jet engine – leading ultimately to the cruise missile, which had no prior strategic rationale.

Although America's security is best served by building on comparative advantage in technology, it is possible that the military industrial complex so distorts allocations in the search for local goals as to push the rate of advance and hence the level of military expenditures beyond the optimal. The complex is in principle no different to any others such as health and education, which compete for resources in the political market place.[125] In fact, however, it is sufficiently different to warrant special concern. Although defence disbursements are less than federal spending on welfare, military spending has a more resounding economic and technological impact. It is different in being more decisively geared to procurement, and thereby involves some of the largest oligopolistic profit-seeking corporations in the political market-place. Nor should it be assumed that the civilian motivation is exclusively profit. Powerful unions, private foundations and universities also have an interest in increasing military expenditures.[126] There exist differences, often severe, between and within the different components of the complex. More spending for one service may mean less for another. A contract for one firm is a contract lost to another. On the whole, however, the 'bewildering intimacy'[127] between the Pentagon and its contractors creates a self-generating cycle of obsolescence and renewal. Through the revolving door businessmen and members of the armed forces move easily between sectors cementing a powerful personal bond. In one three-year period in the 1980s, 2240 senior military and civilian Department of Defense officials took jobs with major defence contractors,[128] the largest numbers being concentrated in those aerospace companies most dependent on military contracts. Given the embodied human capital, migration between sectors is economically as well as politically rational. Others establish themselves as consultants selling to the contractors their inside knowledge of Pentagon practices.

Senators and Congressmen who serve on the key Armed Services committees and Defense Appropriations sub-committees tend to be conservative and favour increased military spending on bases and in factories in their districts. There is, in general, however, a surprising lack of statistical support for the widely held view that defence installations systematically affect voting patterns in the House. Correlation between voting and expenditure patterns is low.[129] This does not indicate lack of influence, however; quite the reverse, for the low correlation is explained by the lack of stable forces in the Congressional system working against high defence budgets. Those who do not benefit do not oppose higher spending, in the expectation of compensating support elsewhere at other times. Congressional support is even so more powerful than the quantitative analysis implies for, unlike the membership as a whole, committee chairmen and senior members who because of their position have discretionary power over the federal budget, do systematically support military expenditures.

The military–industrial complex also differs from other bureaucratic groups in that some expenditures are for activities which are classified and by their nature evade democratic control. In November 1988 the Pentagon acknowledged the existence of the F1117A stealth fighter plane, 52 of which had been delivered, largely financed from the so-called 'black budget', almost inevitably the result of huge levels of expenditure. (The tendency to conceal programmes and their expenditures is not exclusive to the USA as the belated revelation of the British Chevaline programme showed).

Critics conclude that since defence expenditures do not add to civilian wealth or welfare, do not increase security correspondingly to costs, and almost certainly push weapons technology beyond optimal, that the military–industrial complex has a large and pernicious effect on American society and economy.[130] High and expanding expenditures, it is argued, maximise the local interests of the complex rather than the global national interest.

A simplistic correlation between interest and outcome is however not wholly valid. The fact of benefit does not in itself prove causality, and since there are no objective criteria, judgements that expenditure is excessive are clearly value laden. A defence quotient of seven per cent is excessive if a lesser one would suffice, but is not in itself sufficient to prove the existence of the garrison state, especially since the trend until recently has been downward. The complex has been unable to sustain military expansion in the face of political opposition or apathy. The high degree of variance shows that extremely high rates can be sustained for comparatively short periods, largely in response to perceptions of particularly acute external threat. Since the peak peacetime ratio of ten per cent in 1955, the proportion of the nation's resources denoted to defence declined to just over five per cent in 1979 and has also periodically declined in real terms.

Nor is it obvious that profits are excessive by civilian standards, though because the Internal Revenue Service does not require publication of profitability on a contract or programme basis, the evidence is incomplete. Because of contractual cost-plus pricing agreed profit levels should be easily monitored and controlled by Congress, and therefore not excessive, and there are numerous instances of large contractors experiencing lean times, low profits and laying-off workers.[131] One study of return on investment showed profit in the defence industry to average 11 per cent, compared with 15 per cent in civilian industry. Another investigation of 145 major contracts showed a return of 26 per cent. In the aerospace industry the return on equity was 17 per cent, compared with ten per cent for all US industry.[132]

Though contracts specify closely controlled profit levels, the renegotiation which is so characteristic of many programmes gives

Table 2.2   Percentage of total expenditure to major programmes

	1967	1977
Top 5 programmes	11	24
Top 10 programmes	13	35
Top 20 programmes	14	40

Source: J. Gansler, *The Defense Industry* (MIT Press, 1980) p. 33.

leeway to contractors to evade profit controls. When the North American Co. was prosecuted for quite separate reasons, close analysis of its books showed profit levels of 612 per cent and 802 per cent for two years, despite a contractual agreement to eight per cent.[133] Other 'creative accounting' techniques also enable defence contractors to evade congressional norms.[134] Profitability as a percentage of sales is not a good indicator, since so much physical capital and equipment is paid for and risk borne by the government. As profit levels are guaranteed, and high costs do not penalise, profitability may be less significant than absolute profits given barriers to exit and entry.

Competitive outcomes clearly cannot prevail where one-off contracts, often hugely expensive, seeking high technological norms with great uncertainty, and detailed regulation, dictate market structure. Although about 28 000 prime contractors and 50 000 sub-contractors are engaged in defence-related research, development or production, over 50 per cent of prime contracts are awarded to just 33 firms.[135] In 1980, 12 firms contracted more than $1bn. worth of business with the Department of Defense, which for five of them amounted to more than 50 per cent of total business (General Dynamics $3.5bn., 74 per cent; McDonell-Douglas $3.25bn., 54 per cent; Hughes Aircraft $2.8bn., 59 per cent; Gruman $1.3bn., 76 per cent; Northrop $1.2bn., 74 per cent.[136] By 1985 the number had increased to 23. Large scale contracting leads inevitably to a high degree of economic concentration.

The top 12 programmes account for 50 per cent of total procurement, and the Pentagon, it is argued, creates more monopoly in one day than the Anti-Trust Division can undo in one year.[137] Nevertheless the degree of concentration in the defence industry is not excessive by economy-wide standards, and with the exception of a few firms American industry is not especially dependent on military contracts.[138]

Oligopoly structure conventionally leads to less than optimal out-comes, despite possible economies of scale, because of assumed levels of X-inefficiency. The degree to which markets are contestable, that is, the ease with which firms can enter the industry if rewards are sufficiently enticing, or leave the industry if performance is sufficiently poor, also influences the degree of competition. By both criteria the defence industry is inefficient.[139]

Despite a legal requirement that defence contracts be awarded on the basis of competitive bidding, the Pentagon recognises 17 exceptions. Up to 58 per cent of contracts are awarded on a sole source basis, and another 30 per cent after a perfunctory investigation. Ninety per cent of contracts are awarded as a result of bilateral negotiation where design and performance are more important than price.[140] Given the relative unimportance of price, and the need to quickly meet advanced techonological norms it is entirely rational for the Department of Defense and the services to prefer dealing with firms with which they have previously done business, which have the overhead capital and skills and are familiar with the particular and unique requirements of the military market. For complex development and production programmes, where either side faces a large element of uncertainty, the conventional distinction between supplier and demander is destroyed. Success or failure cannot be measured by conventional market criteria but by the degree to which contractor meets imposed norms. Successful firms are those which manage the regulated political markets effectively, which require different skills to ensure success in free markets. Defence contractors have proved highly unsuccessful in penetrating civilian markets on the occasions they have sought to diversify their business.

Firms seek to assemble a range of unique skills and capital, to become national assets which allow them to bypass normal regulatory control. Since 1958 the Department of Defense has on more than 6000 occasions bailed out defence contractors facing bankruptcy and therefore the prospect of leaving the industry. It is as difficult for defence contractors to leave as it is for new firms to enter the industry, and the Pentagon, to ensure the survival of key contractors, is often induced to replace programmes being phased out.

The consequences of the unique defence market are high, perhaps excessive, technological progress, high prices and cost overruns, programme slippage and industrial inefficiency. More insidiously, its internal dynamic is fed by a culture of procurement. Critics of the internal efficiency of the defence economy have produced estimates of enormous savings which are potentially available from a reformed structure, up to $44bn. in a two-year period.[141] Whether the American defence budget is too high or not is ultimately a matter of judgement. The mechanics of how decisions on the level of budgeting are reached give powerful *a priori* support to the hypothesis that spending is excessive.

3 The Soviet Defence Economy

Socialist states, some Bolsheviks argued, had no need of a standing army.[1] Once the revolution had been secured the army could be disbanded and replaced by a people's militia – Trotsky for instance claiming that after issuing a few decrees he could then retire. The reality of invasion in 1919, and systemic capitalist hostility to the revolutionary state, showed the notion of a large socialist nation without a regular army to be nothing more than a chimera.

In 1927 the Party published a Five-Year Plan outlining proposals to bring the Red Army up to the requisite strength and technological level, but the decisive phase coincided with the great and traumatic industrialisation and collectivisation programmes of the 1930s. The first Five-Year economic plan was accompanied by a Five-Year Plan for the development of the Red Army. In 1929 the Politburo voted to increase the pace of military production to manufacture more tanks, aircraft and artillery than its capitalist enemies.[2] Soviet doctrine envisaged the surrender of space for time so that the inventory of armaments in being required an industrial infrastructure which would enable the industrial branches to increase the output of war material and to convert civilian plants to military production prior to and, if necessary, during war. From the outset therefore Soviet leaders conceived a synergising relationship between economic and military power, the latter being after the mid-1930s perhaps the decisive motivation for the intensity of the industrialisation drive up to the outbreak of the Second World War.[3] It was no abstract spirit of economic competition with the more advanced capitalist states which motivated industrial and agricultural policy and organisation in the 1930s but military necessity. From the beginning economic planning coincided with Five-Year Military Plans for types and volume of weapons production, organisation and training.[4] Unlike the USA therefore the integral symbiosis of the military with the civilian community predates the bilateral arms race between the nations. Throughout the 1930s weapons production increased prodigiously.

The quantitative indices were matched by an equally impressive improvement in the quality of weapons. After 1935 for instance heavy tanks replaced the original light models and the numerical

Table 3.1   Soviet arms production 1930–40

	1930	1933	1936	1940
Aircraft	899	2992	3770	10555
Tanks	170	3509	4800	2794
Artillery pieces	952	4368	4324	15300
Rifles	126	241	403	1461

Source: M. Harrison, *Soviet Planning in Peace and War 1938–1945* (Cambridge: Cambridge University Press, 1987, p. 8.)

decrease in production in 1940 concealed an equivalent increase of 80 per cent over 1937.[5] The increase in the quantity and quality of weapons could not have been achieved without a corresponding expansion of the military–industrial base, more remarkable in that it competed for much the same array of investment goods which were at the heart of the civilian industrialisation programme. In 1938 military-related activities absorbed fully 26 per cent of total industrial production and 16 per cent of transportation turnover.[6]

Real expansion required an equivalent commitment of monetary resources, and though prone to high margins of error, data for the state budget show the degree of burden shouldered by an already impoverished society.

Such headlong expansion could not be sustained indefinitely and post-war military expenditure grew at a more modest secular rate of four to five per cent per annum, though with short term and cyclical variations around the trend. The secrecy with which the Soviet Union cloaks its military affairs precludes an exact measure of current defence expenditure. The Swedish-based SIPRI has recently refused to publish data[7] but according to the American ACDA expenditure in current dollars in 1984 was $264bn. The CIA estimated real expenditures (in 1984 prices) at $245bn.[8] equivalent to 15 per cent to 17 per cent of GNP,[9] though this has been challenged as being excessive.[10] Conceptually consideration of whether Soviet expenditures optimally meets its security requirements is little different to the USA. In practice however there are distinct problems of methodology and of calculation.

Despite a likelihood of technological overkill, there is no compelling evidence that American security is bought at the expense of severe civilian economic inefficiency. Rather, allowing for differences in market structure and in the inherent characteristics of military and

Table 3.2 Allocations to defence in the state budget

Year	Total budget expenditure m.r.	Expenditure on defence m.r.	Defence as a % of total	Annual increase of exp. on defence (prev. yr. = 100)
1923/24 to 1927/28				
1923/24 F.	2 267	379	16.7	–
1924/25 F.	2 918	426	14.3	112
1925/26 F.	3 932	570	14.5	134
1926/27 F.	5 186	651	12.6	114
1927/28 F.	6 353	765	12.0	118
The First Five-year Plan				
1928/29 F.	8 105	880	10.9	115
B.	7 737	874	11.3	
1929/30 F.	12 329	1 046	8.5	119
B.	11 591	1 047	9.0	
1930 Sp.Q.F.	(4 635)	434	9.4	
1931 F.	23 069	1 288	5.6	123
B.	21 774	1 290	5.9	
1932 F.	30 740	1 296	4.2	101
B.	27 542	1 279	4.6	
All FYP1 F.	*78 878*	*4 944*	*6.3*	
The Second Five-year Plan				
1933 F.	40 153	1 421	3.5	110
B.	35 011	1 450	4.1	
1934 F.	50 795	5 019	9.9	353
B.	48 879	1 665	3.4	
1935 F.	66 391	8 186	12.3	163
B.	65 401	6 500	9.9	
1936 F.	81 827	14 883	18.2	182
B.	78 715	14 815	18.8	
1937 F.	93 921	17 481	18.6	117
B.	97 120	20 102	20.7	
All FYP2 F.	*333 087*	*46 990*	*14.1*	
The Third Five-year Plan				
1938 F.	124 039	23 151	18.7	132
B.	131 138	27 044	20.6	
1939 F.	153 299	39 181	25.6	169
B.	155 478	40 885	26.3	
1940 F.	174 350	56 752	32.6	145
B.	179 913	57 066	31.7	
1941 B.	216 052	70 866	32.8	125
All 1938–40 F.	*451 688*	*119 084*	*26.4*	

Notes: B. Budget as approved by government
F. Actual expenditure
Source: J. Cooper, *Defence Production and the Soviet Economy*, CREES
Discussion Paper No. 3, University of Birmingham, 1976, p. 35.

civilian goods, factor mobility across industrial sectors makes gross discrepancies in efficiency and productivity unlikely. Although comparisons of civilian and military static and dynamic efficiency are fraught with methodological and empirical problems, there is widespread agreement among Western scholars that for the USSR the level of attained economic performance in defence has been achieved at the expense of the civilian economy, for the functioning of central planning in the Soviet Union offers evidence of gross static and dynamic microeconomic inefficiency.[11]

To meet absolute standards determined by a more efficient and dynamic international competitor, Soviet planners have been obliged to guarantee priority status to military producers, and to protect them by formal and informal barriers against the more debilitating consequences of central planning,[12] without which the defence sector could not have achieved the level of performance it has attained. To a degree absent in capitalist societies therefore economic efficiency depends on the perspective from which it is assessed. For the military the process by which it has historically been able to extract such a high proportion of the nation's resources must be considered efficient. The protective barriers allow a level of performance which otherwise could not be achieved and therefore increase the security of the state, as was shown in the Great Patriotic War. For civilian producers and consumers the barriers are not efficient for they impose costs and burdens which otherwise they need not incur, and which must therefore reduce the level of output, productivity and welfare. The Soviet Union has impressed the West by a high level of military economic performance from a primitive technological base.[13] But by the same token, one explanation for the continuing underdeveloped level of civilian technology is the very fact of military priority. The balance of judgement is therefore necessarily subjective.

Although protected from certain aspects of the civilian economy the defence sector cannot be independent of it. Military–industrial research, development and production is vertically structured along ministerial lines, and workers, managers and administrators respond to similar, exogenously determined incentive structures, and their performance is similarly monitored. The organisational structure did not emerge ready formed from a socialist blueprint however, but reflected a dynamic response to problems and opportunities as they occurred. Although the structure of military production is not immutable, new ministries having being created in 1954 and 1962, the basic

Table 3.3   Ministries in the defence industry group

Ministry	Output
Aviation	Aircraft, missiles, spacecraft
Defence	Conventional ground forces, ballistic missiles, anti-tank guided missiles
Shipbuilding	Ships, submarines, naval weapons
Electronics	Electronic equipment
Radio	Radar communications, special purpose computers
Medium machine building	Nuclear weapons, lasers
General machine building	Conventional ordnance

Source: CIA, *Soviet Weapons Industry. An Overview*, reproduced by the Department of Commerce, Washington DC, 1986, p. viii.

format was largely in place by the beginning of the Second World War. Currently defence production is largely concentrated in eight ministries which compromise the separately constituted defence industry, and such ministries as Tractor and Agricultural, Chemical, Automobiles and Instrument-Making, which though producing mainly for the civilian markets also produce some military equipment.

The defence industry ministries share common features which distinguish them from the rest of Soviet industry and comprise an economy within an economy. Formally the defence industry group is directly answerable to a Deputy Chairman of the USSR Council of Ministers who is usually a member of the Presidium of the Council, but in the bifurcated Soviet system the lines of command are often confused. Ultimate authority in military as in other matters resides with the Politburo,[14] but though it takes a more active and decisive interest in military–economic affairs than is usual in more democratic societies, the effective regular oversight of security is in the control of the Defence Council, chaired by the General Secretary, whose other members are the Ministers of Defence and Foreign Affairs, the Chairman of the KGB, the Politburo member responsible for defence–industry affairs and the Chief of the General Staff.[15] Below this level are specialist institutions which provide expertise and guidance to the Party and the government. The most crucial is the Military Industrial Commission, whose status and function, however, is still unclear to Western observers. Some believe it to be a key policy-making body which brings together at the apex of military affairs the crucial confluence of political, military and economic interests represented by the General Staff, the Defence Industry, the Ministry of Defence, scientists engaged in weapons research and planning experts from GOSPLAN, the state planning organisation.[16] Crucially it has the authority to resolve major disputes over competing claims for resources, and thus wields a decisive impact on how broad political guidelines are transformed into procurement or development programmes. Others believe the MIC to have a strictly operational role, co-ordinating at a more technical level the supply of products and equipment to and from the different branches.[17]

Nominally the Ministry of Defence, within broad doctrinal guidelines determined by the Party, initiates and approves proposals for weapons procurement in response to force requirements and performance criteria worked out by military officers.[18] In fact, as in the USA though to a different degree, procurement is influenced by what is technologically and economically feasible, and at an early stage in research or procurement military representatives co-ordinate with the scientific and economic communities. In addition to Five-Year Plans for military development which coincide with those for economic expansion, there are one-year operational and longer term plans.[19] A special section at GOSPLAN is responsible for co-ordinating military industrial demands with the nation's economic capabilities,[20] and in conjunction with the Ministry of Defence and the General Staff, plan defence production and reconcile inconsistent demands which are finally transmitted to the production ministries in the form of concrete proposals. Within ministries planning committees co-ordinate at a more technical level production of military equipment and complete a highly formalised institutional command structure. As in the USA, the control mechanism itself influences military–economic outcomes in the sense that a different structure would produce different outcomes.[21]

In the USSR, as elsewhere, there are no objective criteria to determine how much is enough. Allocative decisions are essentially judgemental and therefore political. There is some advantage in consistency and benefit therefore to those societies such as the USSR where all allocations are essentially political over democratic states where the public and private sectors coexist in some uneasy symbiosis, each responding to different constraints and inducements. The Party which, through the Politburo, retains ultimate political control and regularly decides on major allocative decisions sustains and is sustained by an ideology which eliminates the separation of the military and civilian spheres.[22] In principle, therefore, the civilian–military trade-off is no different to any other which the Politburo is obliged to make. It is accustomed, indeed required, to systematically and regularly assess in the broadest terms the benefits and costs of alternative allocations.[23] Given also that the rationale of central planning is in broad terms to move the economy in preferred directions, the trade-offs between military and civilian objectives are in principle clearly articulated. In deciding at the macro level how much to allocate to defence at the expense of civilian expenditures foregone, the Politburo must assess costs and benefits of alternative allocations and is forced to make explicit choices, in contrast to democratic societies where legislation is often piecemeal, responsive to different public and private pressures and where no unified view of means and ends exists. The Soviet system offers an internally consistent structure of scrutiny and control within a perspective which provokes intense preoccupation with the security of the state. The Politburo, with professional advice and assistance, has historically accumulated a degree of expertise in military affairs, often of a quite technical nature, which in general far surpasses that which obtains in democratic societies.[24] It has the incentive and the skills to make effective choices between and within competing sectors, capable of distinguishing the valid claims of the military from the spurious, the essential from the peripheral.

The Soviet system is also efficient in that the collective leadership is not responsive to the often fickle demands of a democratic electorate. Soviet political leaders are accustomed to plan and to direct the economy in pre-determined directions, rejecting the arbitrary outcome of markets for long term objectives. Multi-year funding which commits resources to specified programmes at an early stage[25] and which are therefore secure, stabilises military budgets and therefore weapons development and procurement programmes, and not the least impressive characteristic of Soviet military expenditures has been the long steady expansion over a period of more than 20 years, in contrast to the greater variance in the USA. Although direct comparisons between the two countries are only partially relevant, the short term variance in American military expenditure and the failure to stabilise long-term planning objectives is estimated to increase costs by up to 20 per cent.[26] High variance leads to programme stretch-outs, failure to invest in the capital stock, cutbacks in inventories, and if the down phase is sufficiently deep and protracted, to shedding skilled and unskilled labour and the break-up of specialist research teams. Continuity has allowed the Soviet Union to avoid some of these costs. As old weapons systems are phased out, new ones are phased in,[27] guaranteeing continuity, the efficient utilisation of resources, and successful conclusion of long term programmes of which the expansion of the navy to a blue water capability is one impressive example. Indeed, despite systemic microeconomic inefficiency, the capacity to mobilise resources for large clearly articulated development programmes, where marginalist calculations are not crucial, is one of the superior characteristics of central planning, which applies to the defence as much to the civilian economy. The Soviet Union has always responded to large scale challenges to its security and has surprised the West by the speed and skill with which it overcomes problems and constraints.[28] It may even be the case that if it is forced to respond to an American SDI challenge, the likelihood of a successful conclusion may exceed that in the USA,[29] where funding will have to be sustained over three administrations, which historically has been difficult. Long term central planning also allows surge capacity to be invested in plant which facilitates rapid expansion of production in the event of an increase in tension, to meet export orders or to replace allied weapons destroyed in war. Since the 1930s Soviet military plants have also produced civilian outputs to usefully employ buffer capacity, which currently amount to 15 per cent or so of capacity. The military contribution to civilian industry has been and remains substantial.[30]

Despite the technical rewards, long production horizons are not wholly advantageous in that decision-making may easily degenerate to little more than routinised and marginal adjustments to achieved levels, which inhibit flexibility and innovative responses to new opportunities and constraints. Furthermore, although the overlapping phasing of expanding and declining procurement cycles maintains full employment of resources, it also institutionalises the follow-on more systematically than in the USA,[31] inhibiting the redistribution of resources from less to more productive plant or branches. In the absence of commercial inducements to change, the new is necessarily discriminated against.

Efficient central planning requires decision-makers to be fully informed about all possibilities and about the consequences of their decisions. Prices convert the array of real and performance characteristics of goods and services into a single measure. Despite well-known imperfections of monopolies and externalities, prices in market economies are in the main sufficiently responsive to competitive forces to broadly reflect real social and technical opportunity costs. This is not the case in the USSR where prices other than wages are by and large accounting devices. They are not used to determine and guide, and therefore contain little economic information. Surrogate prices used in command economies distort and destroy economic information such that, however consistent and comprehensive the decision-making structure, Soviet leaders are only approximately cognisant of economic rationality.[32] Although major macro choices, especially those embodying a large investment component or rapid technical progress, are only marginally influenced by the lack of a proper price mechanism, objectives can be achieved more or less efficiently. It is at the operational level that inappropriate measures lead to misallocation of resources. The arbitrariness and costliness of the Soviet command structure is of great and growing concern to Soviet politicians and planners disturbed by the failure to devise systematic choice mechanisms and by the burgeoning cost of research, development and procurement.[33]

One requirement for an efficient price mechanism, even if for accounting purposes only, is that similar goods be equally priced in all sectors of the economy.[34] Not even this minimum requirement is met in the Soviet Union, where prices are deliberately discriminatory. Defence goods are systematically subsidised and their true cost to society undervalued to the degree that central planners may be quite unaware of the degree of compensation necessary to calculate true trade-offs. The subsidy extends across the entire array of military goods and services. Commodities which have dual use capacity such as trucks tend to be cheaper for the military customer.[35] Overhead costs, which can account for up to 45 per cent of total costs in dual capacity plants, are systematically charged to the civilian departments.[36] Military producers do not pay full opportunity costs for factors of production, especially those in short supply, and the policy of equalising salaries and wages to meet social objectives of equity reduces wage differentials, which do not reflect skill differentiations. Since military research and development is perhaps the major employer of specialist engineering and scientific skills, and military production capital intensive, the true cost to society is considerably undervalued.[37] Finally, conscription reduces the real cost of labour to the armed services.

Despite its deep collective penetration of military affairs, the Politburo has neither the time nor the detailed expertise to determine more than broad macro allocations or major weapons decisions. In spite of a support system of advisory bodies, military affairs have until very recently been monopolised by professional military officers. Not only does this differ to the USA, where the Secretary of Defense is a civilian, and where other civilians both inside and outside the Department of Defense have critical inputs into the decision process, it is also contrary to the norm in the USSR itself. Although the role and importance of the General Staff does not remain unchanged, its special status is guaranteed by a political decision to centralise the key military functions in the army command, and not create a complementary/competitive civilian institutional structure for military affairs.[38] This is unique in the otherwise bifurcated Soviet system, where the Party exercises control partly by means of a cadre of specialists parallel to the professional experts. The Ministry of Defence is headed by a military man and the administrative structure is manned by military personnel. The political leadership has created and is thus dependent upon a monopoly producer of professional expertise, which the military jealously guards on the grounds that it alone is competent to deal with military matters. Controlling access to specialist information, especially as it relates to issues which are intrinsically complex, is a major capability by which bureaucrats sustain status and power. Although military doctrine remains the domain of the Party, military science has until very recently been the exclusive concern of the General Staff and the military academies. By its very nature, doctrine is seldom other than broadly articulated, capable of diverse interpretation and implementation. Policy, unless the Politburo directly intervenes, is effectively the domain of the military. The army controls the collection and dissemination of military information and also the process of weapons acquisitions. It determines the quantity and type of weapons to be deployed, which in a race so dominated by technology, gives it effective control over broadly based policy formally located elsewhere. The relationship between the General Staff and the Party has historically not remained unchanged, but even in the period of greatest conflict with Stalin and Khruschev, the military monopoly was not undermined. This has recently been eroded to a degree by the emergence of civilian experts who have been involved in the arms control process, are not financed by the ministries and who are by and large less committed to exclusively military solutions.[39]

Given the technological complexity of modern warfare, and the keen desire of the Soviet leadership to improve the weapons selection process, the role of the professional is almost inevitably enhanced.

Although Gorbachev has for good reasons involved himself force-fully in military allocations, there is no evidence of concern to restructure the basic framework, and to reduce the role of the professional military in matters of military science.

Even so favoured a sector as the military requires bureaucratic allies who are similarly motivated to maximise the defence budget. These are the conservative ideologues and the defence industrialists whose motivation is economic.[40] In the relatively open USA it was just such a coalition that gave the powerful domestic dynamic for military expansion. In the bureaucratic Soviet structure alliances of separate constituencies are equally necessary, and where effective, powerful. Formally the military and industry are linked through such organisations as the MIC, but a more organic cohesion grows from their mutual interest in higher defence spending at the expense of other social and economic claimants. The formal structure whereby, within Party guidelines, the military identifies the major require-ments for military equipment which are sequentially transmitted to the industrial ministries, is in reality more complex because of the internal dynamism of technological change. The industrial ministries, design labs and R and D shops in fact delimit what is feasible[41] and the coalition of interests are more mutually supportive than the formal structure might seem to indicate. The close working liaison between the industrialists and the military officers has melded to create an interdependent identity of interests in which industrialists may be quite as influential as the professional military.[42] The milita-ry–industrial complex through a shared identity of interest in maxi-mising defence expenditure exists in the USSR as in the USA, but in view of the different organisational interests its essential relationship differs. Instead of being a special interest group outside the formal structure bringing pressure to bear on the legislative process, the Soviet complex is an integral organic component of the command structure itself. According to Soviet theory, the bureaucracy unites the civilian political and the military function such that the distinction between economics and politics has been largely eliminated[43] and the defence industry is not motivated by and dependent on capitalist profitability. This is not however to infer a totally cohesive single actor.[44] Unlike the USA there is no interchange of personnel be-tween the two sectors and the career structure of the military is quite distinct. The military prefer to buy cheap, high quality, the indus-trialists to produce expensive, low quality equipment. They are also likely to differ over the degree and pace of technological progress, and latterly over the pace and direction of economic reform. Nevertheless the identity of interest clearly and substantially transcends the divisive issues.

The traditional acute concern with the security of the state has been translated into special organisations which cement the unique role of the military–industrial complex. The lack of parallel civilian supervision has been decisive, and until the very recent reforms in the machine tools agro-industrial and energy branches, the Military Industrial Commission was the only command organisation which cut across ministerial boundaries.

The complex had high, though not exceptional, levels of representation on important state and Party bodies[45] but the real source of its extraordinary claim on the nation's resources has been the unique empathy with which the political leadership until very recently identified with its activities and objectives.[46] The Party, anxious to foreclose a Bonapartist reaction to the revolution, has always been careful to hold the military in check even to the degree that when, as in the case of Marshal Greschko, a military officer assembles exceptional political authority in his own right, he is removed from office. The Politburo exercises ideological control through a system of political commissions under the main political administration, and there is no sense as in the West of the military being an adjunct to the civilian community.

The pursuit of power is coterminous in essential detail with that of civilian welfare; indeed some Western analysts discern a preference for the military.[47] The political power buys off the military by giving it priority status and, by Western standards, an extraordinary ratio of the nation's resources. Despite periodic disagreements, which historically the military usually win, it has not struggled against the system of civilian control for it is its most lavish beneficiary. The logic of the Soviet system resides not so much in the special institutional priority of the military–industrial complex, but rather the extreme difficulty of those institutions or sectors which oppose it.[48] Priority is not a function of structure, but structure makes it easy to manifest political preference and is to that degree efficient. The complex's influence is not absolute, however, for within the five-year cycle the defence ratio varies, increasing in the middle few years and falling at the beginning and the conclusion of the plan. The pattern exists, it is argued, because planners must be seen to meet consumer targets in the high visibility early and later periods, and only when these pressures abate in the middle period can the military–industrial representatives push for higher than average allocations.[49] Such a pattern explains only marginal variations about an average level of expenditure and not, far more important, the level itself.

The slowdown in the growth of military expenditures since 1976 is a more potent example of incomplete power. In 1983 the CIA revised downward its estimate of Soviet defence growth from 1976 onward from its original figure of four per cent p.a. to two per cent, due almost entirely to a virtually static trend in real procurement.[50] The Pentagon, which argues that the CIA overstates the degree of slow-down, explains the essentially temporary adjustment which it accepts did occur as an inability to embody new technologies into new weapons. Procurement programmes in consequence had to be stretched out, and the slowdown did not indicate a fundamental change in policy.[51] It is a fact however that the cutback in growth coincided with a dramatic worsening of almost all the economic indices from around 1976 or so onward[52] and increasingly public concern by Soviet leaders about the weight of burden.[53] Although there is no direct proof there is a strong presumption that the slowdown was as much a matter of decision as of constraint.[54] The Brezhnev style of consensus government was to share economic misery rather than provoke a serious political clash, and the defence sector had to bear its share of the cost of adjustment to lower economic potential, in contrast to previous periods when economic problems did not lead directly to substantial reductions in the growth of military procurement. The military–industrial sector could no longer isolate itself from the constraints of the civilian economy.

Allocated resources must be utilised efficiently within and by the microeconomic agents to maximise their military economic impact. Technical efficiency has two characteristics: *(a)* outputs are maxi-mised for given inputs or inputs to produce given outputs are mini-mised; *(b)* consumer preferences are met.

In addition to not paying the full costs of factors of production and resource inputs, plants which produce wholly or mainly military equipment receive priority treatment from the Soviet planners. So-viet enterprises are classified according to how much of their output is distributed to military end use. Those enterprises which produce exclusively or mainly for defence are included in the first planning round and are guaranteed first claim on resources.[55] Those which produce wholly or mainly for the civilian sector are relegated to the status of residual claimants, where quality is lower and supply uncertain. If despite the priority status, supply of a specific input for the first echelon of plants is short of requirement, that for the bottom category may be diverted to make up the shortfall. More informally the most efficient managers, the most skilled workers, the most modern equipment or the highest quality materials are allocated first to defence producers. In a constrained economy where, other than low quality goods, demand always exceeds supply, mechanisms to make manifest the leadership's priority is in terms of that priority efficient, though always at the expense of higher costs elsewhere, and with due consideration to whether that priority could be otherwise and better achieved.

The ministerial system organises the flow of information and command vertically, inhibiting lateral movement which is the essence of market systems. Ministries are reluctant to lose resources to others, especially if they are in short supply and there is no immediate prospect of compensatory gain. In a supply constrained economy, even in high priority sectors, resource inputs are sometimes in short supply, may be late in arriving or may fall below acceptable quality. To ensure supply is adequate in terms of quantity and appropriate in terms of quality and timing, ministries create in-house facilities which make them less dependent on uncertain centrally allocated supplies. Although for the enterprises branches' and ministries' supply is more dependable, in-house production reduces the benefits of scale and specialisation. A recent survey showed that in the aircraft industry, GOSNAB, the central supply organisation distributed only one-third of the items needed, the other two-thirds being produced within the branch ministry.[56]

Managers of enterprises in the defence sector respond to the same incentive structures as those in the civilian economy. They meet most expeditiously those norms which pay the highest bonus if fulfilled. One recent investigation identified over 20 centrally-set plan goals,[57] and norms and managers are induced to trade-off one against the other such as to maximise their and their workers' rewards. Despite many attempts at reform the most important norm remains gross output. Enterprises are therefore induced to maximise production at the expense of qualitative criteria, to behave in short as output maximisers.[58] For security goods which have high priority this inducement may not have been unwelcome to the political planners. Soviet enterprises are prone to X-inefficiency however because of the sequential nature of central planning. Bonus is tied to fulfilment and overfulfilment of plan norms. Managers are induced to conceal from planners the true capacity of their plants in the expectation of being given norms easily reached. To the degree managers are successful resources are underutilised. However plan overfulfilment also leads to higher norms which are more difficult to meet in succeeding rounds. Current success may be brought at the expense of lower rewards in the future and managers and planners are faced with a temporal problem of maximising over time. Decision rules can be theoretically devised to maximise output or whatever is the preferred parameter over time,[59] but in a bilateral bargain between the managers and the planners, both with incomplete information, one of whom at least is motivated to concealment, the outcome is unlikely to be efficient.

The degree of X-inefficiency is probably a positive function of discretionary power and enterprise autonomy.[60] In this respect the defence enterprises differ from those in the civilian economy, in being more highly monitored. Deadlines are tighter and quality controls stricter. The Politburo is more actively involved in military affairs and a system of military inspectors, whose allegiance is to the service rather than the ministry guarantees that more information is revealed to higher authorities, supply inputs arrive on time, and quality control is high. Production norms are fulfilled and X-inefficiency, though not eliminated, is less virulent than in the civilian enterprises. It is also the case that defence plants more completely respond to their consumer's demands than is typically the case for civilian enterprises. This is partly due to better management and materials but most importantly to the countervailing presence, in the form of the Ministry of Defence, of a powerful, knowledgeable and discriminating customer.[61]

In a supply constrained economy in which enterprise norms are predicated on the assumption that planners inputs will be delivered, customers are reluctant to reject deliveries which fall short of their requirements. Inferior inputs may be adapted, used for something else, stored against a future shortage or even bartered for preferred inputs through the Tolchaki system. Suppliers know that whatever they produce will be accepted by their customers, and since producing high quality goods is more costly and troublesome, there is little incentive to meet customer satisfaction. Hence the generally low quality of Soviet equipment. The military customer cannot be party to such a nexus however. Unlike equipment produced for a largely autarchic, domestic market the quantity and quality of weapons must match those available to a dynamic, competitive rival, and ultimate fear of attack gives a high degree of leverage to a tough and demanding customer.[62] Doctrine, strategy and tactics are interrelated with and therefore depend in some degree on there being an appropriate quantity and quality of weapons. The military customer cannot afford to be casual about accepting equipment of a quality lower than specified, and rejects that which does not meet its requirements.[63]

Because of the leadership's intense preoccupation with security it has the leverage to discriminate between what is acceptable and what is not, and through the system of military inspectors the means to monitor and ensure high quality control. In contrast to the civilian sector the defence industry produces equipment of high quality, highly responsive to customer demands.[64]

Even in the Soviet Union where defence has been so favoured, resources are not unlimited. The conflicting pressures of a dynamic competitor and a smaller, less productive economy, limit the degree to which the armed forces gold plates its weapons systems. As a cost conscious sector the Soviet military in contrast to its American counterpart seeks austere outcomes[65] consistent with its preference on other grounds for simple, sturdy weapons. Soviet civilian living standards fall far below those in the USA and these are projected onto military demands. Lacking private profit-seeking corporations which benefit materially from adding to the complexity of new weapons there is no economic inducement to gold plating. Rather quite the reverse. Additional nice-to-have characteristics which do not improve performance almost certainly require more complex production methods, better-quality inputs, greater monitoring, more staff training and are more likely to break down. Since enterprise bonuses are unlikely to increase correspondingly, baroque weapons tend to be resisted by the industrial sector.

The inducement to austerity and economy is illustrated by the Soviet choice of quantity/quality mix. Although it is unlikely to be monocausal, one reason why the Soviet Union tends to produce more units of relatively simple weapons in preference to those requiring expensive R and D with uncertain outcomes, is economy.[66] Given there may be various means of achieving a strategic objective, a preference for quantity over technological complexity offers many advantages to a comparatively low productivity economy. Soviet production runs for roughly equivalent weapons tend to be longer than in the West. Soviet tanks for instance are produced on a scale which has been described as 'inconceivable' in the West.[67] In 1980 for instance the Soviet Union produced 500 new planes compared with 230 for the US. Large scale production generates learning curve economies which in some cases reduce per unit costs by 20 per cent or so.[68] Soviet superiority, to the degree it exists, may be due as much to the tendency towards gold plating in the USA, and its lack in the USSR as to higher spending by the Soviet Union. The weapons style is also consistent with Soviet economic planning, which is most adept at fulfilling simple, quantitative targets, and since the defence sector for all its particular characteristics is embedded in the civilian economy a defence style which departs too far from civilian norms might easily create disfunctional dissonance to the detriment of both.

Given the USA's preference for technological excellence, perhaps the most critical criterion of Soviet military–economic efficiency is the degree to and the manner in which it has matched America's technological challenge, for despite some dramatic achievements, the pace and the direction of military technological progress in the post-war period has been essentially determined by the USA. 'The economy's pace is set not by internal but by international competition spurred by the urge for survival and expansion'.[69] The first problem as always is data, to know how big an effort the Soviet Union has made to meet the American challenge. Official data of expenditure, or the number of scientists who work on military-related R and D, are far too low to account for what is known of the technological output.[70] Western estimates based on inadequate data and uncertain methods vary substantially. The CIA is least confident of its R and D estimates, which, however, suggest during the 1970s a substantial increase in funding to a figure of $30bn.[71] A separate rouble calculation based on official Soviet data estimated expenditure in 1965 to be most likely of the order of 2.5 to 2.9bn. R, equivalent to 29 per cent of total expenditures on R and D, and around eight per cent of total military expenditure. Extrapolation to 1984 on this basis suggests a most probable figure of 8.7 to 9.9bn. R, somewhere between 23 per cent and 39 per cent of total R and D expenditures.[72] Up to 60 per cent of Soviet scientists and engineers may work in the defence sector.[73] There is general agreement that for systemic, environmental and policy reasons the Soviet Union's civilian technological record has been at best modest.[74] Central planning is especially inimical to genuine innovation which in the West is largely entrepreneurial. In terms of military outputs an essentially non-innovative system has historically been obliged to compete with a more dynamic society on terms detemined by the latter.[75]

However great its reluctance to compete in an area in which it is at a comparative disadvantage, the USSR cannot allow the USA to

progress so far ahead that quantitative compensation would be prohibitive or impossible. Given the inferior technological base the
Soviet performance has been highly effective.[76] The average level of
technology embodied in military equipment exceeds that of civilian
goods and more nearly approaches its American counterpart. In a
variety of weapons systems Soviet technology is equal to or even
surpasses that in the USA. Such is the case, for instance, with
electro-magnetic casting to produce aluminium ingots, electro-
impulse de-icing, refining techniques for producing high purity metals
with good ballistic impact properties and the technology for welding
thick titanium plate which is all important for weapons production.[77]

A Pentagon investigation of relative technological levels in deployed military systems shows the USSR equal in 13, ahead in four
and behind in 17.[78] Many American officials have recently expressed
alarm at what they claim to be an erosion of America's security
position by virtue of the USSR's superior performance in the
1970's.[79] The Soviet lead where it occurs is however often due to the
USA choosing not to compete, rather than being unable to do so, and
after the increase in military R and D spending under President
Reagan the relative position of the two countries has in all likelihood
been restored. The USSR lags by four to six years in micropro-
cessors, between four and five years in mini-computers, seven to
eight years in mainframe and five to ten years in software, and in the
20 technological areas identified by the Pentagon as being militarily
the most important the USSR is equal in five and ahead in none.[80]

The Soviet military R and D system differs from the USA in that
the research institutions are by and large part of the formal ministerial planning structure. Some basic scientific research is undertaken
by the Academy of Science, and the Ministry of Defence operates its
own facilities for research with a more specifically operational or
military application. Most R and D of military significance is done in
specialised organisations linked to specific services and financed
through non-repayable grants. For those weapons where traditionally
the pace of technological progress is evolutionary, such as tanks and
conventional army equipment, the R and D establishments are
tightly controlled by the production enterprises, but in the more
innovative aircraft and missile sectors the R and D shops have more
autonomy, are freer to experiment and take risks without incurring
economic costs. Even so the degree of latitude is limited, for a
characteristic of military R and D is the degree to which it is
responsive to user demand.

Research institutes and design bureaux are vertically organised, military demands being transmitted downwards to be transformed into prototype weapons. Although doctrine cannot be independent of the technological environment, to a degree exceptional by Western standards technological progress is determined by doctrine, and hence by military demands.[81] In the 1930s Soviet officers rejected a strategy based on small, mobile, technologically advanced weapons, and eventual victory in the Second World War sustained and justified the military preference for cheap, relatively simple and abundant weapons. Although some weapons designers have been brilliantly innovative and have reaped high economic reward and social status, the procedures by which military scientific demands are converted into prototype weapons enhance the tendency to conservatism. In keeping with planning norms technological innovation occurs in response to exogenously determined developmental milestones and schedules. R and D organisations are rewarded by how effectively they meet pre-determined guide posts,[82] and planners are induced to set norms which are easily monitored, measured and rewarded. These by their very nature are quantitative, and truly innovative changes more responsive to entrepreneurial skills tend to be abjured. This is at least consistent with the Soviet preference for evolutionary change based on known engineering precepts.

The economic component also prefers conservative change. Weapons manufacturers have no incentive to innovate, for new products and processes often require retraining, during which productivity is reduced, and new suppliers have to be arranged, with no guarantee of a corresponding increase in economic reward. One Soviet report estimates that in the machine tool industry which is heavily orientated to military production, a plant which introduces new products will fall behind for three or four years.[83] Managers seek soft plans preferring to produce weapons to existing designs and engineering parameters where production problems have been ironed out. There is in short a powerful endogenous drive for conservative evolutionary change.[84]

The conservative weapons style is by many criteria efficient. It reduces opportunities for gold plating. American experience, which may not however be entirely appropriate, shows that the probability of technological failure, of cost overruns and time delays is directly related to the level of complexity of new weapons system. Incremental change, often using common components, allows for longer production runs and economies of scale. It increases the profitability of exports because marginal costs are low, plants can re-tool quickly, and Soviet weapons have a reputation for sturdiness and reliability which serves the Soviet Union well in those countries which do not seek the most advanced and hence expensive weapons. Technological followership facilitates borrowing from the leader (the USA) which reduces the costs of progress, a perfectly rational process for a less developed country. Although the USA tries to prevent the export of militarily useful technology, there are legal and illegal loopholes in the embargo system which enables the Soviet Union to economise on time and resources. American experience also shows that complex weapons tend to break down more frequently, take longer to repair and in general have lower sortie rates. Simpler weapons moreover are compatible with the low training and education levels of Soviet soldiers, sailors and airmen. Although the relationship between the Party and the military and between doctrine and technology is complex and multi-directional, the Soviet style has the overriding virtue of being controllable and directed by the political authority. The Politburo screens out the 'mad momentum' which characterises American military technological progress.

The virtues of the Soviet style are however the very causes of its drawbacks. As a technological follower, the Soviet Union is forced to race on increasingly disadvantageous American terms. Despite a preference for conservative evolution it must respond to American initiatives and occasionally quickly ingest a large amount of new technology. Changing a technological style is expensive[85] and although the Soviet Union has historically always matched American challenges the cost of so doing cannot be known, but is probably high. One explanation for the slowdown in procurement after 1976 was the difficulty of embodying complex technology into the new generation of weapons.[86] As American finance for R and D and military technological progress increases and Soviet economic constraints become more binding the quantity–quality trade-off becomes increasingly costly. The hierarchical structure inhibits innovative technical progress, by blocking horizontal flows of information, knowledge and ideas. It is also conducive to a more insidious inhibition to technological progress, secrecy.[87] Progress which depends on innovative assemblage of apparently unrelated technologies and which cuts across scientific and administrative boundaries, is increasingly replacing the conceptually simpler linear mode. There is always the temptation to take successful design beyond the stage of effectiveness, which it is argued is true of the T-62 tank[88] whose lineage extends back to the Second World War.

The major critique of the Soviet model is that because there are so few endogenous incentives to innovate, genuine, new-in-principle progress is too often dependent on the initiative of the political centre.[89] National styles impose choices and opportunity costs on political and military leaders. Technological dynamism in the USA has as its counterpart 'mad momentum'. Political control in the USSR has as its counterpart technological conservatism. If the Soviet style is deliberate it may be an entirely rational response to national objectives and abilities. It may however not be exclusively one of choice but may partly be a consequence of failure to sustain a more dynamic response to American competition, in which case its rationality is less beneficial.[90] The distinction between choice and compulsion is never wholly stark and elements of dynamism and conservatism coexist in the Soviet Union as elsewhere. The rationality of the existing model can be variously interpreted depending for instance on the time horizon. Given the relatively low inducement to innovate in the civilian sector, a weapons style which does not require innovative progress is in the short run rational. In the longer run however the inhibition of innovation constrains choice, and leaders are obliged to accept the consequence whether they choose them or not.

Military and political leaders are deeply concerned at the increasing burden of meeting the American military technological challenge.[91] The Soviet defence quotient is increasingly irksome, given the slowdown in Soviet growth and productivity since 1978, the modest recovery therefrom, and the intensity of competing claimants. The extensive model traditionally applicable to military as well as to civilian production is increasingly unresponsive, inefficient and costly. The process is too dependent on exogenous political will liable to arbitrariness, and in view of the irrational price system there are no parameters to guide decision-makers in quantifying the costs and benefits of alternative choices. Soviet leaders acknowledge the need to endogenise the choice mechanism and to economise on the resources necessary to attain their objectives. Within the armed forces the debate between modernisers and conservatives[92] over military–economic reconstruction must influence the degree to which, and the cost at which, the USSR will be able to sustain the arms race into the next decade. More significant for the pace of the arms race is the degree to which Mr Gorbachev and the civilian leadership can impose their military civilian preferences upon – what must be assumed – are reluctant reformers.

4 The NATO Alliance

In 1949 the bilateral arms race between the USA and USSR was internationalised when the USA agreed with Canada, Belgium, France, Luxembourg, the Netherlands, the United Kingdom, Denmark, Iceland, Italy, Norway and Portugal, that an armed attack on one or more of them in Europe or North America would be considered an attack against them all. Subsequently Greece, Turkey and West Germany have joined the North Atlantic Treaty Organisation and France withdrawn. In 1955 the Eastern bloc followed suit, with the creation of the Warsaw Pact. Despite the different, enduring problems which have beset the two alliances since their formation, both, in contrast to most alliances which historically tend to disintegrate once the initial conflicts which gave rise to their creation have disappeared,[1] have remained an instrumental part of the arms race. Systemic conflict between capitalism and socialism and great power hostility between the USA and the USSR have transcended the historical reluctance of countries to tie themselves to a semipermanent alliance, in the case of the USA, to that very part of the world against which Washington and subsequent leaders have railed.

Although the NATO alliance grew from a European initiative which reflected a regional concern with the problem of West Germany once the USA was induced to throw over its traditional hostility to entangling alliances, NATO was rapidly Americanised, and took on the preoccupations and became an instrument of American foreign policy.[2]

Given the basic requirement of an overriding common interest, alliance cohesion requires the greatest possible realisation of the principles of equal risks, equal burdens and equal security,[3] in economic terms an appropriate balance of efficiency and equity. An alliance provides collective security more economically, but at the same time induces nations to cheat at the expense of others. Defence is perhaps the quintessential non-excludable, non-rival collective good, where one nation's security can be extended to another without diminishing the amount available to the first.

In Figure 4.1 each country produces civilian and defence goods. Production of one good increases as that of the other goods falls, but at a decreasing rate. Given a social welfare function CD, efficiency requires, in the absence of alliance, country 1 to produce OY_1 of

Figure 4.1   Economic benefit of alliance

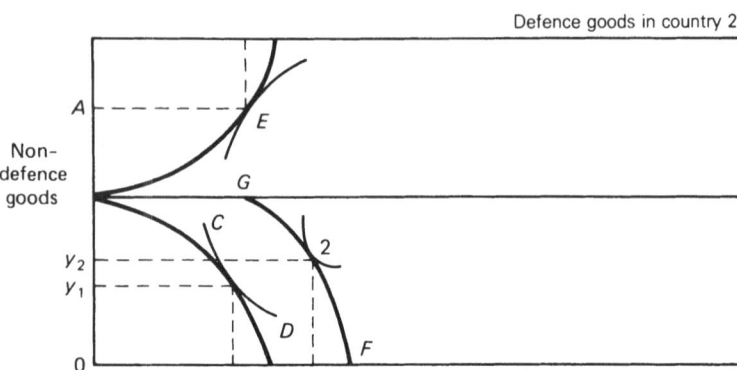

civilian goods and OX_1 defence goods. If the country allies with another to provide defence collectively, spill-in of AE, the amount of defence provided separately by the other member(s) of the alliance shifts the production possibility curve to GF. Given certain reasonable assumptions about normal goods, an optimal position for the country might be at 2, where:

(*i*) total security has increased from OX_1 to OX_2 and
(*ii*) the country has more resources to spend on purely civilian goods, OY_2 instead of OY_1.

If the alliance also increases trade in weapons, additional benefits of international specialisation and of scale will add to the economic gains of alliance.[4] If some benefits are excludable, the collective gains will be correspondingly reduced. In summary form, alliances offer two types of benefits, deterrence, which is a public good – in that deterrence for one is deterrence for all – and protection during a conflict which need not be a public good, that is, one area may be defended at the expense of the other, in which case they compete for the alliance's resources.[5]

Despite the economy of collective security, alliances are limited in number and usually short-lived.

For countries which do not share a common perception of the existence, or the intensity of threat, the potential economic benefits, however large, do not compensate for the costs of giving up some sovereignty, of perhaps being drawn into an otherwise avoidable conflict by a more aggressive or ideologically committed ally. A dominant country may prevent or hinder choice of trading partners as the USA does for export of weapons or sensitive technology to the USSR or to third countries.

For an alliance as a club, optimal membership depends on the relative contribution made by the marginal member against the demands it makes on the collective output, for each new member 'thins' the degree of protection in the event of conflict.[6] In 1949 the UK opposed expanding membership of NATO[7], and the Benelux states the admission of Greece and Turkey in the 1950s,[8] on this ground. As the size of the organisation increases, so also do transactions costs.

Figure 4.1 illustrates one of the confounding issues of voluntary alliance, that of equity between members. Each country is induced to offer the club less than its spill-in benefits in not endogenising the external benefit of its own expenditure for its allies. Because military need cannot be objectively measured, there is a tendency, especially powerful in small states, to free ride by understating the benefits which they claim to derive from the collective alliance, and thus the contribution which they offer in compensation. This either puts an unfair burden on those larger countries which bear the brunt of collective defence, or reduces the level of collective provision below that perceived to be absolutely necessary. The history of NATO is replete with conflict between the hegemonic power and its smaller allies over what the USA regards as their unwillingness to bear their proper share of the total burden. Countries seldom free ride to the degree rationalised by the model, partly because of political solidarity, partly to induce the hegemonic power not to withdraw and partly to draw private benefits. In NATO, the UK has post-imperial obligations and interests, while Greece and Turkey share a deep and abiding antipathy as well as a more immediate conflict over Cyprus which increases their defence spending beyond their 'fair' share. Many European countries finance a defence capability for industrial and technological rather than security benefits, and under some circumstances expenditures are signalling devices. An increase in defence expenditures in one country may indicate its perception of a worsening international relationship and induce other allies to increase and not decrease their own expenditures.

Stylistic economic models assume that members of an alliance are motivated by considerations of microeconomic efficiency and a rational calculation of costs and benefits. In reality, in Europe, no less than in the USA and the USSR, defence spending is as much a function of bureaucratic, political and economic interests which show scant regard for the niceties of economic theory. Theory also fails to identify the enduring conflict over the distribution of economic benefits, such as employment, technological progress or improved balance of payments, a source of continuing and debilitating dissension in NATO. To a considerable degree the economic history of the NATO alliance has been the imperfect accommodation of the conflicting demands of efficiency and equity.

Military affairs, it is argued, are too traumatic to be encapsulated by stylistic theory. Peacetime alliances need a particular sets of circumstances, an exogenous shock and a hegemonic leader before countries willingly forgo sovereignty.[9] It is also beneficial if the burden of membership is clearly identifiable, and however crudely, measurable. Ideological or great power confrontation between USA and the Soviet Union was therefore a necessary but not sufficient condition for the formation of NATO at the end of the 1940s. What the West understood as Soviet expansion was acutely threatening by virtue of the economic and social decay in much of Western Europe and by a perhaps simplistic recollection of economic deprivation and international tension in the 1930s. Economic stability and military security were perceived as complementary goals, the one a prerequisite for the other,[10] part of the single overarching objective of containing Soviet expansionism in Western Europe, and the creation of a unified Atlantic community.[11] Initially the economic instrument, in the shape of the Marshall Plan which facilitated the transfer of the extraordinary sum of $11 and a half bn. to Western Europe for economic and social reconstruction, took priority.[12] America also agreed to a system of regional discrimination against its exports.[13]

By 1950 the period of economic over military priority had passed, hastened by the Korean war. American economic assistance to Europe ceased and trade and payments discrimination were gradually reduced until they were formally phased out in 1958.

Military aid, however, remained an essential feature of the alliance during the 1950s for the very obvious reason that the Europeans were incapable of producing the stock of weapons required to fulfil emerging NATO strategy. With the exception of the UK, most of the mainland European economies had been destroyed to varying degrees by the war, and the UK with substantial though declining commitments to the Commonwealth, diverted some of its military resources to the European theatre. Shortage could only be met by imports from the USA, and to a lesser extent from Canada. In the

USA the Initial Defense Act of 1949 and the Mutual Security Act of 1950 authorised the President to transfer surplus American equipment to the Europeans, and between 1949 and 1962 the US government sold $16.1bn. and gave away $30bn. worth of arms to Europe.[14] American aid took the form of cheap or interest free loans or gifts, for example, the transfer of 70 B-29 bombers to the UK, which though not the most modern of their type were yet superior to any available domestically to the RAF.[15] By 1958 over 50 per cent of European heavy defence equipment was of American or Canadian origin, and to a degree not again realised and due more to necessity than choice, the alliance achieved the collective goals of standardisation.[16] As the European economies recovered, spectacularly in some instances, the justification for continuing aid or subsidy became less compelling. Ironically the defence industries in the larger European countries, based largely on cheaply obtained American licenses, especially in high-tech products, and protected by tariffs and special procurement arrangements, led the economic recovery. Throughout the 1950s European economic improvement coincided with a worsening American balance of payments, aggravated by the deficit on the service account consequent on the expense of supporting approximately 20 000 servicemen and women and their families in Europe. The apparently invincible dollar which had occasioned so much anguish to western Chancellors weakened and eventually required support. The European partners could not justify continued American military aid on the traditional pattern, and in 1961 President Kennedy put the transfer of armaments between the USA and Europe on a commercial footing. Henceforth European countries had to pay for American arms and equipment. Even so, American armaments were so technologically and economically dominant that despite heavy protection of European defence industries, by the end of the decade the imbalance of trade was on average over 10 : 1,[17] the USA selling $86bn. of military equipment to Europe and importing $700m. in return.

Despite an overriding common threat, NATO remained an alliance of sovereign states unwilling to forgo their sovereignty. It effectively took the form of a series of bilateral arrangements in which countries sought to maximise private gain to the degree that the obligations of membership allowed.[18] It was not organised such as to allocate military–economic tasks between nations, which though more efficient, would have diminished European control over what they regarded as high politics. There also exists in the USA an enduring and in some periods compelling view that American involvement in the entangling alliance should be temporary and limited. Too structured an organisation might on the one hand tie the USA too permanently into the alliance, and on the other make the Europeans too dependent on an ally whose ultimate interest could differ from their own.

Inevitably America's strategic vision, by virtue of its economic and military power, dominated: a vision to which the European states voluntary conformed to a greater or lesser degree. They have often been reluctant to support American foreign policy outside Europe, and, despite American objection, more eager to trade with the Soviet bloc. Domestically they have sustained or rebuilt, as appropriate, autonomous military production and R and D capabilities. After the Lisbon conference in 1952 identified force levels higher than those which the alliance was collectively prepared to supply, the domestic parameters took on a more compelling saliency especially for the larger economies. For France the primacy of national goals could only be sustained by withdrawal from the alliance, but de Gaulle was only expressing in more extreme fashion a view widely accepted by all Europeans.[19] For France, the UK, and later West Germany, and to a smaller degree other European states, independence in high politics was more feasible with a secure domestic military–economic base. Despite a common adversary the European nations, by virtue of different geography, history, size, and technological and economic development, could not sufficiently agree on the nature and intensity of the threat to subsume national aspirations for a collective programme of procurement and development. In the final analysis countries which joined voluntarily could leave voluntarily, and members required some domestic guarantee against being made vulnerable by the withdrawal of one or more key countries.

There was in addition a purely economic rationale for military–economic nationalism. Although economists have failed to uncover a monocausal explanation, there was a general perception that economic prosperity is positively related to the level and pace of technological progress. Europeans argued that the USA's economic superiority is positively related to the amount of resources it allocates for R and D.[20] High-tech industries were usually prerequisites for weapons and defence equipment, and by what in retrospect can be seen to be simplistic reasoning, military R and D came to be widely perceived as a stimulant to technological progress in the civilian economy. Historically defence had contributed to technological progress[21] and casual empiricism demonstrated the civilian spin-offs from radar, jet engines, electronics, etc. A domestic capability might also eventually improve the balance of payments by reducing imports from the USA and economising on what initially was a small reserve of dollars. After the defence industries in France, Germany and the UK grew to be sizeable employers, industrial and employment considerations gave a further powerful rationale for indigenous production.[22] Thus states insisted, as far as their local economies allowed, on some defence capacity related to national strategies, which inevitably reduced the consensus on common tactics, training programmes and weapons stock. Each country insisted on its separate operational role, and there was little strategic impulse to industrial specialisation.[23] Mutual military dependence was not matched by an acceptance of its industrial logic of collectivising and therefore economising on the resources which guaranteed security. By 1974, NATO had 22 types of fighter aircraft, seven battle tanks, nine armoured personnel carriers, 22 anti-tank weapons, 35 normal fire control mechanisms and 20 different calibres of small arms ammunitions.[24]

National programmes had a cumulative impact on the level of international specialisation. The larger the inventory of indigenous weapons, the greater the practical difficulty of restocking and integrating compatible weapons from non-national sources, and the greater the domestic economic dislocation of a programme to internationalise NATO procurement. National procurement cycles responded to a domestic rhythm of obsolescence and renewal, often difficult to co-ordinate with the temporally quite different cycles of other countries.[25]

Tariffs, up to 30 per cent,[26] and preferential procurement arrangements which protected European firms against American competition, offered *a priori* evidence of substantial gain from free trade. Protection was not exclusively European, however. Highly subsidised research and development supplemented by the Buy American Act, which required the Department of Defense to buy American weapons unless foreign equivalents – which exactly matched American requirements – were 50 per cent cheaper, also reduced two-way international trade. Protection alone could not guarantee commercial viability to European firms which were by and large too small to exploit the economies of scale available to large and growing defence markets, and in a number of countries governments subsidised mergers of otherwise uncompetitive domestic firms.[27] Economic nationalism gave priority to individual, at the expense of collective, benefits. National weapons stocks reduce international inter-operability and increase costs, that is, are both militarily and economically inefficient.[28] For civilian goods, free trade provided a powerful stimulus to the exceptionally fruitful export-led growth which characterised many of the European countries.

Evidence on technological capabilities is scant, but some European firms, by avoiding the high overhead costs typical of their giant American counterparts, which in defence production can account for 40 per cent of the total, can produce some weapons systems cheaply and efficiently, and at low levels of production compete effectively with American firms. In the UK, the Plowden Report estimated that to produce just 100 units of a high-tech weapon, American costs could exceed an exact British equivalent by five to 15 per cent.[29] American learning curves (the fall in unit labour cost of production for each doubling of output) were far steeper, however, and since production runs were on average three times as great, the eventual American cost per unit could be lower than the British equivalent by around ten to 20 per cent.[30] American firms, geared to large scale production, were more able to exploit economies of scale, and to undercut European competition. Schematically the analysis may be illustrated in Figure 4.2. A typical production run might be 300 to 500 in the UK, for example, the Harrier, and 2000 in the USA, such as the F-16.[31]

If Britain were to buy 300 units domestically, price would be C_1 compared with C_2 if she bought 300 units on top of the 2000 that the USA produces for its own services. The level of output at which the two curves intersect depends on the initial cost difference and the relative steepness of the two learning curves. If the UK cost curve exceeded the American at 300 units, the benefit to the UK from free trade would be even greater.

Authoritative investigations suggest that free trade in NATO might reduce costs by 20 to 30 per cent, given the large differentials which are observed in the national price of defence goods or civilian equivalents.[32] The potential gains from trade are especially large, in that because of protection, the range of manufactured equipment is similar in most countries which increases the benefits of a customs union.[33] Under free trade, economic forces would in all probability lead the USA to concentrate on weapons which were research intensive and/or produced in large numbers and where economies of scale were abundant, and the Europeans concentrate on the pro-

Figure 4.2 Economies of scale in defence procurement

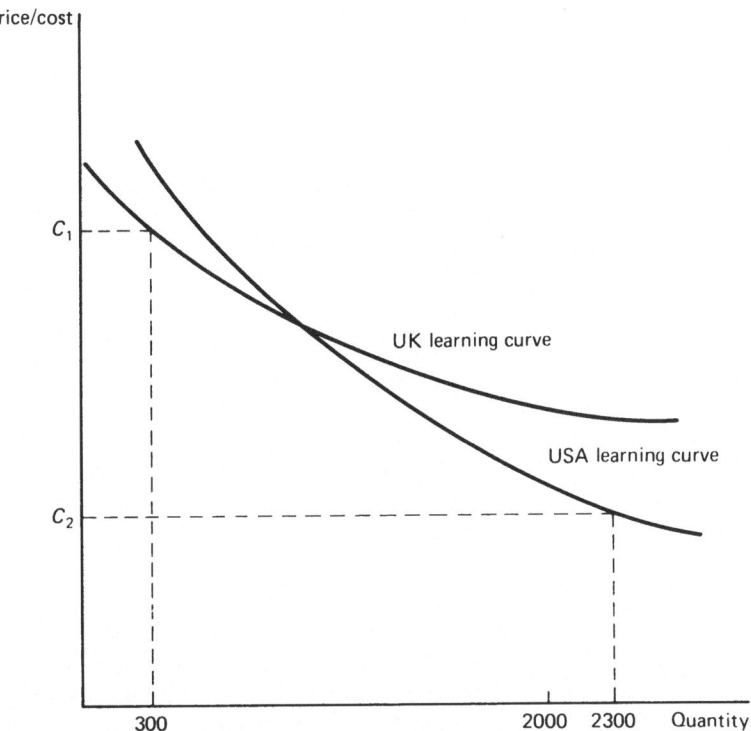

duction of weapons where scale and initial research costs were less dominant. To those European countries which had only small defence industries, the logic of free trade, buying off-the-shelf, was even more compelling. Despite the economic and, because of cheaper equipment, military benefits, free trade as a coherent alliance strategy was rejected, imposing, according to one calculation undertaken in the mid-1970s, an additional collective burden of $10 bn. p.a., and a reduction in military efficiency because of lack of inter-operability of up to 35 per cent.[34]

The rejection of the cost effective model by the Europeans was partly strategic and partly economic.[35] Buying off-the-shelf meant accepting into the domestic inventory a weapon whose operating parameters were already developed, and which might be less than optimally calibrated with the stock in being. Free trade would eliminate inefficient firms, but international competition would keep in check the monopoly power of those remaining, though dependence on a single monopolist or small group of oligopolists might leave some countries dangerously exposed to economic blackmail.

Theoretical musings on hypothetical market outcomes were of little concern compared with the fears of Europeans that in the real world the industrial division of labour would militarily and economically benefit American, at the expense of the European, firms. Investigations of OECD countries suggests that American firms have the greatest comparative advantage over their European rivals in high technology products, many of which are closely associated either directly or indirectly with military equipment, in particular aerospace, where American firms account for the great majority of the world civilian aerospace market. Free trade therefore could be predicted to result in an American dominance of high-tech weapons, with Europeans being relegated to the position of industrial helots.[36] The one example of relatively free trade in weapons, that between Canada and the USA, a consequence of the USA–Canada Defence Equalisation Act, produced just such an outcome. Although trade between the two countries is in rough balance, Canada exports by and large standardised and generally low-technology parts and components to the USA.[37]

R and D is widely believed to be an important input to economic expansion, interruption to which could create a gap not easily made up. For the larger European nations, military technology was deliberately nurtured as a mechanism for increasing civilian productivity via technological spill-ins,[38] and governments which were concerned to optimise allocations between economic sectors and different time horizons were willing to compensate loss in specific sectors for overall economic gain.

America's R and D expenditure exceeds by up to three times the amount spent collectively by the European nations, even after adjusting to a specifically appropriate rate of exchange. Fifty per cent of American federal-funded R and D is allocated to defence, a ratio approached only by the absolutely far smaller expenditures for the UK and France.[39] Furthermore, since up to 90 per cent is allocated for product development, American firms are well placed and highly motivated to incorporate new technologies into modern weapons. The European companies operate at lower levels, with longer research cycles which inhibit competitiveness, but for the larger, and even some smaller, European countries which have, or seek, a high-tech capability, the global gains from free trade are less important than their distribution. Defence equipment, in short, is and was perceived to be different. Giving up technological capacity, either voluntarily or through market readjustments, would relegate Europe to even greater dependence on the USA. Periodic disputes raised the ever present, though usually dormant, issue of American commitment to Western Europe. Should the USA withdraw from Europe, due perhaps to a retreat to traditional isolationism or accommodation with the USSR, Europe, without the technological resources to defend itself, would be doubly prone to blackmail. For European countries an autonomous capacity to produce armaments is indispensable to political independence and national security.[40] Thus strategic and overall economic consideration merged to elevate technology into a fetish which a perhaps more rational view would demystify.

Despite the assumed importance of technology to growth and welfare, economists have been unable to explain the causal relationship. Investigations which show an apparently high statistical contribution simplify what is, in fact, a complex relationship, technological progress often being the term used to collect together those explanations which cannot be explicitly modelled. The relationship between technology and economic progress is not unidirectional as some simplistic statements imply. It is not obvious that a high rate of technological progress in one sector necessarily benefits others. Spill-in effects may be difficult to consummate and America's declining productivity growth and international competitiveness has been traced to excessive expenditures on military related R and D.[41] Nor is it certain that Europeans have an inbuilt comparative disadvantage in all high-technology areas.[42] American superiority stems as much from economies of scale due to the size of the domestic market, and an unfettered market in defence equipment might well benefit more efficient European firms, leading them to concentrate on basic research which could be sold as licences to American firms, which would produce the equipment on a more economical scale. Even in the unlikely event of American disengagement from Europe, American firms would still, in the absence of a wholly unimaginable hostility between Europe and the USA be commercially motivated to export to what remains the largest single military market outside the USA and the USSR. Conventional European defence of economic nationalism usually fails to clarify the specific issues of military production and overall economic prosperity. If indeed it is the case that technology and high R and D expenditures are prerequisites for economic growth, the rational solution is to invest directly in civilian technology which offers the prospect of good return, to which the Japanese growth strategy seems to point, rather than hope for an accidental spill-in from defence R and D.

Whatever the validity of the theoretical arguments, in practice the Europeans refused to contemplate free trade in weapons, influenced by the special pleading of the European equivalent of the military–industrial complex which, as elsewhere, was powerfully entrenched in the political–bureaucratic decision-making structures.

Even though the Europeans had rejected free trade, narrow economic nationalism was costly, and becoming more so. The apparently inexorable increase in costs characteristic of American weapons was also true of Europe. In Britain the TSR$_2$ supersonic bomber was cancelled in 1969 after expenditure tripled, and £159m. spent on this one project. In France the Atlantique naval patrol aircraft was estimated to be up to ten times as expensive as its 1950 precursor, the Alize.[43] Despite the high growth rates achieved by many European countries during the 1950s and 1960s, increasing welfare demands by richer and more demanding European electorates squeezed the resources available for defence, which in Britain forced a fundamental reassessment of its global and regional role.[44] One potential source of economy was international collaboration between roughly equal partners. The benefits could be both economic and military. International collaboration, if it resulted in a higher degree of standardisation, offered the possibility of economies of scale, international specialisation and the elimination of duplicate R and D without loss of independence. Military collaboration increased inter-operability, common stocks of weapons and components and, if sufficiently integrated, a common infrastructure which, given the impact of technology on doctrine, created unified Atlantic as opposed to national military strategies.

The benefits of a standardisation had been understood from the outset, and in 1948 the American Joint Chiefs of Staff identified it as a major alliance objective, though highlighting even then the potential political tensions, for they understood it to mean accommodation to American norms.[45]

In the initial period *de facto* standardisation was imposed on much of the NATO market as a consequence of American military assistance. Even so, standardisation was not complete, especially in the UK whose defence industry, though in disarray, was largely intact. The Americans exported surplus weapons and equipment and through the Military Assistance Program, offered credits and other forms of material support. They also provided licences to embody American technology in the burgeoning European industries. In addition, the Americans sought dynamic process standardisation within the NATO framework, though were usually thwarted by the organisation's unanimity rule. Within NATO the Military Production and Supply Board, and the Defence Finance and Economic Committee were between them initially responsible for the technological and economic aspects of European-wide weapons development. In 1951 the two agencies were replaced by the Defence Production Board, to co-ordinate production on an alliance-wide basis, and the Military Agency for Standardisation, to ease the process of standardisation between the different countries. The practical benefits were meagre, the Atlantique naval patrol aircraft being the only standardised weapons system. In 1954, a further institutional initiative the Defence Production Committee had, like its predecessors, little practical impact, as did subsequent organisational reforms.[46] Such standardisation as was achieved was due mainly to bilateral American assistance to individual countries outside the NATO framework.

American concern for a more integrated weapons stock, of which it expected to be the greatest beneficiary, increased with the worsening balance of payments problems, and the shock which the Sputnik launch in 1957 gave its military and scientific communities. Five American systems were standardised through NATO, the M-44 torpedo, the F-104 fighter, and the Hawk, Sidewinder and Bullpup missiles.

Despite the organisational reforms, which included the NATO Basic Military Requirement which lasted from 1959 to 1966, and the Conference of National Armaments Directors, NATO's contribution to alliance standardisation remained peripheral, limited very largely to the exchange of information – useful, but not crucial. NATO was an alliance of voluntary members and the central organisation had little influence on whether or to what degree countries should co-operate in a collective venture. It failed to establish the supranational operational research staff, budget or decision-making procurement agency essential for a co-ordinated institutional approach.[47] Countries concerned to protect and to establish an indigenous capability were not prepared to concede their bargaining power in a formal process which might pre-determine the distribution of costs and/or benefits of weapons standardisation, but preferred to operate outside the formal framework on a one-off basis with countries of similar technological styles which allowed them a degree of control.

Bilateral or trilateral agreements increased the potentiality and the range of feasible projects. Weapons systems which European countries could not research, develop or produce individually and therefore, in the absence of collaboration might not be deployed, if collectively funded increased the total stock of alliance-wide weapons. Although they or their equivalent might be available off-the-shelf, given European reluctance to become too dependent on the USA, collaboration offered a potentially greater diversity of weapons. The potential benefits to the participating countries were two-fold; sharing the increasingly expensive R and D costs, and exploiting economies of scale by producing for two or three rather than one market. Although the gains per project were probably less than buying off-the-shelf, collaborative programmes had, for the European nations, the supreme advantage of preserving, even expanding, their technological base. Collaboration was especially desirable in systems where development costs as a ratio of total programme cost, or the risk of failure, were high, and was therefore especially prominent in aerospace, missiles, for example. In joint projects the collaborating country participated from the beginning, could influence the configuration of the weapon's parameters, and therefore the outcome to its own preference. They increased the likelihood of a controlled transfer of technology between countries of similar technological capabilities which did, however, require each to make available to the collective effort its own, perhaps unique, skills. The German defence industry, in particular, expanded a great deal on the basis of collaborative projects, which account for 60 per cent of its procurement, and increased its competitiveness compared with France and the UK, which initially had a technological lead. Collaboration widened the benefits of scale, not only by increasing the size of the total market, but also through increased specialisation. In the MRCA Tornado, UK companies manufacture the nose and rear fuselage, German companies the centre fuselage, and Italian companies the wings.[48]

During the 1950s and the 1960s, internationalisation was still suspiciously regarded, and the numbers of collaborative projects, were small. In the 1970s the pace quickened, and by the late 1970s, in addition to the German ratio, 20 per cent of the British budget was spent on collaborative programmes, though more than half involved American firms. Many successfully put into NATO service advanced weapons which European countries alone probably could not have sustained. One analysis of three important collaborative efforts undertaken during the 1960s – the Atlantique naval patrol aircraft, the Hawk missile system and F-104 Starfighter – concluded that international collaboration projects could be successfully managed and brought to fruition.[49] Although the problem of counterfactual assumptions is always present, it was argued that production time and quality of product equalled equivalent national programmes and, above all, produced weapons which no one country, other than the USA, could have produced alone, thereby increasing the degree of commonality. Although NATO did not play a leading role in initiating or seeing the collaborative programmes through to their conclusions, its organisation did help.

Despite modest success, the costs of bilateral or trilateral collaboration became increasingly prominent. Successful collaboration requires agreement between two or more countries on sharing the total budget, between two or more services about the weapon's operating parameters, and between two or more defence contractors about industrial costs and profitability.

One presumed benefit of international collaboration over buying off-the-shelf is that a country can influence the configuration of performance parameters of the new weapon to match its existing inventory. Because of different histories, members of the alliance have different strategic requirements, so that a country concerned to develop a new weapon must not only find a country wishing to manufacture a new system with the same broad strategic function, but also one which is prepared to compromise over detail. A further constraint on agreement is that the two or more potential partners must also be prepared to phase in the new system at much the same time. Finding partners who meet all the requirements is time-consuming, consultations alone sometimes lasting two to three years. Since it is unlikely that each partner's requirements exactly match, either the finished product is a compromise which in military terms is less than optimal for either country, or one country concedes to a stronger bargainer, which is even less desirable to the weak bargainer. Alternatively, the weapons will have to meet both sets of requirements which, even if possible, is expensive and often militarily unsatisfactory. The final outcome may be as much due to bargaining power, the number of units which one country is prepared to buy, or the relative intensity with which the two countries claim to need the new weapons, as military, technological or cost considerations. In the MRCA Tornado programme Britain had to make major concessions over the plane's role and performance characteristics to induce agreement with the Germans. From the British point of view, the multi-role aircraft was too complicated and its role overlapped with the Jaguar aircraft already in being.[50] If services refuse to compromise, the weapons must incorporate multiple characteristics, which makes it more complex, often not compatible with existing technology and sometimes eventually cancelled. This latter was the outcome of the attempt to produce an American–German tank. The project, which began in 1963, finally collapsed in 1969, after joint expenditure of over $400m., due eventually to a failure to agree on compromise requirements for the respective armies,[51] and in 1987, Britain, West Germany and Italy finally agreed to cancel a 14-year collaborative project to produce a self-propelled howitzer.[52]

The economic inhibitions to joint collaboration have been as daunting as the military. High and increasing costs of new technology have kept down the number of major new programmes being developed or produced. Collaborative weapons as a consequence of extra complexity took longer to complete and were usually more expensive. Because the number of new contracts was small, each one was economically significant, and each country sought to negotiate as large a share as possible of the final contract for its own defence contractors. One method of avoiding potential conflict was, as in the case of the Anglo–French Martell missile, to allocate production in proportion to the amount of money each country was prepared to buy.[53] Nationalist economic consideration usually precluded the creation of a prime contractor which would be financially responsible for the viability of the entire project, and thus strongly induced to impose tight management control on national sub-contractors. In the absence of a single overall contractor, management is dissipated, especially at the second and lower tiers of contractors and subcontractors, where arrangements depart – often considerably – from those consistent with economic efficiency. Orders might be awarded to the domestic firm or consortium with leaner order books rather than the one most likely to bring the project to fruition most economically.

Because there has never been a central body party to all agreements, collaborative projects have by their very nature been one-off ventures. There exists no mechanism for centralising costs and benefits to gather and disseminate acquired knowledge to the wider community. In particular, there has been no clearing mechanism to transfer costs and benefits over more than one project. Each joint development has been self-contained,[54] having to be calculated anew. For each country, the cost of each project had to be compatible with benefits. There was no guarantee that the partners to one project would agree to collaborate on another, or if they did agree, the balance of costs and benefits might be so distorted by the passage of time as to be incalculable. Collaborative ventures also increased the problems of exporting to third countries, in that the major exporters often pursued policies which inhibited sovereign action. Although national negotiating teams learn by doing, much information is inevitably dissipated and has to be learnt anew. Sometimes a one-off venture does lead to more permanent arrangements, for instance Britain's decision to buy the MILAN system from the Euromissile Group led to the British contractor, British Aerospace, joining its French and German counterparts to create the European Multi-lateral Defence Group, but such organic development tends to be exceptional.

Experience of collaborative projects showed that attained economies of scale were almost always less than theoretically possible, for even if weapons were produced to a common design, they were often modified at the production stage to meet indigenous norms, which required re-jigging and smaller runs than were technically feasible. This was the case, for instance, with the Jaguar aircraft, where British requirements differed from the French. Thus, despite savings to individual companies and countries, there was, by the end of the 1960s, growing appreciation that for the alliance as a whole collaboration was costly and time-consuming, both increasing more than proportionately as the number of collaborators increased. Bilateral projects, it is argued, take 40 per cent more time to complete and are 25 per cent more expensive. Trilateral projects take 70 per cent longer and cost 40 per cent more.[55]

For smaller European countries, where collaboration was less often feasible in view of their limited facilities, buying off-the-shelf was more acceptable. Where, for various reasons, they rejected free trade, a preferred alternative was to produce under licence a weapon developed by another country. Licensed production offered a compromise to those countries which could not finance a large R and D programme but sought to retain some production capacity. In reality, licensed co-production was usually a one-way trade, European firms manufacturing equipment designed in the USA. The terms of agreement varied, but as an example, the European consortium of countries buying the F-16 plane produced on the basis of (*i*) Ten per cent of the initial US order = 65; (*ii*) 40 per cent of own order = 139; (*iii*) 15 per cent of sales to other countries, an arrangement which in practical terms allows the European manufacturers to produce 80 per cent of their total purchasing requirement of 279 aircraft. Licensed production was not costless, however, for manufacturing costs are almost always higher in the licensee country, and spreading production between the participating countries reduces the gains from trade, from specialisation and scale. The additional costs can be substantial, for the F-16 up 20 per cent to 25 per cent higher than buying off-the-shelf from the American producer.[56] Furthermore, for the licensee, exports to third countries are likely to be proscribed or controlled for either commercial or political reasons.

Although intellectual awareness that collaborative programmes were expensive grew, pressures for a more integrated international market in NATO mounted throughout the late 1960s and 1970s, though for different reasons, on either side of the Atlantic. From the European countries the motivation was mainly though not exclusively economic. In the face of mounting costs and constrained budgets, especially after the mid-1970s, all countries faced, though to different degrees, the same fundamental choices: a reduced security posture reflected in a smaller number of or cheaper weapons programmes; more buying off-the-shelf, usually high-tech weapons or equipment from the USA, or increased collaboration. Despite higher global costs and time delays, the advantage to each country individually was such that, in principle at least, most countries chose the latter option.

In 1968, long term economic trends combined with a series of political events to induce the European countries to take formal steps towards institutionalising international collaboration. American involvement in South-East Asia coincided with a politically insistent demand that the Europeans bear a greater share of the collective burden, most graphically highlighted in the first of a series of amendments by Senator Mansfield to reduce American troops in Europe.[57] The Soviet invasion of Czechoslovakia increased political tension and also highlighted the growing importance of conventional, and costly, weapons, especially in light of increasing strategic parity between the two superpowers. The Europeans felt obliged to look more to their own salvation. Budgets could not, politically, be increased, and in 1968 a group of ten nations (not including France) formed the Eurogroup, to co-ordinate and standardise wherever possible defence procurement, as well as providing a forum for European affairs, which eventually might become sufficiently cohesive to argue a distinctly European view in bilateral negotiations with the USA. As well as creating a series of subgroups, the group in 1972 issued what has since been described as 'revolutionary' Principles of Equipment Collaboration, whereby for the first time members formally agreed to decrease defence barriers to European weapons collaboration, to exchange information on future needs and on the timing of procurement, and to co-operate on logistical support.[58] The arrangement did result in some successful ventures, such as the FH-70 and the SP-70 howitzer. The fundamental and continuing European refusal to accept the hard logic of cost cutting standardisation is highlighted in Eurogroup's first review, which refers to the need to explore methods of defence co-operation and to carry out equitably and at least cost the increasing demands of defence provision, objectives which were in practice likely to be incompatible. Even though the Eurogroup assisted in the organisation of some bilateral agreements with the USA, in particular the purchase of the F-16 fighter planes for the air forces of Belgium, Netherlands, Denmark and Norway, it polarised the conflicting Atlantic interests in collaboration and standardisation. Despite a more secure European technological base, the import–export ratio between Europe and the USA had not fundamentally changed. In the period 1965–74, the ratio for the UK was 3.1: 1, for West Germany, 21.0: 1, and for France 2.8: 1, and for single bilateral deals individual European firms were almost inevitably overwhelmed by their larger, more aggressive American competitors. American firms, on the other hand, despite protestations to the contrary, were concerned at being excluded from competing more effectively in European markets by what they argued were unfair protection and procurement practices. European–American relations worsened, reaching a nadir in style as much as substance, in Kissinger's abrasive and condescending Year of Europe speech in 1973. President Carter insisted in his 1973 State of the World speech that Europe should more positively redress the American balance of payments problem which in many European eyes was due mainly to America's reluctance to trim its domestic and hegemonic objectives and which, moreover, increased inflationary pressures around the world to the detriment of all. American frustration with what many Congressmen saw as European reluctance to share the burden equitably finally bore fruit in the Jackson Amendment to decrease American forces in Europe by the same proportion that Europeans failed to offset the costs of paying for American troops. The administration, to head off a more serious revolt, accepted the Amendment. 1973 was also the year of the Nixon–Brezhnev accords which inaugurated an era of greater American–Soviet accommodation which not only excluded Europe from the negotiations, but in European eyes raised the ever-present possibility of the marginalisation of Europe in American policy. It was in addition the beginning of a period of serious discord between the USA and Europe over the appropriate response to the oil embargo when, according to some Americans, Europe deserted the USA,[59] and was the proximate cause of the Jackson Amendment.

Europeanisation was taken a stage further in 1975 when at a special meeting in November, members agreed to explore further the potential for widening co-operation in European armaments collaboration in an independent forum open to all European members of the alliance. At this time a European Defence Procurement Secretariat was established. Formalised European co-operation within an exclusively NATO framework was inevitably limited, for France – one of the major European powers – was not a member. A European solution without France was clearly partial. It was necessary to establish an organisation which France could join, which had therefore to be outside the formal NATO organisation. In 1976, the European members of NATO and France agreed to the creation of the Independent European Programme Group, which still however reflected irreducible nationalist tendencies in that it was organised as a standing conference without a formal secretariat.[60] Its work was concentrated into three main groups; to bring about a greater harmonisation of replacement schedules, to suggest possible areas of co-operation to improve procurement procedures, and to establish criteria to identify problems for improving co-operation in defence procurement.

The essential rationale for the formation of the IEPG was the long held belief in the need for a co-ordinated European response to American scale and technological superiority. European firms simply had to be bigger if they were to successfully compete in the international market place, which they could only do on the basis of European-wide collaboration. Wholly European firms would also be free of American restrictions on arms sales to the Third World.

The Group's activities were not initially successfully, dogged by the ever-present resistance to forego national benefit. It was also cautious of American resentment at being excluded from its most lucrative market and therefore of retaliation, especially the continuing threat of troop reductions.

The American response to European integration was, however, with certain reservations positive, for President Carter and his advisers were also concerned to improve international collaboration, though from a slightly different perspective. Although American firms as always sought to avoid exclusion from the European market and Congress to reduce the American burden, governments by and large, confident of the industrial dominance of American corporations, had traditionally been less concerned with the industrial and macroeconomics of alliance procurement. They were more concerned that the alliance be able to contain the Soviet threat and therefore with the military consequences of national economic policies. General Goodpaster argued that lack of standardisation reduced NATO military effectiveness by up to 30 per cent and that consequently its military posture was inconsistent with its policy.[61] Although NATO spends more on defence than the Warsaw Pact, it buys less security,[62] a deficiency due largely to the far lower degree of standardisation and inter-operability among the NATO forces.

A more efficient European defence economy was especially desirable in view of the real decline in the volume of resources allocated to defence in the USA following the conclusion of the Vietnam war. In 1979 defence spending as a ratio of GNP fell to its lowest post-war quotient of five per cent. At the same time, and despite the brief period of East–West detente, expansion and modernisation of Warsaw Pact forces made greater European expenditures on conventional weapons more urgent. After 1974 European and American economic growth declined to an intensity and duration deeper and longer than the normal down phase of the business cycles, and defence budgets became increasingly constrained. Costs, on the other hand, maintained and even accelerated their inexorable rise. The Americans were willing to accept the smaller evil of discrimination as they had in matters of international trade for the greater benefit of more military resources to collective security. Although many, especially in the business community, argued that free trade was optimal, American leaders recognised that, politically, Europe could not accede to a policy which jeopardised their domestic industries. More European standardisation and collaboration was therefore a half-way house, a vital pre-requisite for the Atlantic dimension which they ultimately sought. The Americans were prepared to make concessions to European interests, but within a wider Atlantic framework. In 1975 Public Law 93–365 instructed the Secretary of Defense to develop a list of standardisation actions to improve NATO performance, and in FY 1976–7 the Department of Defense Appropriations Authorisation Act instructed the Secretary of Defense to waive the Buy American Act, perhaps the greatest stumbling block to effective standardisation. In the same year the Nunn–Culver Amendment laid down instructions for greater standardisation, or at least inter-operability, for American troops in Europe.

Economic and military demands mounted as in 1977 President Carter unveiled his concept of a Long Term Defense Program, which sought a commitment by each member to increase spending in real terms by three per cent p.a. for ten years, and a more efficient international market to reduce wasteful duplication. Greater equality in transatlantic trade, it was recognised, was possible only if European firms were more competitive, thereby establishing a more equitable balance. Congress, traditionally more protectionist than the Executive, and concerned lest American forces be required to buy costly, technologically inferior armaments, insisted that European weapons should not be more expensive than their American equivalent and should meet American technical standards, which effectively reduced the likelihood of potential European penetration of the American defence market. Congress preferred a more organic system of licensed production, secure that American firms would keep the technological lead. The concept of a rigid two-way street was modified to a less restrictive view of a family of weapons,[63] whereby both sides agreed to procedures to identify and apportion new weapons systems between them on the basis of comparative advantage in different models. Although highly contrived, the family of weapons had the virtue, to European firms, of keeping a technological presence in Europe. This initiative did at least lead to the AMRAM/ASRAM agreement between the USA and Europe, but even in this single instance the USA eventually failed to commit itself to the European ASRAM.

The American initiative over the two-way street and the family of weapons shifted the focus of debate back to NATO, which established an Armaments Planning Review and a Periodic Armaments Plan to improve the mechanism for alliance-wide co-operation.

The European countries, because of their differing military and technological requirements, responded differently to the American initiatives. Smaller European countries were as apprehensive of being overwhelmed by the larger European powers in a formal

European pact as they were of the USA,[64] and buying off-the-shelf had at least the merit of reducing costs. Norway, for instance, had a long and strong Atlantic orientation and welcomed the American initiatives. The UK, with its claim to a special defence relationship with the USA, and Germany – especially vulnerable to American troop withdrawals – were ambivalent. While recognising the logic of the American initiatives, they were as always concerned with losing domestic capacity. France as usual was most hostile to the American proposals. Before the two-way street concept could be institutional-ised the European position had to be clarified. As the political commitment to more standardisation and collaboration in the weapons economy solidified, the IEPG assumed a wider capacity to speak on behalf of European interests. In 1984 the first full ministerial meeting of the IEPG coincided with a West European Union decision to end armaments restrictions on Germany (other than chemical warfare). The influential Klepsh Report pushed a strongly European line, that because of the disparity between the USA and Europe, NATO was not at that time the most appropriate forum for transatlantic dis-cussions, and that there was real need for a separate European pillar before two-way street agreements could become significant.[65] By 1988 agreement had been reached on five collaborative programmes, as well as a number of important political developments. At the time of writing around 20 collaborative ventures are under active consider-ation. Numerous political and military committees, some under NATO, and thus excluding France, others outside NATO, are in being to investigate and identify problem areas and to recommend how they may be resolved. Most governments have expressed in principle a commitment to greater co-operation to achieve the ben-efits of standardisation and commonality, and for perhaps the first time agreement on specific collaborative projects for reasons of economy are being merged with considerations of and provide a dynamo for overall political and economic integration in Europe. The diversity of weapons currently in operation reflects stocks re-tained from past procurement policies, and is not in itself indicative of current practice, and in any case weapons diversity may be posi-tively beneficial. It can imply competition between manufacturers and hence a tendency towards technical efficiency, though that argu-ment would be more convincing if the weapons had been produced and bought in a free market unencumbered by tariffs and other protective devices. Diversity of weapons also increases costs to the adversary. Despite the inhibitions to collaboration, 60 per cent of West German, and 20 per cent of British procurement, not insubstantial ratios, are collaborative.

However, after 40 years of effort, the results of international collaboration have not been impressive. Even the most prestigious European initiative, the European Fighter Aircraft, has been beset with national problems after a promising beginning in which the four participating countries, Britain, France, Germany and Italy agreed on outline details. In 1985, the project ground to a halt in the face of two conflicting concepts when the French Dassault company put up an alternative to the apparently agreed British, German and Italian version.[66]

In the USA, despite the formal ending to Buy American, little effective progress has been made, and initial enthusiasm in Europe in the wake of the successful Roland missile sale was dashed when, after considerable expenditure on modifying the missile for American services, it was cancelled. The basic imbalance in American–European trade remains, though the ratios for some individual countries vary over time. In the period 1979–83, the French ratio was 36.0: 1, the German ratio 7.9: 1 and the British ratio 3.5: 1.

Despite the public rhetoric and the by now well-known costs of economic nationalism, practical achievements on the twin issues of European collaboration and transatlantic trade have not been impressive, and NATO has been described as a military museum.[67]

NATO has not in general successfully resolved the conflicting demands of military economic efficiency and economic nationalism. Neither has it been able to solve to the satisfaction of all members the issue of equity.

Economic theory predicts that small countries in an alliance are induced to conceal their true preference for the public good and shelter behind the non-excludable umbrella of larger, especially the largest, members. As free riders they contribute not only absolutely but also proportionately less than large states. The alliance leader bears a disproportionate share of the collective burden. Small countries seek to manipulate the balance of costs and benefits, to undervalue the benefit which they claim to obtain from the alliance and therefore reduce the cost they should incur in exchange. Because of real differences between members of the alliance in the evaluation of external threat, it is virtually impossible to distinguish between genuine justifications for low or lower contributions and those contrived in consequence of the non-excludable component of the public good. Europe, due to its geography, ideology and history, traditionally holds a less apocalyptical and confrontationalist view about the nature of the Soviet threat, in which case the benefits it obtains from an alliance may be less, as therefore should be its contribution to collective security. On the other hand war, should it occur, will be fought on the European mainland. The cost of failure is likely to be incalculably higher in Europe and on that basis the European partners should pay a greater share of the collective burden.

From the outset, problems of equity have undermined alliance solidarity, sometimes occasioning much diplomatic and political disagreement, even animosity, but never yet sufficiently dominant to unravel the centrifugal forces which give the alliance its integral cohesion. American support, even when it acknowledged that Europe was unable to unilaterally defend itself, was predicated on the assumption that eventually the Europeans would bear their equitable share of the total burden. That share might initially be small, but the Americans, not unnaturally, sought some recognition that collectively the Europeans accepted their responsibilities to the alliance. As the economic fortunes of the two sides of the Atlantic diverged, American payments deficits and low growth of GNP and productivity being matched by economic recovery, sometimes spectacular in Europe, so to America the disproportionate burden appeared increasingly unjust. Implicitly, however, demands for equity assume a knowledge of what is fair. There is in fact nothing more difficult to assess than the true effort each country makes, or should make, for joint defence.[68] Logically, equity requires the alliance to estimate global expenditures necessary for the desired level of security and to calculate contributions in the ratio that each country benefits. Distribution is not independent of the total level of expenditure. In reality such a logical procedure is not workable. There is firstly no agreement on the degree, the likelihood or the nature of Soviet threat. Although Europeans do exploit differences of history, culture and geography to conceal their true preferences, these genuinely do exist and do influence the assessment of threat and the appropriate response to it. Even if there were broad agreement on the nature of the threat, there need not be on how it is best met. Less ideological members of the alliance might legitimately prefer a more diplomatic accommodating approach to East–West affairs than a military expenditure race. Since national trade-offs between civilian and defence goods are intrinsically political, the rationality implicit in the two-stage process seldom occurs, for even at the macro level the alliance has been unable to allocate the level of resources consistent with its own strategic requirements. There exists an ongoing dissonance between what is required and what is available influenced by failure to agree over an equitable distribution.

Notionally, balance is equitable when it 'approximates burdens that are equal in relation to differences in economic capacity',[69] and also in relation to differences in benefits. In such a formula all costs and benefits should be included. For instance, a country might incur low expenditures either absolutely or relatively, but offers its territory as a base for foreign troops which, for instance, is true of Iceland. Some countries near the front line bear high psychic costs in being more likely to bear the brunt of attack if and when it comes, although by the same token an alliance which deters also provides high benefits. In the collective search for equity and efficacy, it could be argued that countries which are relatively efficient at producing military goods should incur a higher burden, but also enjoy a disproportionate share of the economic and technological benefits which accrue to military producers.

Alliances provide also private benefits which each country internalises and are even more difficult to calculate. They are, for instance, means by which hegemonic states exercise leadership. NATO, it is argued, is an instrument of the *Pax Americana* which encompasses economic as well as military means and ends.[70] Economic prosperity and military security are indivisible, part of the seamless web of capitalist democracy, and as the hegemonic leader the USA derives benefit, and therefore should incur costs.

Intangible benefits and costs by definition are not quantifiable, and by default political disputation between the allies focusses on cruder but more measurable economic criteria. Comparison of military expenditures measured in domestic currencies are influenced, often distorted, by purely financial forces, such as exchange rates. As these vary so do the relative contributions of different countries: those whose currencies are appreciating increase their apparent share of the total burden, and vice versa. Absolute sums are also affected by domestic prices of military inputs, particularly by conscript wages, which seldom equal the market value salary of professional volunteers. According to national defence quotients the USA bears a disproportionate share of the burden and, not unnaturally, is the criterion to which American politicians turn in defence of their view that the USA bears and has borne a disproportionate cost. In 1985, for instance, the USA allocated 6.7 per cent of its GNP to defence, compared with an average of 3.9 per cent for the European members of NATO. Judging one nation's contribution in terms of a reference country – the USA – is flawed, however, in that it is implied that expenditures in the reference country are in some sense correct. If that is not the case the comparison is necessarily invalid. If the reference country spends too much on too little, then the alliance as a whole might spend too much or too little. Nevertheless the defence quotient has the virtue of being easy to understand. Politicians in those countries which benefit from the current arrangements as well as academic analysts argue that national burdens should approximate to differences in economic ability to pay. Economic capacity however need not equate to benefit, and there is no necessity for the two criteria to require the same absolute and relative statistical adjustments to the crude defence/GNP quotient based on per capita income. The apparent disparity between the USA and Europe is further reduced if an additional adjustment is made for that ratio of American spending, mainly strategic and some naval forces, which is not designed for NATO protection, which the Pentagon calculates may account for up to 58 per cent of total USA expenditure.[71] This however raises in stark form the *raison d'etre* of the American force structure and the real nature of the Soviet challenge, in that without NATO the USA might not have built the Central Area Strategic Force to its present level, for massive retaliation derives from its commitment to the European landmass. That commitment may simply reflect a generous American response to threatened and needy allies bound by tradition of friendship and a common culture, in which case American spending on NATO is a luxury which it does not have to incur. If this is the case it is unfair, as well as unwise, to lean so much on an ally which incurs real and in its own view unnecessary leadership costs. NATO, on the other hand, may be a necessary instrument of the hegemonic *Pax Americana*. American leaders argue that as the security of the USA is affected by out of area expenditures, so is that of Europe. They should therefore support American activities in areas vital to Western interests such as the Gulf, which provides a smaller proportion of American energy requirements than many other NATO countries, or Latin America, where the Soviet challenge is more indirect, but where the tardy material response is matched by grudging diplomatic support, and often outright opposition to American initiatives.

Although there is nothing more difficult to assess than the true effort each country makes for joint defence, a series of American Department of Defense reports in the early 1980s concluded that the Europeans were shouldering 'at least' or 'roughly' their fair share of

Table 4.1   Troops and trade

	US troop presence	Defence spending as percentage of GNP	General trade balance (billions)	Military trade balance (millions)
Belgium	3325	3.0%	$ +1.2	$ −40.5
Canada	541	2.2	−23.3	+416.0
Denmark	70	2.2	−1.1	−0.5
France	81	4.1	−3.4	−191.4
Greece	3488	7.1	Parity	+117.1
Italy	15 082	2.7	−6.5	+28.0
Luxembourg	12	1.1	NA	+2.0
Netherlands	3072	3.1	+3.5	+69.1
Norway	223	3.3	−0.2	+159.9
Portugal	1630	3.1	Parity	+206.1
Spain	9136	2.9	−0.3	+150.8
Turkey	4923	4.5	+0.5	+478.9
United Kingdom	29 458	5.2	−4.6	+190.0
West Germany	246 852	3.2	−15.6	+114.5
Total NATO	317 893	3.4	−49.8	+1700.6
United States	1 677 787	6.9	NA	NA

Source: 'Sharing NATO's Burden', *National Journal*, vol. 14, May 1987, p. 395.

the collective burden.[72] In the final analysis, judgements on equity are political. While Europeans must always be attentive to external parameters, they cannot plan to increase expenditures, even if formally required, if this were to create domestic dislocation.[73]

Definitional and statistical niceties carry little weight with the American public and its Congressional representatives. In the late 1980s Congressional pressure to redress the imbalance is again mounting,[74] fuelled by the overall trading imbalance between Europe and America, despite a positive trade surplus in the latter's favour (see Table 4.1).

Transatlantic friction is nothing new. Hitherto, the centrifugal demands of overriding common security have bound together the disparate parts of the alliance. Current disagreements between the USA and Western Europe are different in terms of scale and complexity and threaten to undermine the fragile collectivity of Atlantic relations. NATO, it is argued, is in the grip of a systemic crisis of the Western economic and political order.[75]

5 The Warsaw Pact

The Warsaw Pact, the Eastern bloc counterpart to NATO, was formed in 1955, not so much as a military response to that organisation, which after all had been in existence since 1949, but to the incorporation of West Germany into the Western alliance system.[1] It was from the beginning as much political as military in conception[2] though its ultimate rationale necessarily influenced the structural relationship between the members.

The first problem in assessing Warsaw Pact military economics is, as with the Soviet Union, that of inadequate data. According to some experts, the dimensions of the problem are so acute, and the gaps so substantial as to preclude a detailed assessment of the quantitative dimension of the East European burden.[3] East European governments nowhere publish in a form easily accessible in the West definitions of what their published data include. They almost certainly include the direct costs of maintaining military personnel, the cost of equipment and supplies and maintenance of the capital stock. They most probably exclude military R and D, spending on which is hidden away under items of the civilian budget.[4] For most of the nations the exclusion of R and D costs does not seriously distort the global data as research and development activity is small.[5] For others, in particular Poland and Czechoslovakia, its exclusion is more serious (especially in recent years).[6] The data is also distorted by the probably wide, though imprecisely quantified, subsidy of military economic activities.

The divergence in Western estimates is reflected in the data from different sources.

Table 5.1   Defence expenditures in the non–Soviet Warsaw Pact countries (measured in $bn.)

	1975	1980	1985
ACDA	28	31	47
SIPRI		12.6	13.9

Source: Arms Control and Disarmament Agency, World Monetary Expenditures and Arms Transfer, (Washington, DC); SIPRI, *World Armaments and Disarmament* (London: Taylor & Francis).

99

Table 5.2   Military expenditures in local currencies

	1965	70	75	80	82	85
Bulgaria (m. leva)	230	324	848	866	967	1010
Czechoslovakia (m. crowns)	9618	1471	184458	21269	22270	27500
East Germany (m. marks)	3255	5998	7512	9873	113315	13041
Hungary (m. forints)	5757	9484	11811	17700	20200	23300
Poland (m. zlotis)	23552	36174	52293	74118	182903	315000
Romania (m. lei)	4735	7472	9713	10394	10773	12113

Source: T. Alton *et al.* 'East European Defence Expenditures 1965–82', in *East European Economics: Slow Growth in the 1980s, vol. 1, Economic Performance and Priorities*. Selected papers submitted to the Joint Economic Committee, Congress of the United States, Washington DC 1985, pp. 477.

ACDA estimates are based on a methodology similar to that used by the CIA. Independent estimates using the same data source and methodology conclude that expenditures in 1981 amounted to $32bn[7] divided between the various countries as follows:

Poland	$9bn	Romania	$5bn
Czechoslovakia	$6bn	Bulgaria	$4bn
East Germany	$5bn	Hungary	$3bn

The data for selected countries, in local currencies, are shown in Table 5.2.

Because of the index number problem there is a difference, sometimes large, in the estimated defence burden measured in dollars and in local currencies – with the discrepancy usually negatively related to the level of economic development.

Compared with an estimated dollarburden of 15 per cent to 17 per cent for the USSR, the East Europeans spend on average approximately 5.4 per cent of GNP for defence purposes. In local currencies, the crude average is around 3.1 per cent. The discrepancy between the USSR and the East Europeans both absolutely and as a proportion of GNP replicates the NATO pattern whereby the smaller nations free ride under the defence umbrella provided by the hegemonic power.[8] If however the Soviet Union is excluded from the comparison there is no correlation between the size of the remaining members and their defence quotient. The defence burdens of the individual East European countries reflect also their different bilat-

Table 5.3   Defence burden measured in dollars and local currencies 1982 (percentage)

	local currencies	dollars
Bulgaria	3.2	10.1
Czechoslovakia	3.5	5.2
GDR	4.2	5.8
Hungary	2.2	4.5
Poland	4.0	7.0
Romania	1.4	4.6

Source: Alton *et al.*, 'East European Defence Expenditures 1965–82', *East European Economies: Slow Growth in the 1980s, vol. 1, Economic Performance and Priorities*. Selected papers submitted to the Joint Economic Committee, Congress of the United States, Washington DC 1985, pp. 478–479.

eral bargaining power with the USSR,[9] the degree to which they can exploit strengths and weakness to avoid an undue share of the collective burden. The lower defence quotients also reflect lower force modernisation and expenditures on expensive technology and only partial identification with Soviet (and Russian) interests. Whereas the USA pays for 66 per cent of NATO security, the USSR pays for 85 per cent to 90 per cent of Warsaw Pact security.

Burden is greater than just the proportion of the nation's resources which are allocated for collective defence. Nelson identifies two components of burden.[10] The extractive burden is measured by the proportion of GNP allocation for defence purposes, and of the population in national service. The performance burden is measured as the level of arms exports, Pact military exercises on home soil and the number of soldiers on active duty abroad. There is no correlation between the weight of the two dimensions of burden and based on his own quantification Nelson estimates the extractive and performance burdens as shown in Table 5.4.

The Soviet burden far surpasses that of the other countries. A further burden, quite impossible to measure, is the degree to which the economies of the East European states have been distorted, and inefficient outcomes imposed by having to accede to Soviet demands for military economic outputs.[11] The cost is almost certainly large.

Generally speaking military growth in Eastern Europe has matched economic growth, hence the small to modest quotient

Table 5.4   Rank ordering of Warsaw Pact members on extractive and performance burden

	Extractive	*Performance*
USSR	1	1
Bulgaria	2	6
Czechoslovakia	3	4
Poland	4	2
East Germany	5	3
Romania	6.5	7
Hungary	6.5	5

Source: D. Nelson, *Alliance Behaviour in the Warsaw Pact* (Boulder: Westview, 1986) p. 93.

measured in local currencies. The growth rates in general fluctuate much more than is the case for the Soviet Union, reflecting not only indigenous domestic factors, but also pressures or inducements from the USSR when its leaders decide that the Soviet burden is especially onerous. In 1965 when the Soviet Union called for a greater effort from its allies, they responded enthusiastically. When in 1978 in response to NATO's long term modernisation programme it again asked for an additional rate of increase of three per cent p.a. the response was much tardier[12] due it is assumed to the poorer economic performance of most countries in the late 1970s. Paradoxically however growth of military expenditures, with the exception of Romania, has been particularly high in the 1980s despite fragile economies. Even Poland, which for a few years achieved negative economic growth, showed the same high trend in military expenditures. One possible explanation for the paradox might be the high and increasing costs of modernisation, required of the East Europeans by the Soviet Union; for non-personnel expenditures currently account for 42 per cent of the budget compared with 39 per cent in 1968[13] and, despite their small roles, expenditures on the air forces of all countries have increased faster than on the ground forces in recent years.[14]

Although quantitatively the East Europeans contribute less to collective defence than do the European members of NATO, they have been more organically integrated into the Soviet military economic domain.

Unlike the West Europeans who, as voluntary members, are free to leave NATO if they wish, the East Europeans have no such right of egress: and the Pact, reflecting as it does Soviet interests in the main, does not tolerate an indigenously independent defence policy. For the Soviet Union bloc defense is regarded as an extension of internal policy,[15] a key justification for the pre-eminent role of the political leadership and the Party. Preservation of the East European bloc has been one of the basic foundations of Soviet domestic legitimacy.[16] Given the different institutional histories of the various national forces and the always problematic question of reliability, the Soviet Union has made effective use of the overall Pact forces.[17]

Force co-ordination has been matched to a significant degree at the economic level, yielding substantial resource benefit to the Pact. Before the Second World War the Czech and German armaments industries had high reputations in Europe and provided the basis for expansion within the Soviet bloc. The Soviet Union, initially through a system of personal representatives but later more systematically, effectively inhibited the expansion of independent indigenous armaments industries, and national industries were forcibly integrated more or less successfully into the Soviet defence economy. Although a few European countries are modest producers of armaments, and in the case of Czechoslovakia a significant lower echelon exporter, the pattern of arms production has been forced into a complementary and dependent relationship with the Soviet Union. Czechoslovakia, Poland and Romania do manufacture weapons to their own design which are sometimes exported to third countries, usually as appurtenances to larger Soviet deals[18] but the Czech L-29 jet trainer is the only non-Soviet weapon to have been widely adopted by the USSR.[19] In the majority of cases East Europeans produce weapons of Soviet design, or based on Soviet licence. As the Soviet Union phases in new, technologically more advanced weapons systems, licences for older models being phased out are transferred to the appropriate East European producing nation.[20] The Soviet style of evolutionary design and high commonality facilitates the transfer of technology internationally. Such a high degree of standardisation yields substantial economies of scale benefits to Soviet and non-Soviet producers. The Soviet Union tends in any case to produce large quantities of arms to compensate for Western technological superiority. When East European exports and those to third countries are added to the domestic output – for example in the case of tanks – the consequence is production on a scale far in excess of the West. Exports to Eastern Europe lower unit costs by spreading overheads which sometimes amount to 40 per cent of the total over larger production runs. Since production is inevitably to Soviet technical norms, it benefits most from common engineering standards.

Moreover the Soviet Union has imposed a modest degree of specialisation on Pact production. Czechoslovakia and Poland tend to concentrate on the production of tanks, armoured fighting vehicles and aircraft, East Germany on naval vessels and Hungary on transport equipment.[21] The greatest element of specialisation however is the dominant Soviet control of military R and D. Although Czechoslovakia, Poland and Romania in particular undertake some R and D, technological progress is firmly in the control of the Soviet Union which has, when convenient, not hesitated to use for its own benefit such technological skills as the East Europeans have developed. It has for instance directed Hungarian and East German computers, optics, chemicals and robots to Soviet military needs.[22] In this respect it has achieved a high level of international trade and specialisation which Western theorists have long argued would be beneficial to NATO. The Soviet Union is guaranteed large export orders to reduce the costs of expensive R and D, and the East Europeans obtain access to technology relatively cheaply. The Soviet Union can also exploit the civilian spill-in benefits of military technological progress, though the systemic inhibitions to the dissemination of new knowledge, especially that emanating from the military sector, reduces actual benefits below potential.[23] Given inadequate data it is impossible to quantify the benefits of the undoubtedly high degree of standardisation which Soviet practice has imposed on the Warsaw Pact.[24] Investigations of potential NATO benefit conclude that they could be substantial.[25] Qualitative assessments by Western observers suggest that this may well be true of the Warsaw Pact. In terms of manpower, greater standardisation enables the Warsaw Pact to field larger fighting forces with approximately the same number of men in the field. The Warsaw Pact fighting man requires one man in support compared with two for NATO forces. The degree of benefits from greater standardisation has been estimated to be roughly equivalent to the military superiority of Warsaw Pact over NATO forces, and has convinced some that it is winning the resources war.[26]

Nevertheless the level of standardisation is far from optimal, and that which does exist is often inefficiently attained.

Because the East Europeans only imperfectly identify with Soviet interests they resist where possible total assimilation into the Soviet system. Bilateral trade agreements which exclude the Soviet Union give some economic reward to indigenous production, and outside the field of weapons the degree of standardisation has not been especially great,[27] though often this has been due as much to Soviet preference not to press the issue as an inability to do so.[28] The degree of standardisation and the economic benefits derived therefrom have not been larger because of the systemic inefficiencies of the command economies. In economies which – though less rigid than the Soviet Union – have not been stimulated by market competition, especially from foreign firms, the incentive on the one hand and the compulsion on the other to maximise the economic reward of specialisation and standardisation are limited. The degree of standardisation lower than optimal also reflects the lower and often different levels of modern-isation attained by non-Soviet forces.

The greatest source of Pact inefficiency is however Soviet insist-ence in keeping to itself the overwhelming portion of R and D work, and therefore of expenditures. Although the sheer bulk of the Soviet effort necessarily yields comparative advantage, the benefits of special-isation are maximised if brought about by competitive market forces which directs research and other activities to the most productive and efficient sources. Soviet technological pre-eminence in East Europe has been obtained through the negation of competitive forces. Apart from the scale of the research and development effort, the Soviet Union is not, compared with its East European allies, inherently more efficient in the creation and dissemination of new technology. A more equitable sharing of the R and D burden might well yield at the margin greater technological/economic rewards than has hitherto been achieved. For the East Europeans, technological followership keeps them firmly in a position of dependency, ill-organised to exploit for their own civilian economies the benefits of military technological progress. The Soviet Union has acknowledged the inefficiencies of the present arrangements by asking the East Euro-peans to bear a greater share of the burden of military R and D,[29] in conjunction with its requirement that they modernise their armed forces. Its own defence burden is increasing, not only by virtue of the quantitative and qualitative demands made on economic and techno-logical resources, but also because of the higher salience of civilian objectives – industrial modernisation and higher living standards – to Gorbachev and the new Soviet leadership. The cost of competing with the USA has increased because of the secular increase in the costs of military technology, and also because of American policy to direct the arms race into areas where the Soviet Union is at a comparative disadvantage,[30] and where therefore the costs of competition are correspondingly greater. It is also the case that many East Europeans produce goods of higher quality than the Soviet Union and have shown relatively high levels of progress in producing and disseminating advanced technology. To ignore such a source of benefit when costs are increasing is inefficient, and the hard-pressed Soviet leaders are increasingly reluctant to sustain current costly arrangements. While higher levels of modernisation impose on the East Europeans a greater degree of standardisation because of the overwhelming influence of technology,[31] greater variety and Soviet dependence on East Europeans will in compensation yield them more economic freedom.[32]

The high though not optimal level of Pact standardisation could not have been achieved without organisations and a structure of power to incorporate the East European defence economies so firmly into the Soviet orbit.[33] Initially organisation was not important. Until Stalin's death Soviet control was enforced through an informal but ruthlessly effective system of personal representatives in key decision-making bodies. These backed by Soviet military might pushed economic development in directions costly to the East Europeans but beneficial to the USSR. Since in his lifetime priority was given to such a high degree to military objectives, the Eastern European economies were obliged, at a high cost, to subordinate national civilian–economic development to Soviet military–economic demands. After Stalin's death his arbitrary personal rule was replaced by a more systematic relationship through the already existing Council for Mutual Economic Assistance (CMEA) and the newly created Warsaw Pact. Despite its ostensibly civilian objectives of enhancing bloc trade and socialist integration, military co-ordination has always had a fundamental place in CMEA planning. In 1969 the Pact created three organically related organisations to deal with the twin issues of increasing technological progress and standardisation, and of co-ordinating military economic production in each nation's planning structures and procedures. The Military Science and Technology Council (MSTC) plans and co-ordinates military technological research, co-ordinates the activities of the arms industries – for instance which new weapons to introduce and which to retire – and prepares guidelines for the standardisation of arms within the bloc. Since most of the officers on MSTC are members of their respective countries' Defence Councils, it offers a high level link between the Pact and national defence decision-making bodies.

M.S.T.C. decisions are implemented by the Technology Committee (TC), which is directly linked to the national arms production, supply and acquisition establishments. The Technology Committee:

(i) Establishes the timetable for the replacement of old by new armaments;

(ii) resolves conflict with regard to standardisation of military equipment;

(iii) co-ordinates military R and D programmes.

The TC and the MSTC are in turn subordinate to the Warsaw Pact's Military Council (MC), a high level organ of management and control. The MC has its own staff of high ranking Soviet military officers who are attached to each national military command and therefore provide direct links with the national military economic planning bodies.

Military affairs which are the concerns of the Warsaw Pact must be co-ordinated, both internationally and with the civilian planning organs of each member country. The high level body which undertakes such co-ordination is the Military Industrial Commission of the CMEA. The MIC is an economic institution which deals with military economic allocations through its direct links to the principal national economic planning and management institutions. Nevertheless Soviet efforts to integrate military production on a single bloc basis have been only modestly successful.[34]

Because the non-Soviet members cannot voluntarily leave and are forced to accept a degree of standardisation greater than they would probably voluntarily choose, questions of equity which have been problematic in NATO assume different forms in the Warsaw Pact. The Soviet Union compensates for the lack of choice by incurring a higher proportion of the collective budget than is true for the USA in NATO and by economic subsidy.

During Stalin's rule formal organisations were as irrelevant to the conduct of economic as of military relations with the East Europeans. For the USSR autarchy, though not economically efficient, was not prohibitively costly given its large internal market and abundant resources. For the East Europeans however autarchy was illogical and costly, totally at variance with their pre-war histories. The collapse of the German economy which had so dominated Eastern Europe pre-war created a vaccuum into which the Soviet Union quickly moved as the hegemonic power. The East European economies were distorted to the Soviet model of economic and social organisation, their trade directed towards the Soviet Union quite at variance with their history of trading with capitalist Germany. So uneconomic was the resulting pattern of international trade, that according to Western calculation, neither the Soviet Union nor its allies benefitted.[35] As the victor in the Great Patriotic War the Soviet Union exercised its claim to reparation payment from in particular the GDR, but also from the other countries, even its wartime allies. The reparation payments which in the main took the form of material and equipment transfers to the Soviet Union and the creation of joint stock companies in the host nations, amounted to $32bn. between 1945 and 1955 of which $19bn. was extracted from the GDR.[36] This pattern is consistent with a simple theory of economic warfare where powerful countries extract tribute from the weak. In general terms a country's power to exact unequal benefit depends on the absolute and relative contribution of trade to GNP, the pattern of trade and the ease with which alternative markets and sources of supply can be found.[37] According to all these criteria the Soviet Union was well placed to demand tribute. International trade accounted for less than one per cent of GNP at the end of the war, and its exports were largely of hard goods which could easily be sold elsewhere in the international economy. For the East European nations however international trade with Western Europe had traditionally been important in the wealth creating process, but after the war they were forcibly absorbed into the Soviet economic orbit. They became dependent on the Soviet Union for raw materials, interruption to which could seriously jeopardise growth and welfare, and could sell their own low quality exports only to the Soviet Union. For the Soviet Union the military and economic cost of empire was small.[38] Stalin's arbitrariness could not however long survive his death.

Since in totalitarian states individuals have no effective political input, the legitimacy of the regime comes to be determined to an unusual degree by economic success.[39] Although political disturbance is never entirely economic in origin, the arbitrary exclusion of economies from the material benefits of capitalist trade and investment, and the squeeze on personal consumption consequent on the command model, provoked riots and revolution in Poland, the German Democratic Republic and Hungary, and forced upon the Soviet Union a reappraisal of the utility of savage exploitation. After 1955 it reversed the net flow of capital, paying back around $2.6bn. of previously expropriated reparations and cancelling what it claimed was its right to a further $9.2bn. which allowed it to claim a real contribution to the recovery of Eastern Europe of the order of $12bn.

Stalin's personal rule was replaced by international organisations designed to formalise and to make more systematic the Soviet Union's political, economic and military dominance. Soviet insistence that the East European countries restructure their economic systems to replicate the Soviet model suggests that it was prepared to sacrifice secondary economic benefits of empire to military security.[40] The empire, which in the Stalinist era of tribute yielded economic, political and strategic benefits, was in the fluid post-Stalinist period more constrained. Poor economic performance – especially in meeting consumer demands – increasingly forced the Soviet Union to trade-off military for political and economic benefits. Since security dominated, and the Soviet Union was not prepared to compromise on the inefficient, planning mode, it had to make concessions in its international economic relations with the East Europeans. Their very weakness gave them leverage with the Soviet Union,[41] allowing them within systemic limitations to free ride.

In societies constrained by absolute scarcity the price of a single commodity imperfectly captures the net transfer of resources between traders, for a high price for one commodity might be compensated by a low price elsewhere, or a low price by forced purchase of commodities countries do not really want to buy. The irrational price system which prevailed in the command economies made the systematic calculation of costs and benefit of international exchange, and the settlement of net deficits and surpluses almost impossible. Efficient trading and settlement required an acceptable common unit of account, which in the absence of a socialist alternative, was agreed would be the appropriate world price for each commodity. The Bucharest pricing procedure established intra-Comecon settlements on the basis of the world price for the goods in the previous five years. The actual settlement diverged from world price to a greater or smaller degree by purging such capitalist elements as capitalist profit and as a consequence of the relative and specific bargaining power of the countries. Though nominally based on world prices, Comecon practice allowed considerable divergence.

Despite Moscow's apparent superior bargaining power intra-Comecon terms of trade were consistently adverse. On average until the mid-1970s the price of East European manufacturing exports exceeded world price by 20 to 40 per cent, while Soviet exports of energy and raw materials exceeded world prices to 20 per cent,[42] and the Soviet terms of trade are estimated to have deteriorated by around 20 per cent over the period. The Soviet sacrifice was greater than a simple price comparison might indicate for Soviet exports of petroleum and raw materials were of a quality which could be sold for hard currencies and used to buy high quality imports from competitive capitalist countries. Protected and hence low quality East European manufactures could only be sold to the Soviet Union or within the CMEA generally. That is high quality, low priced Soviet hard currency exports were exchanged for low quality, high priced East European soft currency imports.

The Soviet Union was also unable or unwilling to exploit its apparent bargaining power to impose on its allies its vision of the optimal pace and degree of socialist integration. In 1962 Khruschev proposed an ambitious programme of supranational management through a series of co-ordination agreements to integrate economic planning in each country, and in 1966 additional further measures were proposed by the Soviet Union. These were successfully resisted by the East Europeans,[43] as by and large were all Soviet initiatives for deeper integration.

The CMEA was not without economic benefit to the Soviet Union.[44] Eastern Europe was forced into a complementary trade pattern which guaranteed secure markets and sources of supply which served Soviet quantity planning and were not liable to interruption by unpredictable markets or by embargo. Although they resisted formal integration, the East Europeans were prepared to participate in joint investment schemes where these promised eventual payback in the form of energy, power or raw materials. The 'Peace' electricity grid and the 'Friendship' oil pipelines were tangible results of intra-CMEA investment in this period.

Soviet subsidy up to the mid-1970s was not consistent with the predictions of the simple warfare model. Its behaviour in the second half of the decade appears even more paradoxical. Energy reserves are unevenly distributed in Eastern Europe. The Soviet Union has abundant reserves of all energy resources, the GDR and Poland produce and export coal and lignite: but apart from Romania, the Soviet Union is a monopoly producer of oil. Over a period of years the energy deficient countries increased their dependence on Soviet imports, as they as well as the coal producers diversified their energy balance to a greater dependence on oil, which was also a basic input into the chemical industry which many of the industrialising countries had identified as a leading growth industry. As a consequence of bilateral long term agreements between the USSR and the other countries Soviet exports increased throughout the 1960s at an average annual rate of 12 per cent and by 1970 totalled 38m. tons.

So long as oil was cheap and abundant, East European dependence though perhaps strategically undesirable, was economically rational. When however in 1972 the Soviet Union in response to the growing opportunity cost of selling to soft currency markets urged its allies to seek alternative sources they quickly responded. The tenfold increase in the price of oil in 1974 and later in 1979 effectively destroyed Comecon plans for diversification. The Soviet Union could not, without disastrous consequences, relinquish its role as the guarantor of energy to the socialist community. From 1970 to 1979 Soviet exports accounted for 90 per cent of the increase in energy consumption in Bulgaria, the GDR and Hungary, and for 85 per cent in Czechoslovakia. Exports increased at an annual average rate of 7.2 per cent.[45] By the end of the decade exports of energy had increased to around 80m. tons p.a.

The Bucharest pricing principle, which in 1975 tied prices to those prevailing in the world economy in 1966–70, imposed intolerable burdens on the USSR. In 1971–74 it forewent a potential improvement in its terms of trade of 35 per cent,[46] and in 1976, a year ahead of schedule, it not only increased prices but induced the CMEA to accept a new pricing formula. Under the 'Moscow' principle intra-COMECON prices were to be based on a rolling five-year average of world prices, so they would change annually but with a lag. This also was an instance of the Soviet Union failing to press home an apparent advantage for it initially proposed the elimination of any time lag, and then one of only three years.

Nevertheless the Soviet benefit was instantaneous and large. In 1975 its terms of trade improved by 11 per cent and by 1980 a full 40 per cent yielding a gain to the Soviet Union of over $2000m. in four years.[47]

The increase in energy prices was the source not only of the greatest windfall profit for the Soviet Union but also paradoxically its greatest opportunity cost. Even though the terms of trade moved so decisively against the East Europeans they nonetheless benefitted from Moscow's highly accommodating stance. The Moscow principle postponed the crippling price increases for a few years, giving the East Europeans a breathing space to adjust to the new economic circumstances, and the terms of trade deteriorated much slower than if they had to pay world prices. For the USSR however, slower adjustment meant price increases foregone. This implicit sudsidy has been estimated to be of the order of $43bn. Though the terms of trade improved by 40 per cent or so, the USSR forewent another 30 per cent and in 1981 Soviet oil was 70 per cent below the world price.[48]

The Soviet opportunity cost was greater even than this calculation alone indicates, for in selling to East Europeans rather than to world markets it forewent sales of hard currency. It obtained less for its exports and with what it got, bought inferior quality goods. This sacrifice was not the result of economic abundance for Soviet economy performance worsened over the period. The cost of raising oil increased as did the net hard currency debt to the West from $1.6bn. in 1974 to $12.4bn. in 1981.[49] Traditionally CMEA trade was cleared bilaterally but in view of the enormous increase of Soviet surplus with its allies, instead of following conventional practice it allowed them to accumulate large and unredeemed deficits. From a relatively modest figure the Soviet surplus increased in three years to $1.9bn. and by 1983 total East European debt in transferable roubles amounted to almost $30bn.[50]

Estimation of the total subsidy to the East Europeans is controversial, depending on a number of often questionable counterfactual assumption. One estimate suggests that between 1973 and 1980 alone the subsidy might have totalled $60bn.;[51] $26bn. due to paying higher than world prices for East Europeans manufactured goods and $34bn. because it subsidised energy prices. Estimates based on different assumptions increase the figure to $133bn.[52] Whatever the 'correct' figure the scale of the opportunity cost is quite at variance with the exercise of economic compellance.

For the Soviet Union despite an apparently unassailably powerful position the economic costs of the intra CMEA trade and investment far exceed potential economic gain. The Soviet Union, like all other countries, was caught unawares by the magnitude of the OPEC price increase in 1974 and later in 1979, and the net consequence may have been partly the outcome of happenstance.[53] Subsidy may also in part reflect the undoubted economic benefits to the Soviet Union of compatible and secure trade and investment with the socialist commonwealth, though the degree of plan co-ordination which the Soviet Union has occasionally sought to achieve has by and large been weak and ineffectual.[54] The alliance clearly offers non-economic benefits to the Soviet Union of which the military (though not exclusively) were critical.[55] These have been variously described as creating a buffer zone against invasion, preventing complicity in invasion from third countries, forward defence, addition to Soviet military capabilities and a means to funnel support to third countries.[56] Despite these and other benefits it was the very weakness of the East Europeans which enabled them to extract economic concession from the Soviet Union's intense preoccupation with national security.

Russia's lack of natural boundaries and history of invasion have traditionally motivated its leaders to give high and enduring priority to the defence of the homeland and current policy is no departure from norm.[57] The Czars and their advisers sought to enhance the nation's security through the extension of empire and a system or more or less formal alliances, and the Warsaw Pact is a formalisation of what has been described as 'a uniquely organic imperialism'.[58] Soviet theories of capitalist encirclement gave added impetus to the need for external protection. This however can only be achieved within an organisation which accepts the inevitability of Soviet hegemony. Given what Soviet leaders would view as reactionary resistance in Eastern Europe to socialist ideology and practice, old style voluntary alliances were insufficiently secure. Co-operation had to be imposed upon recalcitrant allies. When Stalin was alive accommodating behavior could be ruthlessly imposed by force with little concern for the sensibilities of the allies. They had no effective bargaining power and the economic price which the Soviet Union had to pay in compensation, reward or bribery was small. After Stalin's death however, brute force – though never abjured – was not enough. As the systemic consequences of their forced adherence to the Soviet model became increasingly painful so workers and elites had to be bought off. A price which the Soviet Union had to pay therefore for alliance cohesion was the opportunity cost of trading with the CMEA at inferior terms. Economic subsidies carried by petroleum exports are one of the few effective foreign policy instruments at the Soviet Union's disposal towards its East European allies,[59] and it was the tight integration of economic and military interests and instruments, through common membership of the Warsaw Pact and the CMEA which facilitated the military–economic trade-off. Soviet subsidy to its allies broadly reflects each one's contribution to its security. For various and quite different reasons Poland and the GDR are especially vulnerable to counter-revolutionary tendencies, and it is no accident that these two countries have received the highest subsidy both as a reward and as an inducement to continued support and loyalty.[60] Ironically the drastic fall in energy prices in the 1980s not only reduces Soviet hard currency earnings but also the opportunity cost of alliance. Indeed in a period of falling world prices those prevailing in intra-CMEA trade exceed world prices because of the delayed lag inherent in the Moscow principle. The Eastern Europeans for a brief period may subsidise the Soviet Union, but to the degree they pay in soft currencies and fail to settle their bilateral debts the net resource transfer to the Soviet Union is reduced.

Soviet hegemonic dominance in Eastern Europe is eroding, the military–economic subsidy an indication of weakness not strength.[61] The source of Soviet dominance in Eastern Europe has historically been largely military, but as economic issues in the Soviet Union and between it and its allies become more salient, so do the economic costs of current arrangements in the socialist commonwealth. Although the Soviet Union continues to dominate militarily, it has been obliged to accept a greater degree of economic independence for the East Europeans, more variety in economic organisation, more trade with the capitalist nations,[62] not only to reduce its own burden of subsidy but to induce allies to undertake a greater share of the alliance defence costs, through higher R and D and weapons modernisation. Like NATO the Warsaw Pact is changing from simple hegemonic domination to a more complex and demanding relationship, and some East Europeans have taken advantage of Mr Gorbachev's recent initiatives to reduce their own economic contributions to alliance security.

6 The Defence Burden

In the popular imagination the burden of defence is production and consumption of civilian goods foregone. In a static economy more of one means less of the other; and in the absence of more embracing measures, the defence quotient, the ratio of a nation's resources spent for military purposes, is a conventional and convenient metric of the static burden. In a growing economy the relationship between civilian and military outcomes is less pre-determined, for more of one category of goods need not necessarily reduce the amount of the other and in some societies military based values and institutions or R and D if successfully implanted in an otherwise sluggish civilian economy may even increase economic potential.[1] Military investment – R and D and procurement – does compete directly for the same human and material resources as civilian investment, usually necessary though not sufficient for economic growth and its net effect on economic progress is generally perceived to be detrimental.[2]

Implicit in the concept of burden is the assumption that defence goods yield no welfare benefits[3] or at the very least less than would equivalent expenditure on civilian goods. The validity of the assumption in a world of certainty is vitiated in the anarchic real society of states where security is a valid component of a nation's preference function. Though not exclusively, military burden can be justified in real and monetary terms only to the degree necessary to enjoy the benefits of civilian investment and consumption. It is excessive only if the resources invested exceed what are strictly necessary, due perhaps to a domestic dynamic in which civilian claimants are unfairly disadvantaged.

Military services are similar to others centrally supplied in that there are no objective determinants of how much is enough, but are uniquely different in that more inputs do not necessarily yield more of the final output, security. Even if because of bureaucratic bargaining public spending at the margin on, for instance, education is excessive in the sense of yielding a lower return – be it material or psychic – than elsewhere in society, the excess is unlikely to reduce educational benefits or standards. Military spending however may so provoke an adversarial response, however opaque or delayed, as to reduce rather than enhance security in the initiating country. Because of the security dilemma, defence spending is profoundly and uniquely

115

ambiguous.[4] No country can finance riskless security and political leaders are obliged to choose what, within their bounded rationality, is the optimal trade-off between risk and welfare over different time horizons. Within countries over time as well as between countries the calculation of a hypothetical optimal is not temporally consistent, such that the utility of the defence quotient as an indication of burden varies with the international and the domestic environment. Domestically the intensity of burden depends on whether, for instance, aggregate economic activity is demand- or supply-constrained. If demand-constrained, characterised by un- or underemployment, the burden may be small, if as a consequence of reduced military spending resources released from the production of military equipment find no alternative employment, but merely increase to the pool of unemployment.[5] Indeed there may well be circumstances when military employment and production is positively, though not necessarily optimally, virtuous. The defence quotient also overstates the weight of burden if transferred resources find employment in occupations where productivity and or salaries are lower than those prevailing in the armed forces. The balance of benefit is of course influenced by whether serving personnel are volunteers or conscripts. Furthermore the Keynesian one-commodity macroeconomic model in which economic resources are assumed to be instantly and completely fungible overstates the degree of substitutability in most economies and hence the potential short term economic benefits of reduced military expenditures.[6] Skilled factors of production and specialised equipment are often specific and if released from one job may for a time remain unemployed or be employed in lower productivity employment before being reabsorbed into the active economy at maximum productivity and reward.

The generic concept of burden conceals what is in fact a complex and often interdependent assortment of budgetary, resource and performance costs. The budgetary opportunity cost is civilian public expenditures on, for instance, health or education foregone, or conversely the additional taxation required to finance military activities, which reflect political choices. The resource cost is private goods and services foregone, the dimension of which depends on a complex interaction of microeconomic factors. If resources in a supply contained economy are not mobile between sectors lower defence spending may not increase civilian output to a corresponding degree. The resource cost depends also on the absolute size of the economy and on its propensities to import. Countries which have a large, indigenous defence industry are more likely to benefit from defence expenditures than smaller countries, where they are dissipated in imports. Whereas over 95 per cent of American military expenditure is spent domestically the ratio for other NATO countries falls to 80 per cent. A given three per cent increase in military expenditures increases the American burden by 3.2 per cent, the Norwegian burden by 3.8 per cent and the Danish burden by 4.4 per cent.[7] Although precise data are unavailable, a similar pattern for the Warsaw Pact distinguishes the Soviet Union from the other Pact members.[8] For less developed countries with no or poorly developed manufacturing sectors the degree of dissipation is even larger. The resource costs depends *inter alia* upon the technical substitutability of factors of production and resources which in the short term are unlikely to equate to social or political preferences. The performance cost is indicated by macroeconomic indices. Civilian investment or R and D forgone adversely impacts long term growth potential, competitiveness or economic stability. Inflation, balance of payments and employment can also be affected.

The diversity of trade-offs and different time horizons makes the calculation of the defence burden difficult. It is almost inevitable that statistical analysis will not reveal consistent patterns of choice which must be influenced by a diversity of historical, cultural, geographical and economic experiences.[9] For instance the budgetary trade-off between defence and an array of welfare services – health, education, social security, and so on – has historically been more sharply drawn in the USA than in European countries which have been generally more supportive of welfare objectives.[10] Even within countries, radical governments of left or right depart from traditional norms – clearly the case for instance of many governments in the 1980s ideologically unsympathetic to established welfare concerns. Where, as in the USA, a high proportion of the federal budget is predetermined because of prior entitlements, the competition for uncommitted funds is more intense and the burden more sharply focussed. Choices between budgetary, resource and performance criteria are seldom exclusive, so that though a simple statistical analysis of a specific pair of diatonic variables may show only weak or no significant correlations, over the entire range of outcomes the consequences of military spending may be highly pronounced. In expanding societies where trade-offs take the form of lower growth of some variables rather than absolute declines, simple formal statistical tests may undervalue the real costs.

In the short run factors of production are fixed, but in the long run are flexible and the resource opportunity cost, as measured by increased civilian production consequent on a marginal decrease in military production varies over different time periods. If in the short run resources released from defence related activities remain unemployed or are forced into less productive occupations the opportunity cost will be small. In the long run when all resources are fungible and the range of alternative choices theoretically infinite the cost is greater. Indeed the calculus of costs and benefits may move in different directions over different time horizons. In economies where resources are un- or underemployed an increase in recruitment may reduce unemployment or an increase in procurement create higher demand for manufactured goods.[11] Since the manufacturing sector is an engine for growth in capitalist economies the growth potential of the economy may be increased. In the long run civilian output growth will be held back by resource and factor constraints. Evidence of the type and degree of burden can even be affected by an ostensibly technical choice between cross-sectional and longitudinal statistical tests.[12]

Before the Second World War military expenditures were almost universally believed to impede growth and reduce welfare.[13] In conventional analysis they cause budget deficits, and 'crowd out' more productive civil investment. As a proportion on GNP they seldom exceeded two per cent. The economic history of the industrial states and the Keynesian intellectual revolution before and during the Second World War wrought a sea change in the perception of the economic benefit of military spending. Germany, guided by a powerful rearmament programme in the 1930s, recovered earlier from the Depression, and it was rearmament rather than civil investment which finally pulled the democratic societies into full employment. Economists, influenced by the experience of the capitalist economies after the First World War forecasted a sharp decline in peacetime from the high levels of economic activity which prevailed during the war years. Thus military Keynesianism propagated in the UK by Keynes's powerful presence in the Treasury quickly took root. In the USA the decisive single event was the publication of the classified, but none the less widely circulated NSC-68 in 1950.[14] Although NSC-68 was primarily important in laying the guidelines for America's foreign and defence policy in the Cold War, economically it provided the crucial rationale for military Keynesianism. The perceived Soviet threat could be contained only by a massive increase in military spending, but conservative critics of budget deficits had to be assuaged by pointing to the success of military expenditures in pulling the economy out of depression during the war. Economists who forecasted a post-war depression appeared to be vindicated by evidence of falling GNP, industrial production and employment in 1948 and 1949. Not only would military spending not damage the economy, but would inject a positive stimulating boost to flagging economic activity. The beneficial Keynesian consequences were endorsed by influential members of the economic establishment – particularly Leon Keyserling, then in process of being confirmed as Chairman of the Council of Economic Advisers. Although its economic arguments and conclusion were not immediately and universally accepted NSC-68 did explicitly if crudely formulate for the first time the beneficial consequences of military Keynesianism. In economies with substantial domestic, invariably protected armaments industries, higher expenditures stimulate the demand for manufacturing output, within the USA a multiplier of 1.5 to 2.0 for employment. Military training might also increase the skill levels of the working population. In the USA for instance 60 per cent of the nation's vocational educational teachers work directly or indirectly for the military.[15] For countries where overt intervention in the macro and micro-economies is politically unacceptable defence expenditures may be and have been so used by American governments in a counter cyclical capacity[16] and as a surrogate for industrial policy. The current $600m. project to develop third generation computers and artificial intelligence is a case in point.[17]

The military economy can also boost technological progress and thereby economic growth. Wartime research and development accelerated such key technologies as jet engines, radar and electronics – and even penicillin, which subsequently spilled-in to the civilian economies. In the UK the influential Plowden report on the aerospace industry concluded that 'no other single industry would have such a pervasive effect on the technical progress of the nation'.[18] As early as 1965 the report identified materials, digital computers, high pressure lightweight hydraulic systems gas turbines and electronics as having benefitted from the technological fall out from aerospace.[19] A later and wider British investigation added liquid crystals, aeroengine propulsion, carbon films air terminal to the list of civilian spill-ins.[20] In France military technology is supported by governments precisely because of its contribution to technology and to public welfare and the conventional wisdom of guns or butter has been transformed to a

positive 'more butter because of more guns'.[21] A wide-ranging historical enquiry by a British economic historian identified both specific
and general stimuli to technological progress. Gun castings improved
general foundry practices. Armaments increased demand for machine tools, which could also be used for civilian production, for
munition firms were seldom exclusive, and they were instrumental in
promoting and disseminating new alloys and metal innovation. Because of the need for inter-operable parts, standardised and large
scale production of rifles preceded and showed the way to commercial sectors.[22] In the USA defence spending is claimed to have made a
'substantial contribution to technical developments of great importance to [the] economy'.[23] Although military-related research and
development is undertaken elsewhere, the sheer magnitude of expenditures in the USA allows it to dominate the pace and the pattern of
technological progress. Military technology is influential in two ways.
It forces the pace of technological progress in constantly seeking state
of the art developments. The Pentagon is the only national organisation rich enough to finance experiments on all scientific fronts.[24]
Furthermore the urgency with which the military community seeks to
incorporate scientific advance in new weapons, the degree of progress which is usually sought, the importance which scientists believe
their work to be to national security and the economic reward to
important constituencies all combine to push forward progress at a
prodigious rate. The Pentagon sustains its scientific commitment to
technological excellence for both military and economic reasons. The
current $600m. strategic computing initiative, for instance, aimed at
matching the Japanese challenge in superspeed supercomputers and
artificial intelligence, is justified as a vital contribution to the future
wealth of the US economy. Even when military related R and D does
not originate state of the art discoveries, the Pentagon can behave as
an economic incubator in offering an initial market for products
which commercially might not be viable.[25] Demand is sustained and
research stimulated until eventually costs are reduced to levels where
they become commercially viable to private corporations. Integrated
circuits, the scientific breakthrough for which occurred in civilian
laboratories, when first produced were too expensive for commercial
exploitation, and in 1967 100 per cent of output was bought by the
federal government almost entirely for the military. A guaranteed
demand – despite the high price – stimulated the additional investment which reduced costs and increased reliability to the degree that
military demand now accounts for less than ten per cent of industry

output. The incubator factor has also been important in developing satellite communications, small mobile terminals, on-line computer time-sharing, computer networks and microwave spectroscopy[26] all of which eventually spilled-in to civilian markets. For those who argue that indirect support to technological advance is inefficient compared with the Japanese policy of targeting, which though not foolproof has historically been successful, resources in countries such as the USA, the UK or France might not, because of political and economic inhibitions, be forthcoming at all.[27] Military R and D it is argued does not so much supplant as add to similar research and development.

More indirectly military spending has been an essential, for some the only, basis for great power status in the international system – [28] and for many leaders civilian welfare or growth foregone is a small price to pay for international power and prestige.

Impressive though the economic benefits of military expenditures may be, their mere recital does not address the fundamental issue of whether they are efficiently achieved. Defence in the final analysis is not primarily an economic activity and a different pattern of allocation might achieve the same or comparable benefits at lesser cost.

In a static economy the budgetary trade-off is most acute between defence and the other major claimants for public funds, health, education and social security, and early studies appeared to show that in some economies all three were sensitive to variations in defence spending.[29] As defence expenditures increase so do those for health, education and social security decrease. A more elaborate investigation of choice, specifically between defence and public health expenditures in the USA also gives more weight to the hypothesis that a trade-off exists between the two variables in that country than one of no trade-off.[30] As expenditures on health increase absolutely and proportionately, and therefore become politically salient the trade-off is likely to become more pronounced. The form and the dimensions of the trade-off however are seldom uniform or simple. Competing expenditure programmes are seldom effectively compared in the legislature process, coming before the relevant bodies sequentially and often made in isolation of one another.[31] Governments or legislatures which are not strongly motivated for or against particular categories of spending tend to fudge the choices in favour of compromise outcomes. In the USA for instance, choice between defence and welfare at the appropriations stage of the budgetary process is more acutely drawn than at the allocation or final expenditure stages, suggesting on balance a greater Congressional commitment to welfare and reluctance to make budgetary choices which might adversely influence the prospects for re-election.[32]

The incidence of war, not surprisingly, influences the intensity of choice,[33] and there is a strong displacement effect, which is incompletely made up in the succeeding period of peace. When wartime expenditures are removed the statistical evidence for a significant degree of choice between defence and welfare services disappears. Sometime the trade-off is negative as predicted, but significant. At other times the correlation is positive.[34] Evidence from the major industrial states shows welfare, widely defined, to have increased continuously in absolute terms since the conclusion of the Korean war, and until the 1980s in the USA to have increased as a proportion of central budgets and of GNP. As countries grow they have, by and large, been able to avoid having to choose between security and welfare. Social goals have become more important up to but not, in some countries, through the 1980s, and as social spending hardened into entitlements governments found it politically inadvisable to make large adjustments between spending patterns. A single systematic pattern of trade-off does not emerge.

The lack of a statistical trade-off does not indicate the absence of choice, for many statistical techniques cannot account for the additional expenditures which might have been made had defence spending been less.[35] The domestic determinants of defence expenditures tend therefore to be the political limits on total expenditures rather than distributional choices between budget heads. Some hitherto thought secure have been challenged. Since 1980 defence spending in the USA has been obtained at the expense of welfare and guns *v.* butter has again become a dominating political issue.[36] Civilian publicly funded goods have however been sacrificed as much to conservative distaste for the ideology of welfare as to the need to release resources for higher spending on defence.

Budgetary choices may also indirectly take the form of fiscal policy. Although monetary expenditures on all major social categories have increased over the post-war period, their distribution has changed, with consumption, education, health, etc. absorbing a higher proportion of national income. In the USA the distribution of federal funds are as shown in Table 6.1.

In the short term increased defence expenditures especially in the form of higher procurement, increase demand for manufacturing inputs, and via the accelerator effect stimulate investment. On average around 14 per cent or so of durable manufacturing output in the

Table 6.1   Outlays share percentages

	Welfare	Defence
1962	24	43
1981	36	23
1984	39	31

Source: Hearings before the Subcommittee on Economic Goals and Inter-governmental Policy of the Joint Economic Committee, Congress of the United States, October–December 1982, p. 19.

USA was sold to the Department of Defense, and since in capitalist nations growth and productivity are positively associated with manufacturing output, the stimulating potential to economic performance is considerable. The net effect on economic activity will however depend on the macroeconomic circumstances of the economy, on how the expenditures are financed and on the degree of micro-economic substitutability between industries and sectors. In periods of specific shortage the net effect is sometimes detrimental, for example Korean re-armament in the UK increased demand for metal goods beyond capacity and held down domestic civil investment and exports.[37] In the long run however specific shortages, with perhaps one or two exceptions are unlikely to be the major problem.

In societies characterised by full employment and/or slow growth increased defence expenditures will almost certainly adversely affect investment. For much of the post-war period powerful political constituencies in the democratic nations have successfully defended consumption's share of the national wealth. Investment which is consumption postponed has been less secure. At the margin therefore competition for economic resources has been intense between the two investment categories, private capital formation and defence,[38] in which defence has certain in-built advantages. In the USA the Defense Production Act gives priority to defence firms in the commercial market place,[39] while the common practice in defence contracting of cost plus pricing makes military contractors less responsive to conventional commercial considerations of economy, and more prepared to absorb and therefore to offer higher prices for inputs. The defence investment trade-off is also acute by virtue of competition for similar inputs especially if the supplying industries are at or near full capacity and/or factors of production are not flexible in the short run. In the longer period inflation or higher interest rates may also adversely influence private investment. In countries where the two sectors are well integrated and where public sector investment is a significant proportion of the total, the trade-off is almost unitary. Military investment 'crowds out' civilian investment.[40] For both neo-classical and Keynesian economists investment increases growth potential and the degree of resource utilisation. For Keynesians investment increases aggregate demand. For neoclassicists it increases supply, embodies technological progress, eases the adjustment from declining to expanding sectors, increases dynamic economies of scale and maximises the benefits of export-led growth.

Defence also indirectly has an impact on economic progress and welfare. In periods of fixed exchange rates, growth is sustainable over the long period, if the balance of payments is favourable. Historically, export led growth has been potent and dynamic as the post-war performance of, *inter alia*, West Germany and Japan testifies. In the UK on the other hand the external sector has inhibited expansion[41] and even during the period of flexible and managed exchange rates, though less binding than previously, has adversely affected growth. As with so many economic variables the relationship between military spending and external balance is not straightforward, but depends on how large are the expenditures, on how they are distributed and financed and on economic structure. For nations which are highly dependent on manufactured exports, military spending may during periods of exceptional shortage or rapid expansion divert manufactured goods away from international trade. During post-war reconstruction in Britain the trade-off was direct, and throughout the period of fixed exchange rates, the adverse balance of payments was perhaps the major immediate constraint on economic expansion. In the USA too the external demands of the imperious economy adversely affected the external balance[42] and was especially potent during the 1980s.[43] For industrial countries as a whole the statistical relationships – though weak – are in line with the hypothesis,[44] and export shares are negatively related to defence ratios. Normally the resource trade-off, if it occurs at all, is brought about indirectly via price. For nations which have small or modest defence capabilities, a portion of defence spending, usually substantial, will almost inevitably be dissipated in imports from the major exporters. The different impact of a given level of spending on the American and some European economies has already been noted. Even countries with large defence establishments cannot escape from the balance of payments costs of security, as neither the UK nor France despite their high degree of independence manage without access to superior American technology. Whereas membership in alliances allows smaller countries to forego paying their proper share of the collective burden, the trading account is almost necessarily adverse. For larger countries domestic production often cannot be divorced from the requirement to finance troops stationed abroad in which case the service account is made adverse. Thus despite American and to a lesser degree British success in exporting weapons and licences, the service account has remained stubbornly negative, though the foreign trade multiplier does reduce the net imbalance on the foreign account. Indeed the external drain on its resources has been a major explanation for the decline of American hegemony.[45]

Exports of armaments have positive impact on the economies of large producers. In 1985 the USA exported over $10bn. of arms; it also dominates world trade in many military related civilian products, such as aeroengines, whose growth and competitiveness are closely geared to the rhythm of military production. In France and the UK exports offer a powerful rationale for military investment and production.[46] In West Germany too, arms exports by the 1970s exceeded imports, and for a country so geared to export success the military sector plays a useful if supplementary role to the civilian economy. Nevertheless between 1950 and 1970 the net deficit on the external account is estimated to have amounted to $33bn. for the USA and to $7bn. for the UK.[47]

As the number of arms exporters increases, the balance of benefits has shifted towards importers, and arms exports are less profitable to the nation, though still so for the individual exporting firms.[48] Because of increasing competition importers are able to insist on non-price benefits as inducements to buy. In addition to equipment, importers are demanding access to the technology of the exporters, and to offset agreements to reduce the exchange costs. One conservative estimate valued the total number of such agreements at around $1.8bn. between 1975 and 1981. Others have been as high as $5bn. which if correct would amount to 1984 to roughly 30 per cent of US military arms sales that year. The practice has increased to the degree that currently virtually all arms sellers must offer some offsets inducements[49] and to that extent the balance of payments benefits to military exporters are reduced as are the costs to importers.

Econometric investigation highlights the contribution of technological progress to long term economic growth in advanced capitalist nations. Japan, perhaps the most dynamic post-war nation, and to a lesser extent West Germany, are examples of countries which have harnessed the benefits of civilian technological progress to export-led growth and to increase their share of world trade in manufactured goods to impressive levels. In the USA and the UK on the other hand the experience has been to the contrary.

More significant for long term growth potential has been the conflicting trends in market shares for technologically advanced equipment. Definition of this category of manufactured goods is necessarily arbitrary but based on an analysis of the technological intensity of US manufactured goods Judith Reppy has identified ten such industrial sectors ranging from guided missiles to plastic and synthetic materials. Reppy shows that America's market share between 1963–1971 and 1971–1980 declined in eight of the ten sectors including all the civilian based technologies, and for the UK in eight of the sectors.[50] Additional evidence suggests that for the USA the largest decline in market share has occurred in precisely those industries most heavily engaged in military contracting.[51] The UK share of world trade in high-tech exports has fallen from 12 per cent in 1965 to 8.5 per cent in 1984.[52] The Japanese share on the other hand has increased in eight of the ten sectors.[53] In the USA and the UK furthermore, declining market shares have accompanied deficits on the trading account, compared with surpluses in Japan. The poor trade performance of the USA and the UK has to be assessed in conjunction with the proportion of each nation's scientific and technological resources which is being systematically diverted to military purposes. In the USA defence R and D as a percentage of total R and D spending reached almost 50 per cent in 1956, fell to a low of 25 per cent in 1978, before increasing against to just over 30 per cent in 1984.[54] In what have been described as cutting edge technologies such as lasers, artificial intelligence and advanced materials, defence-related projects account for between 70 per cent and 80 per cent of total spending.[55] The Pentagon's share of federal spending increased to 73 per cent in 1986.[56] Whereas the USA spends 1.9 per cent of GNP on non-military R and D, Japan spends 2.5 per cent[57] and less than one per cent of its national scientific resources for military purposes. The American National Science Board, the governing body of the National Science Foundation, has expressed concern about the serious erosion of US dominance in science and technology. The data point, not unambiguously however, to an inverse association between the share of GNP devoted to military R and D and competitiveness. Countries such as the USA and the UK which divert a high ratio of their scientific and technological resources to defence inhibit the pace of adjustment to new industrial sectors in the face of international competition which *ceteris paribus* hold down long term economic growth. In the USA most federal military research does not add to the total research activity but 'crowds out' company financed R and D.[58] Moreover positive spill-in effects once so abundant are increasingly difficult to harness to civilian requirements. The high degree of specialisation, exotic nature and gold plating characteristic of so much embodied military technology has transformed the Department of Defense into a net consumer of civilian technology.[59] Although there are dual use products such as helicopters or computers which are equally accessible to civilian and military markets the obstacles to effective transfer are increasingly severe. Given the emphasis on technological excellence in the American armed forces irrespective of costs, considerations of commercial economy which are of major concern to profit-seeking firms necessarily become secondary. Weapons are increasingly exotic and even the British Ministry of Defence has complained of over-elaboration.[60] The military requirements for technologies which function at extreme condition embody a degree of capability which few commercial firms require, and the practice of paying a disproportionate cost for comparatively small improvement in performance further adds to cost and reduces utility. Military R and D tends to emphasise product at the expense of process innovation[61] and only a small proportion of military R and D is spent on the technological base where potential spill-ins are greatest. In 1985 90 per cent of Department of Defense R and D spending was allocated to developing specific weapons,[62] and over the last two decades only about 20 per cent of total military R and D has been allocated to basic research. A case study of the USA electronics industry identified few products developed for the military which had commercial applications[63] and in key technologies such as integrated circuits the lines of technological development often diverged markedly from the requirements of civilian markets.[64] In many current advanced technological programmes such as the American Very High Speed Integrated Circuit Program and the Strategic Computing Initiative to produce a new generation of superspeed supercomputers, developments may be excessively skewed to meet security needs at the expense of the commercially beneficial growth.[65] In the USA military R and D is highly concentrated, 85 per cent of total expenditure being spent on sectors such as aerospace and electronics compared with Japan where it is more widely dispersed[66] and the Japanese government subsidises private commercial research into technology with a basically civilian as opposed to a military potential. Furthermore, research contracts are narrowly dispersed to a small number of firms, most of which are chosen after only the most cursory search for competitive alternatives, and the array of skills necessary for success in military markets are not those which guarantee success in commercial markets. The internal organisation of corporations geared largely to military markets is ill-suited to internal transfers of scientific and technological knowledge. The civilian departments are often organisationally separate from the military[67] and the endemic secrecy also inhibits the commercial exploitation of new knowledge for at the end of the day the primary purpose of military investment is security not profits.[68] One study found that only five to ten per cent of Pentagon R and D yielded substantial commercial spin-offs.[69] The Pentagon has recently increased from 13 to 20 per cent that part of its budget, the so called 'black budget' kept so secret that the research it finances need not be disclosed. In 1987 this represented a 300 per cent increase over that of 1981, while the Secretary of Defense can forbid publication of approximately 70 per cent of the unclassified research undertaken by defence contractors.[70] For both the UK and the USA the shift in scientific and technological resources to the military has been a major reason for their poor trade and productivity performance. Even in industries where military research is qualitatively and quantitatively important, the USA and the UK have not performed as effectively as might have been anticipated. For both countries their share of the world armaments market has declined, to a low for the USA of 30 per cent in 1985 and for the UK to 3.3 per cent in 1983, though for both countries the ratios have since increased. In the key electronics industry, Britain's trade deficit increased from $181m. to £2205m. and import penetration from 37 to 59 per cent.[71] A recent report published by the National Economic Development Office argues that the British electronics industry faces a crisis of survival due in part to undue reliance on defence contracts.[72]

Because the number of nations which undertake military R and D on an economically significantly scale is small the evidence of its civilian consequences will necessarily be dominated by the experience of a few countries. Nevertheless the concentration so far on the USA, the UK and Japan has excluded from consideration other obvious industrial countries, in particular France and West Germany, whose performances have a bearing on the overall assessment. In France military related R and D has been deliberately fostered to provide an impetus to technological innovation, and the conventional view of defence or welfare replaced by a philosophy which positively relates welfare to military R and D. France, which allocates 25 per cent of its total R and D resources to military, increased its market share in seven of the ten industries including four of the five civilian based technology sectors and declined in only two. West Germany on the other hand which allocates just over five per cent of its scientific and technological resources to defence experienced a decline in its market share in eight of the ten sectors, ironically increasing its share in ordnance and aircraft,[73] sectors which have been identified as military based. The evidence is thus inconclusive. Market shares are influenced by a variety of factors other than the defence quotient but for economies which for other reasons are not competitive in world markets the opportunity cost of civilian scientific and technological investment forgone cannot but aggravate the secular trends.

Total factor productivity in the industrial nations is influenced by the weight of conflicting consequences of military investment, especially in R and D. On the one hand it diverts resources from the civilian economy but on the other yields spill-in external benefits. Cross-sectional data suggest that countries such as Japan and West Germany where the defence quotient is low have achieved higher productivity growth than countries such as the USA and the UK where the quotient is high. Time series data however show no such association.

Given the uncertain and sometimes conflicting consequence of military expenditures on microeconomic and macroeconomic variables it is not surprising that the net effect on economic growth also cannot be conclusively traced. High defence spending, low investment, low productivity countries such as the USA and the UK are also low growth countries, while the opposite tends to be true of Japan and West Germany. The high growth, high productivity countries have also by and large weathered the shock to the international economic system after 1974 more successfully. More systematic analysis involving more countries is less conclusive however. France – which allocates not much less than the UK – has experienced better trade, productivity and growth performance. But even in the case of the UK and the USA recent economic history, although limited to a small number of years, shows higher defence spending in the USA and no lower in the UK to be positively associated with higher growth in

Table 6.2   Defence spending and productivity growth

	1950–60	1960–71	1970–79
USA			
Productivity growth	2.3	2.1	1.1
Defence quotient	10.3	8.7	6.1
Japan			
Productivity growth	–	9.7	4.5
Defence quotient	1.0	0.9	0.9
Germany			
Productivity growth	–	4.6	3.4
Defence quotient	3.9	4.2	3.9
France			
Productivity growth	–	4.8	3.4
Defence quotient	7.2	5.4	3.9
United Kingdom			
Productivity growth	9.0	2.8	2.0
Defence quotient	7.9	5.8	4.9
Canada			
Productivity growth	3.0	2.4	1.3
Defence quotient	5.6	3.3	2.0

Source: Congressional Budget Office, *Defense Spending and the Economy*, Washington DC 1983, p. 40.

both countries.[74] Indeed for some countries the long term effect is beneficial. For a group of comparatively undeveloped Mediterranean states the modernisation consequences of militarism have more than compensated for crowding out.[75]

The performance consequences of high military expenditures are not of course limited to economic growth. The defence sector is directly and indirectly a major employer of military and civilian personnel. In the USA approximately two million people are on active duty and a further one million are employed in military-related service jobs. The employment multiplier has been estimated at 1.5 to 2.0 and total employment associated with defence spending is between nine and 12 million. The benefit to the labour force of changing expenditure depends not on the total or average but on the marginal effect of military compared with civilian spending of comparable magnitude. In the USA an injection of $1bn. in the USA on average creates 35 000 jobs, and $1bn. of military exports 50 000 jobs,[76] and is often important in determining Congressional support for the level and distribution of military spending. The net effect depends upon how spending is distributed. That spent mainly on labour intensive activities such as preparation or readiness has a bigger direct impact on employment than expenditures on R and D. By and large, however, most industries which sell goods or services to the Pentagon create fewer jobs per $ than the average for the American economy. Seven of the 11 industries which sell most to the Pentagon, including the three largest manufacturing industry sectors, create fewer jobs than the media industry.[77] However the net effect on employment will also be affected by secondary consequences. Because military activities are technology intensive the distribution of employment is distorted away from the norm. Defence tends to be a more intensive user of skilled labour such as skilled machinists, metal workers, aeronautical and electronics engineers, scientists and managers than the economy as a whole. It employs more than 20 per cent of total employment of teachers of vocational education, mathematical specialists aero-astronautical engineers, life and physical scientists, engineers and physicists in the USA,[78] while in the UK approximately 30 per cent of scientists are estimated to be employed in the defence sector.[79] Defence employment also tends to be geographically concentrated; in the USA disproportionately in the southern and western states, in the UK in the south-east. Simulation exercises can indicate the employment consequences of spending a hypothetical sum of money in different sectors of the economy. They are however problematic, depending critically on counterfactual assumptions on what it is assumed the equivalent amount of money would be spent. One investigation shows the outcome as shown in Table 6.3.

A study by the Congressional Budget Office concluded that $10bn. will increase employment by a virtually identical 250 000 million in the military and the civilian economy, though if the sum were to be concentrated on military procurement the increase in employment would fall to 210 000 jobs.[80] As the authors note the results – as for all the others – are subject to important caveats, for instance the effects of budget deficits on the long run equilibrating effects of a free market economy.

Finally, it is argued defence spending is inflationary,[81] though not necessarily more so than any other programmes of government expenditure not financed from taxation.[82] Defence spending is potentially inflationary in two ways. Expenditures which are financed from public borrowing or by printing money loosen monetary variables. The precise outcome depends, as always, on the manner in which the expenditures are financed, but can take the form of higher interest

Table 6.3   Employment consequences of $1bn. expenditure '000 jobs

petrol industry	motors	military	median	new public transit	Personal consumption	Education
12	25	30	32	34	58	72

Source: R. De Grasse, *Military Expansion and Economic Decline: The Impact of Military Spending on US Economic Performance* (Armonk: M. E. Sharpe, 1983, p. 23).

rates, budget deficits, or a larger money supply, all of which influence real economic variables. The inflationary consequences will also depend on the degree to which the spending authority can raise taxes and reduce other government spending programmes. In societies where entitlements are strongly entrenched and social consumption difficult to reduce, the demand pull effect will, other things being equal, be severe and difficult to dislodge. Where on the other hand social expenditures are politically vulnerable, as for instance in President Reagan's administration, the direct inflationary pressures are more easily contained,[83] (though of course the record expenditures did make their way through the monetary system in other ways).

Military expenditures also add to cost push inflation depending on the strength of cost push price increases in the military sector and the ease with which they are transmitted to the civilian economy. Military goods and services are prone to higher cost push pressures by virtue of their particular characteristics; the high proportion of new products for which there are no established markets or prices, the bureaucratic bargaining as opposed to the market determination of prices, the speed with which results are incorporated in new products and the monopoly structure of military markets. The practice of single sourcing or follow-on contracts weakens the incentive to be vigorously competitive. High barriers to entry and to exit increase cost push pressures by what is known as cost-pass-along pricing policies.[84] Both prime contractors and component supplies are highly concentrated and consequent inflation in defence equipment *sui generis* tends to exceed that in civilian equipment in the USA by an average of three to ten percent.[85] It is difficult to be precise because some of the excess price changes reflect genuine technological progress which is embedded in defence equipment. Even if cost push inflation is higher, the consequences to the civilian economy depend on how effectively the inflation is transmitted across sectors. Although pass-along techniques flourish in the uncompetitive defence sector they are more difficult to apply in civilian industries more prone to competition from domestic firm and from imports.[86] The consequences will also depend on the absolute size of the defence sector. The statistical evidence as usual is not conclusive. In the UK for instance inflation has varied up to 29 per cent p.a. even though the proportion of the nation's resources devoted to defence has remained reasonably constant, and in the USA the massive increase in defence spending since 1980 has not, despite the worst fears of many of President Reagan's critics, been associated with a build-up of inflationary pressures. A comparison of the inflationary consequences in four OECD countries failed to indicate a systematic and generalised trade-off between military expenditures and inflation for all countries.[87] In some periods where expenditures have increased – for example during the Vietnam war in the USA – the inflationary pressures are severe and immediate. At other times when circumstances are more favourable they are easily contained.

In complex economic systems the failure to identify a single general statistical pattern[88] should not surprise. This should not however disguise the real problems created by failure to reconcile commitments and resources. In the USA this has been revealed in the huge budget and payments deficits, the consequence of which will become apparent only in the future.

7 The Defence Burden in the Socialist States

Conceptually the defence burden is no different in socialist to capitalist societies. In reality, however, different modes of resource allocation and policies effectively exclude some trade-offs and intensify others.

In the command economies inflation and unemployment are largely covert and disguised. Although the more flexible Hungarian economy is more prone to macroeconomic imbalance than the rigid Soviet Union, and in all the socialist societies inflation and unemployment have increased in recent years, in general these are not as responsive to economic circumstances and hence to the level of defence expenditures as they are in capitalist states. Given central control over the volume and the terms of exports, international competitiveness also is more complex and indirectly determined than in capitalist states.

As in capitalist societies the true cost of burden depends on the social evaluation of civilian goods foregone and on the ease with which resources can be transferred from military to civilian production in the event of a change in priorities. The non-Soviet socialist states spend as a crude average six per cent of their national income on defence, measured in dollars, compared with four per cent for the European NATO countries. The USSR spends 15–17 per cent compared with under seven per cent for the USA. On the other hand, because prices systematically understate the real cost of military investment, production and manpower, the true quotient may be greater than conventionally measured. However the index number problem, which overstates the expenditures of one country when measured in the currency of another, is probably greater for the Warsaw Pact compared with the European NATO countries. High defence ratios are not in themselves evidence of greater belligerence but reflect the smaller GNPs of the socialist states. Because such high ratios are drawn from civilian economies in societies where living standards fall below those prevailing in the West, it can be presumed, though it is no more than a presumption, that the defence burden is higher in the sense that consumers would be prepared to spend more on and pay relatively high prices for civilian goods if they were able to express their preferences freely.

The opportunity cost is high also because resources are fully employed, and as a consequence of central planning can be quickly transferred to alternative employment. Planning avoids what Soviet economists aver to be the slow and arbitrary processes of markets. High priority sectors can be targeted and allocation does not depend on factor and commodity prices which are time consuming, and may for an unspecified interim period leave resources unemployed. At a practical level the process is expedited in the Soviet Union by the practice of incorporating a buffer capacity in military plants which in peacetime is usefully employed in producing civilian investment and consumption goods, ranging from railway stock through machine tools to toys and furniture.[1] In such plants substitution of civilian for military goods may, depending on the specificity of the plant, be achievable without extensive re-tooling of plant and equipment.[2]

Central planning is not in this respect without problems however. Even though Soviet military technology falls short of that embodied in American weapons it is still by and large higher than that in the civilian economy due partly to the superior quality of the capital stock. Where equipment is dedicated to specific tasks the adjustment to lower military production will require some once and for all re-training and re-tooling.

A more fundamental problem for central planners derives from the lack of economic information in the price system, which reflects neither marginal utilities nor rates of technical transformation. Economic targeting is therefore necessarily subjective, and there is no way outside of planners' preferences of assessing whether civilian objectives are efficiently chosen or achieved.[3]

Analysis of the defence burden in command economies encounters unique problems of principle and of quantification which are absent from capitalist economies. Despite the lack of proof it is generally believed by Western economists that the Soviet defence sector is a more efficient user of economic resources than is the civilian economy.[4] If true, a first problem is the degree to which the superior efficiency is transferable along with physical factors and resources. If the source of superior efficiency is exclusive to the military sector, it is not transferable and, perhaps paradoxically, the defence burden is reduced, in that civilian production will not increase proportionately as military production declines. If, however, the source of military superiority is not structurally induced and is potentially transferable, the burden of civilian production foregone is greater. If,

Table 7.1   Characteristics of the Soviet civilian and defence space sectors

	Civilian	*Defence/Space*
1. Experimental production and testing facilities	Poor	Good
2. Series production plant	No slack	Excess capacity
3. Vertical integration (ministerial autarchy)	Low	High
4. Design commonality (use of off-the-shelf components)	Low	High
5. New product cycle (research to production)	Long	Short
6. Foreign and domestic competition	Low	High
7. Style of output	Heavy, expensive	Spare, simple, cost-effective
8. Bargaining power of customer	Low	High
9. Target production price at beginning of design	No	Yes
10. R & D costs considered in weighing alternative designs	No	Yes

Source: N. Nimitz, *The Structure of Soviet Outlays on R and D in 1960 and 1968*, Rand R–1207 – DDRE, Santa Monica, 1974, p. 43.

contrary to majority opinion, the military sector is not more but less efficient, the burden is even greater.[5] The assessment of relative efficiencies is necessarily judgemental. Many likely sources of military efficiency are policy induced and are, in principle, transferable.[6] Superior access to raw materials and personnel, tight production schedules, and so on are clearly within the compass of planners to modify.

The most powerful single explanation for superior performance is however unique to the military and therefore not easily transferable. In a supply constrained uncompetitive economy where enterprise targets and rewards are predicated on the assumption that supply plans will be fulfilled, enterprises have no incentive to reject inferior quality inputs, raw materials, machinery, semi-manufactured goods, etc. Customer power is weak, reflected in low quality goods, poor choice and uncertain delivery schedules. In the defence sector this is not the case. International competition with a dynamic innovator forces Soviet weapons and military equipment to approach international standards. Unlike civilian customers, the Ministry of Defence is forced to behave as a powerful and discriminating customer with a strong preference for economy and austere outcomes.[7] Military efficiency therefore reflects a degree of international competition largely absent in the civilian sector. A transfer of material resources alone will not replicate the objective circumstances of military production and to that degree the burden of military production is, in the absence of comprehensive economic reform, reduced.

It is, however, greater than quantitative indicators alone might suggest in that superior military performance has been bought very much at the expense of that in the civilian economy. Military economic superiority, whether structural or policy induced, exacerbates the disadvantages of command economies.[8] The systemic costs of command economies are more onerous on civilian producers than they theoretically need be, because military priority imposes a disproportionate share of the costs onto residual civilian claimants. This is not due to chance. In the 1930s defence priority was a crucial justification for the concentration of economic power implicit in collectivisation. Economic planning was the most effective way of diverting resources to defence – and from 1932 was perhaps the single most powerful rationale for the intensity and speed of industrialisation which so transformed Soviet society.[9] The ultimate burden is not so much the maldistribution of resources between the competing sectors, but the systemic inefficiency brought about by a rigid command economy, which after an initial surge of extensive growth inhibited productivity, technological progress and economic expansion.[10]

In the Soviet Union, as for all societies, defence is not without utility. Indeed, it may perhaps have been the case that only by ruthlessly imposing so severe a burden on Soviet society in the 1930s did the state survive the supreme test of its sovereignty. Some Western observers aver that the ultimate Soviet objective is, and always has been, the maximisation of economic–military power, in which the military component, though not exclusive, has by Western standards an abnormally high weight.[11] Taken to its logical conclusion this implies a preference for allocation which rather than minimising defence spending to a level consistent with the objective security of the state, minimises welfare to the degree necessary to sustain the leadership's power objectives. Such might have been the case for Stalin,[12] but is not so currently.[13]

Nevertheless it is the case that the military is organically integrated into Soviet society and is maintained by a civilian leadership which empathises to a high degree with the values and goals of the military establishment.[14] The Party remains the final arbiter and its identification with military objectives is attested quantitatively by the high defence quotient, and qualitatively by the non-monetary priorities which characterise defence production.

Although an effective programme of civilian education has taken over some of the tasks once undertaken by military schools and colleges, the army still offers technical and vocational training to young men and women. The construction units of the armed services offer, at minimum cost, practical assistance in the form of a mobile labour force which can deal with specific problems as they arise. Construction troops have been employed to complete large construction projects such as the BAM railway in Siberia, to build roads, bridges, schools, and they are also regularly employed to help with the harvests, when state and collective farmers cannot cope with peak demands.[15] Armaments is one of the few industrial branches which is competitive in international markets, and a major earner of foreign exchange. Military demand despite, or perhaps because of, the debilitating economic consequences of military priority, has proved the most effective source of modernisation,[16] though the potential spill-in benefits to the civilian society are not maximised due to the poor incentive systems and institutional barriers.[17]

The army, along with other state and Party organs, has the important but delicate task of making Soviet citizens more receptive to the social and moral obligations of Marxist–Leninist ideology, and army schools provide an arena for political socialisation. The army is a key point of assembly, where young people of different cultural and ethnic backgrounds are instructed in civic as well as military values, for it has been axiomatic of Soviet ideology that training the good soldier is inseparable from nurturing the good citizen.[18] Russian is the sole language of instruction in the armed forces, and provides perhaps the only common bond between the young people of the Soviet nations.

Soviet foreign policy is informed by an aggressive Russian nationalism and an ideology which is reflected in an intense preoccupation with the security and the survival of the state.[19] Russian consciousness of its long land barriers and vulnerability to invasion by stronger nations to the East and West has projected itself externally in an aggressive policy of imperialism and alliances. Russian preoccupation with the defence of the homeland has been given theoretical substance by a Manichean ideology which divides the world into two warring camps engaged in a constant struggle for superiority. To ensure ultimate victory the Soviet people must be constantly vigilant. Ideological fervour waxes and wanes but the basic view that a belligerent and reactionary international imperialism is primarily responsible for the intensification of the arms race,[20] has only very recently been modified in response to Gorbachev's 'New Thinking' on international affairs.[21] It is the world correlation of forces which has kept the imperialist forces in check and the inevitable struggle between capitalism and socialism therefore legitimises the constant improvement in Soviet defence capability. Moreover, socialist states have a positive responsibility to support and inspire revolution in the Third World by providing arms where necessary, and by giving a positive example in withstanding capitalist counter-revolution, though many of these traditional theories are in the process of being modified.

For most Soviet citizens the domestic economic rewards of socialism have been meagre, and the once revolutionary *élan* has declined to a conservative support for the *status quo*. Military might has become the showcase of Soviet achievement, the only arena in which the Soviet Union has been able to compete on equal terms with the capitalist nations. It is the sole basis for Soviet superpower status.[22]

Soviet defence expenditures in short have positive virtues for Soviet leaders. They are not however costless. The economic costs of defence are two-fold. The priority allocation of resources to military spending within the prevailing mode of production, given chronic excess demand, necessarily reduces the quantities available for civilian purposes. But the mode of production is itself not independent of the policy objectives of the leaders. The attainment and, subsequently, the maintenance of military power was from the outset crucial to Soviet leaders, and therefore necessarily an important determinant of the mode of production. Military power on the desired scale and pace required a sectoral distribution of resources incompatible with market determined allocations which had to be replaced by a command system of choice which centralised economic and political power. Forced collectivisation and industrialisation were justified by the defence needs of the state and throughout Soviet history, the material requirements of the armaments industry have decisively influenced the rate and pattern of economic expansion.[23]

In the first few years of the Republic, arms production was relatively neglected as the Bolshevik leaders struggled with the crippling economic and social consequences of war and civil war. By the middle of the 1920s, however, Soviet planners were giving serious consideration to how best to integrate civilian and military production and although the turbulence of the 1920s makes conclusive judgement difficult, it is likely that even in this early period the growth of defence production had deleterious consequences on the civilian economy.[24] The economic dimensions of military production grew phenomenally during the 1930s (Table 3.2, p. 52). Growth at such a rapid pace inevitably imposed a heavy cost on the civilian sectors. In 1935, defence took 15 per cent of the State budget for working capital and investment. By 1939 this had increased to fully 50 per cent.[25] The defence sector absorbed 20 per cent of the output of the machine tool branches, and by 1938 between 33 and 40 per cent of steel output and ten per cent of the output of the chemical industries. The armaments' commissariats competed directly with civilian industries for the output of the metal, engineering, machinery and machine tools branches, which were at the heart of the industrialisation programme. Investment in material resources demanded complementary employment of managers and skilled workers. Throughout the decade periods of higher defence production coincided with a decrease in the overall rate of growth, but was especially acute after 1934. In 1937, when the country began to re-arm, the supply of machinery for civilian investment actually declined, as within four years defence as a proportion of total industrial production doubled.[26] The pattern of industrial development was permanently distorted. Lower quality steels and metallurgical products useful mainly for the civilian branches were relatively neglected which reduced long term productive potential as well as current output. Between 1928–52 funds earmarked for military production increased 26 fold in real terms, a rate of expansion twice as rapid as those for civilian-based heavy industry. Rapid and disjointed growth were especially demanding of managerial skills, perhaps at that time the scarcest of all resources.

Investment in and production of military outputs distorted the allocation of investment goods between competing sectors, but the major burden was borne by the consumer, for excessive claims on the nation's resources could only be reconciled by forcing consumers to the status of residual claimants.[27] Defence had a significantly deleterious impact on the consumer goods sector and even more on the standard of living. The measured increase in total personal income of around 33 per cent or so represented in actuality a large decrease in per capita consumption of between 25 per cent for wage earners, and 40 per cent for the farm workers. The priority provision of food, clothing and shoes to the military meant that in some years civilian per capita income was little more than one half of that attained in 1928. Indeed, so effective was the policy of suppressing civilian consumption that it almost attained the status of a policy objective.[28]

Consumers would not willingly sanction such a level of sacrifice and Soviet leaders recognised that if military production was to grow at the rate and attain the level which they envisaged, the market, which the Bolsheviks in any case rejected as an allocating device, would have to be replaced by a mechanism which would give the Party effective political control of economic resources.

In 1922, the Soviet Union was poor and technologically backward. The short term Bolshevik objective was economic recovery from the depradations of war and civil conflict, which the NEP, with its relatively high degree of economic freedom, achieved to a substantial degree. The long term objective was nothing less than to catch up with and surpass the level of economic development attained by the capitalist countries. The participants in the great intellectual debates of the 1920s were agreed that only through a policy of deliberate industrialisation could that objective be attained within a reasonable period of time.[29]

By the end of the decade, the polar stance of the right and the left had been modified. Bukharin acknowledged the inevitability of discontinuous growth, while Preobrazhenski warned about the risks of too rapid expansion. In the event, Stalin, by a series of manoeuvres, crushed first the rightist and then the leftist factions, and after consolidating his supremacy imposed his own preferences on the Party, which were for a rate of industrialisation and a degree of coercion that not even the superindustrialists of the left faction had contemplated. Stalin accepted the left view that to bring about the transformations which he sought, voluntary exchange, the basis of the market mechanism, had to be destroyed. This objective was made more immediate by a drop in grain procurement in 1927–8 of over 30 per cent, which seemed to justify the widely held belief that reliance on the market would make the state too dependent on the rich peasants whose loyalty to the Revolution could not be guaranteed.

In theory planning can involve various degrees of centralisation, of forced and voluntary relationships between citizens and the state. Whatever the intellectual rationale for indicative planning, it had little relevance for the Soviet experience. Central economic planning came to the Soviet Union as the servant of a specific strategy,[30] to bring about a revolutionary shift in factor allocations between the major sectors. This could be achieved only through a mechanism which would mobilise and concentrate resources on a small number of selected targets and prevent their dissipation to sectors of low importance. The task of the planner, therefore, was not that of technically co-ordinating plans within a consistent framework, but rather to impose on society the vision of the political leadership and to devise the mechanisms which would translate the political objectives into operational outcomes.[31] Soviet central planning was almost exclusively an instrument of mobilisation. The first Five-Year Plan went through numerous drafts, as Stalin demanded more and more improbable targets for steel, cement, non-ferrous metals and machine tools. Consumer goods were inevitably sacrificed, and to avoid the consequences of the goods famine which had so concerned Preobrazhenski, centralised planning had to be accompanied by a comprehensive programme of agrarian collectivisation to force down the living standards of the peasants and enable the Party to expropriate the agricultural surplus to feed the industrial proletariat.

Industrialisation reduced per capita income, and collectivisation brought about a prodigious increase in the industrial labour supply. In 1929, one million households lived on collective farms; by 1930 this number had increased to 14 million. The social consequences of so great a dislocation left even many of the superindustrialists aghast.

The goal of production became, not the maximisation of welfare, but the production of more industrial goods and weapons which was at least consistent with the quantitative objective of catching up and overtaking the capitalist countries. Consumption became little more than a means of production, the allocation to which was determined by the minimum necessary to provide an adequate supply of labour, and to avoid political unrest. In a state governed by terror, that minimum quantity was small indeed.

The one consistent objective was to guarantee to top priority branches the resources necessary to meet their goals. A powerful defence industry was an integral part of the industrialisation programme. Military production provided an irresistible rationale for, and justification of, the massive concentration of economic and political power in the Soviet system of central planning.[32] To the extent that military objectives were important, even decisive, influences on the practice of Soviet central planning, so was defence responsible for the systemic and policy induced inefficiencies which have characterised the planning system since its inception.

Central economic planning is wholly consistent with the Marxist view of the market as inefficient and unjust. Nevertheless, even within a centrally planned framework, politically determined objectives can be attained by more or less efficient methods. Even if planners reject the market as a satisfactory allocative device, there exist capitalist procedures which, suitably modified to the socialist environment, could be used to assist the planners in their allocative tasks. The degree to which such devices are rejected depends upon the ideological perspective of the planners; on the economic distance which they seek to shift allocations away from that which would have prevailed in a free market. Given Stalin's preferences, central planning to the exclusion of economic rationality offered the only way they could be achieved, and was in terms of those preferences, by and large successful. The process was costly, however, for those whose lives were directly touched by the great transformation and those who have since had to accept the economic consequences of lower living standards.

Although planning was sanctioned by Marxist theory and was not in itself irrational, its particular manifestation in the Soviet Union reflected the unique social circumstances of time and place.

The overriding objective was economic growth, the pre-requisite for military–economic power and for catching up with and overtaking the capitalist countries. Other desirable criteria, such as microeconomic efficiency, high consumer living standards or equality were dismissed as either being irrelevant, or had to be postponed until the revolution had been secured domestically and the capitalist counter-revolutionary impulses checked. Realpolitik and Marxist theory combined to give emphasis to the quantitative parameters of planning, and from the outset, physical comparisons with the economic performance of other countries became the touchstone of progress.[33] The tasks of planners and managers were simplified if targets were set, norms agreed and performance monitored in physical dimensions. As a matter of principle and of expediency, economic industrial and military success came to be measured in quantitative terms – more steel, more cement, more machine tools, and, of course, more armaments.

As markets were anathema, so by definition must be everything which made them work. Chief among these was price. There was little attempt to distinguish between their operational functionalism and the social framework within which prices had historically functioned. Although prices in Marxist societies were theoretically to reflect socially necessary labour time incurred in production, it has not been possible in practice to devise a price system independent of the prior evaluation of what is socially necessary. There can thus be no systematic evaluation outside of planners' preferences of the social costs and benefits of the most desired outcomes, or the most efficient way of achieving objectives after they have been determined. Prices do not precede but follow the allocative decision and therefore cannot influence it. The rate of interest and rent were not only the price of capital and land, but also the unnecessary and exploitative portion of national income which accrued to a particular class, due to their possession of a particular array of property rights, rather than as a reward for their essential contribution to economic well-being. These also had to be abolished, especially since, as some argued, interest rates – by artificially raising the price of capital – would lower the organic composition of capital and therefore hold back investment and growth.[34] Thus the monetary basis for rational economic calculation was rejected as *bourgeois* formalism, of little relevance for socialist planners. The function of planners was to work out and improve the technical relations between the economic branches[35] much as if the Soviet Union was one giant factory. The objective was not consistent balance, so that when the input and output plans failed to mesh, which was usual, the practical response would be the transfer of resources from the residual to the key branches. Although solving the immediate problem, such procedures were detrimental in the long run in that they forced Soviet planners into an empiric and *ad hoc* mode of evaluation,[36] which was emphasised by Stalin's rigid prohibition of theoretical debate which might lead to conclusions about desirable economic means and ends other than those he had determined upon. The failure of economists to engage in theoretical debate to increase understanding of how planned economies work, and thereby to add to the disembodied parameters of growth, remained characteristic of Soviet planning long after they had been shown to be inimical to Soviet objectives.

In terms of the leadership's own criteria, central planning was effective though inefficient. It enabled the planners to mobilise economic forces, many of which had traditionally lain dormant or which had been only partially exploited, and by so doing to simultaneously achieve their economic and military goals. The Soviet Union, in a remarkably short period, grew to assume the status of a major industrial and military power and, building upon the industrial expansion of the 1930s, became after the war one of the two military superpowers. It did produce more steel, more cement, more machine tools and more armaments than any other country in the world. (This is not the place to consider whether these were valid objectives or whether they might have been achieved by other means, or even whether the sacrifice was worth it.) The mechanism which had been devised and put into operation in the 1930s served well the interests of the military, and the economic performance sustained those who urged that increasing investment would of itself bring forth the required growth rate. The outcome was partly fortuitous, however, for though planning effectively mobilised resources, it gave little incentive to use them efficiently, and only so long as consumption could be squeezed and the dynamic economies of scale characteristic of newly industrialising economies available, were the economic and military objectives not in serious competition.

Soviet planning did not emerge fully formed in the 1930s and the processes of change did not stop with the Second World War, but the post-war planning system is essentially that which had been created in the 1930s. Defence priority continues to influence economic perform-ance to a high degree and the system designed to bring about such an outcome remains an acute source of economic inefficiency.

The period of demobilisation after the Second World War and of comparatively low spending on armaments lasted only briefly, brought to an end by the Korean War, after which defence expendi-tures grew at a steady, though not excessive, rate. As economic growth declined from the very high rates achieved in the 1950s, the secular expansion of the armaments branches appropriated a growing proportion of the nation's resources. When, in response to inter-national crises, the rate of military expansion increased above the long term norm, the additional appropriations of economic resources by the military branches increased more than proportionately. Each time defence spending increased above the trend, it brought about a 'prompt and unambiguous' effect on the other macroeconomic com-ponents, especially on investment, which declined by nearly the full amount of the increase.[37] Soviet spokesmen admit that consumption has been held back by defence expenditures[38] and that living stan-dards have fallen below the levels prevailing in other countries at roughly similar levels of development. Once the broad sector allo-cations have been determined, the resource claimant most competi-tive with defence at the margin for the output of the capital goods branches was and remains civilian investment. The basic pattern was established early in the 1950s, when increased military spending

Table 7.2   Growth rate of machinery

	All engineering	Defence
1958–68	11%	19%
1970–82	7%	11%

Source: *Allocation of Resources in the Soviet Union and China, 1983*. Hearings before the Subcommittee on International Trade, Finance and Security Economics of the Joint Economic Committee, Congress of the United States, Washington DC, 1984, p. 1.

during the Korean War was accompanied by declining growth of investment which, however, increased again after the end of hostilities. In 1960–63, when defence spending was again pushed above trend, investment growth decreased and the pattern remains to the present day. Above plan growth in investment in 1980–85 from ten per cent to 20 per cent was probably made possible by a slowdown in the rate of military expansion.[39]

Technological improvements are usually embodied in new machinery and equipment,[40] equally important for the production of civilian and military goods. The output of the machinery and equipment sector, the Machine Building and Metal Working branches, (MBMW), is therefore of particular importance to economic growth. Although Soviet statistics do not distinguish between civilian and military end use, it is possible, by the method of residuals, to construct estimates of sectoral appropriations which reveal a clear and unambiguous trend for the growth in military allocations to exceed the overall rate of expansion of durable goods.

Such large differences in overall growth rates must inevitably increase the proportion of durable goods output apportioned for security purposes. The average military share grew from 11 per cent in 1961 to 19 per cent in 1975 to 30.1 per cent in 1980, and to 40 per cent in 1982. The CIA has recently calculated the marginal share of new machinery for defence at a remarkable 60 per cent[41] though this has been challenged as being unrealistic[42] and is in any case inconsistent with other data on the civilian share.

Since the average proportion of durable output allocated for civilian consumption is only ten per cent the measurable decline has been small, and the brunt of the burden has fallen on civilian durable investment goods, the share of which has fallen from 70.2 per cent to 60 per cent of total output.[43] In recent years engineering branches such as electronics, instrument making, radio and communications, most useful to military production, have grown more rapidly than the branch as a whole.

Gorbachev has identified expansion of the machine making branches as of paramount important to his programme of reconstruction and modernisation.[44] Higher quality industrial and consumption goods are not obtainable without more sophisticated machinery and equipment. Although the Soviet machine park is the largest in the world and the machine branches are efficient producers of high volume general purpose standardised tools, up to 40 per cent of machine equipment is 15 to 20 years or more old and in a speech to the Royal Institute for International Affairs in 1987, Abel Abenbegyan stated that 71 per cent of machine tools were obsolete.[45] The draft guidelines for the twelfth Five-Year Plan identified expansion of the machine tool industry as a top priority,[46] especially for computer equipment, instrument making, electric and electronic equipment. As part of the drive to imporve performance, the Council of Ministers in 1985 created a super-ministry, the Co-ordinating Bureau for Machine Tools, on the lines of the Military Industrial Commission, to address one complete problem area, which has ultimate authority to allocate economic resources throughout industry, even to military users. The quantitative and qualitative indices remain modest however. Between 1971 and 1980 machine building grew at an average annual rate of 0.47 per cent.[47] Production of machinery and equipment for some key sectors such as energy fell up to 20 per cent below target and in some individual categories actually declined. Modest quantity growth coincided with an equally modest quality performance.

A special conference called under the chairmanship of Abel Abenbegyan in 1985 concluded that the Soviet machine tool branch lags behind international best practice in the degree to which high quality products are diffused throughout the economy by ten to 15 years,[48] and the lag appears to be positively correlated with the degree of technological sophistication, being greatest for the most advanced tools. Thirty per cent to 50 per cent of the productive potential in new equipment design may be dissipated because of the shortage of high quality cutting tools, and despite the scale of production imports from more advanced capitalist producers have increased from $75m. in 1976 to $700m. in 1980.[49]

Despite its high priority, little fundamental improvement has occurred. Production of highly automated tools and machines has

Table 7.3   Incremental capital output ratios

	1960	1970	1980
Economy	1.6	2.2	3.3
Industry	1.5	2.1	3.8
Agriculture	0.6	1.0	2.9

Source: R. Leggett, 'Soviet Investment Policy in the 11th Five Year Plan', in *Soviet Economy in the 1980s: Problems and Prospects*, Part One, JEC, Washington DC, 1982, p. 133.

increased slowly and customer complaints about quality are widespread.[50]

Machinery and labour are complementary inputs, and the growing allocation of material resources to the defence branches has been accompanied by a parallel movement of labour. Between 1962 and 1980 employment in the civilian machinery branches increased by 35 per cent, but by 62 per cent in the military related branches, which are estimated to employ up to 60 per cent of machine workers.[51]

Quantitative data alone do not reveal the qualitative preference in end use allocations. The defence branches lay prior claim to the best quality materials, the most advanced machinery, and to the most clever scientists, engineers and economic managers. Soviet enterprises, squeezed betweeen tight plans and capital and machinery shortage, have pursued inefficient investment practices, in particular conservative capital retirement and replacement policies, so that not only the quantity but also the quality of civilian investment is adversely affected. Soviet retirement rates, averaging 1.6 per cent p.a., fall far short of the American figure of 3.6 per cent p.a., and whereas 50 per cent of American gross investment is for replacing capital taken out of service, the figure for the USSR is only 23 per cent.[52] The productivity consequences of an ageing capital stock are amplified by inadequate civilian investment in new machinery and equipment, the potent carriers of new technology. The combined effect has been to increase incremental capital ratios (Table 7.3) in all sectors of the civilian economy.

Economists using more formal econometric techniques have sought to measure the effect of defence priority on the major macroeconomic variables and on overall economic growth. The usefulness of the results depend on the reliability of the data and on the appropriateness of the structural relationships specified in the models.

Since the models are based on avowedly capitalist concepts, they are unlikely to replicate Soviet circumstances exactly, but do indicate within broad magnitudes the dimensions of the civilian–military trade-off. The techniques are simple enough in principle. A statistical correlation based on historical data is calculated for military expenditures and the civilian macroeconomic end uses. Assuming that the model remains a valid statistical description of the economy, variations in economic growth, civilian investment and consumption can be estimated for different hypothetical growth rates of the independent variable, defence spending. The technique thus allows a statistical comparison of the beneficial or adverse consequences to the civilian economy of changing the rate of growth of defence spending and, assuming that this is within the control of the political authorities, gives a broad assessment of the outcomes of different policy mixes.

The perhaps surprising conclusion which obtains from most such calculations, is that quite large changes in the rate of increase of defence expenditures have only limited impact on the rate of growth of GDP, industry and of agriculture.[53] If the baseline assumption is that defence expenditures grow at around 4.5 per cent p.a., equal to the long term trend from around 1960 to 1976 or so, the economy will grow at approximately two per cent p.a. If it is then assumed that the growth rate of defence spending declines to zero, and the output of the MBMW branches which would have been allocated for military production is instead redistributed to civilian investment, GDP will grow by only 0.17 per cent faster than the baseline projection. If, on the other hand, defence were assumed to grow by nine per cent p.a., GDP could be expected to grow only negligibly slower. The effects of such severe changes in military spending on civilian end use is more marked, with growth ranging from 0.83 to 2.68 per cent for consumption, which could have a significant effect on improvements in living standards, and from 2.0 to 3.4 per cent for investment. Assumptions about different degrees of resource transfer can be incorporated into the models. If, in addition to MBMW outputs, R and D resources are also transferred, and furthermore it is assumed that defence based resources are more efficient on average than those in the civilian branches, only marginal improvement is obtained over the baseline case.[54] Different models yield slightly different outcomes, but in each case the general conclusion holds that large changes in the rate of defence growth yield only minor direct and immediate costs or benefits to the civilian economy.

The explanation for the comparatively small impact on civilian growth is twofold. In the first place, even though the Soviet defence sector is larger than that in most developed countries, it is still a comparatively small proportion of total GNP. Changes to a comparatively small component of a larger total inevitably have small consequences on the larger variable. In addition, the inefficiency of Soviet investment during the 1970s yields a low output elasticity of capital, so that quite large additions to the capital stock produce comparatively small increases in output.

The inference from such models that defence expenditures have only marginal consequences on civilian output is misleading. Apart from the conceptual and statistical problems with the models themselves, a number of crucial qualifications must be made. Even if it were true that over a brief period of time the trade-off between the civilian and military sector was small, foregone exponential civilian growth over a long period of time is cumulatively large. The models measure the marginal adjustment of economic variables around an average level, whereas a consistently different allocation in past periods would have altered the average level, so that by later periods consumption and investment would be much larger than in fact they are. They assume symmetry between expansion and contraction of defence spending, whereas there is a strong likelihood that outcomes may in fact be asymmetrical, which means that the detrimental impact of more rapid growth of defence spending will exceed the beneficial consequences of lower defence growth because of the effects on bottlenecks, which discernibly reduced growth rates in the tenth and eleventh Five-Year Plans. The models also indicate that the statistical cost to society of a given rate of military expansion has increased. Whereas in the 1970s the economy could simultaneously attain over three per cent p.a. growth in consumption and 4.5 per cent p.a. growth in defence expenditures, by the 1980s, due to more adverse economic performance, a 4.5 per cent rate of increase in defence would constrain consumption to 2.6 per cent.[55]

Policy-makers who have to calculate the security and civilian benefits of alternative allocations at a point of time are less concerned with the historical relationships between economic sectors than with the crucial policy question of how newly created resources are allocated between civilian and military outputs. One item of relevant information is the proportion of investment goods output that may have to be sacrificed for a given rate of expansion of military output. The marginal cost in terms of new resources foregone far exceeds the historical average. If military production were to continue growing at the long run rate of 4.5 per cent, then given certain, not implausible assumptions, the defence branches would, by the year 2000, absorb upward of 25 per cent of new material resources created between 1985 and 2000. Figures for the crucial durable goods sectors show by the same calculations that by 1995 defence would absorb up to 90 per cent of all new durable goods output; that is, virtually no new capital goods of the type most conducive to technological progress would be available for civilian investment – an impossible state of affairs, especially given the thrust of the Gorbachev modernisation programme.

The statistical models are sensitive to fairly modest changes in some of the key assumptions. Variations in the assumed rate of increase in productivity have an especially potent effect on growth and hence on the trade-off between civilian and military outcomes.[56]

Despite the large numbers employed in total Soviet R and D, skilled scientists and engineers remain in short supply.[57] Military R and D accounts for around 50 per cent or so of total expenditures, but 60 per cent of R and D personnel, and of those not working directly in scientific institutes, over 70 per cent are employed in the MBMW branches, a high proportion of whose output is destined for military end use.[58]

Preoccupation with the military usefulness of new or existing technology has often overly determined the pattern of development in key industrial sectors. Soviet haste in developing computer hardware most useful for defence and basic science analysis, instead of that economically useful for planning and management, has been one explanation for the ten-year gap behind Western computer technology which the Soviet authorities are so anxious to close.

Military R and D is bounded with restrictions, which not only reduce the efficiency of information flows between different institutes within the defence sector, but also between it and the civilian branches. Spill-ins effects do reduce the burden of resources foregone to the civilian economy, but the departmentalism endemic in the Soviet economy is specially virulent in military related R and D, where security considerations give an added reason for and justification of secrecy. The sectoral distribution of patents shows there to be less linkages between defence and the civilian sectors than between different branches within the civilian economy.[59] Military spin-off effects have been limited, largely to management techniques which have little security implications[60] and unlike capitalist economies, the lack of a profit-oriented sector seeking to exploit military development for private gain inhibits the flow of information, personnel, materials and technology. The economic incentive from both supply and demand to generate military civilian spin-offs is weak and the administrative mechanisms largely ineffectual.

The adverse consequences of investment foregone is specially critical given that according to Marxist theory extended reproduction requires increasing proportions of the nation's resources. Capital was the catalyst for growth, especially that portion allocated to the capital goods sector. Capital, however, required complementary labour to avoid or at least postpone diminishing returns. Thus, crudely, the intellectual rationalisation for the two revolutionary institutional changes which transformed Soviet society in the 1930s and which has since characterised it. Although Marxian theory, especially as extended in the 1920s, provides a sophisticated analysis of the appropriate distribution between the means of production and the means of consumption, the actual strategy for growth in the 1930s was determined by much cruder considerations,[61] being little more than the identification of a small number of key sectors as being especially crucial for rapid expansion.

The preferred strategy was what came to be described as extensive growth, based primarily on mobilising underused resources to produce the investment goods necessary for extended reproduction. The economy was richly endowed in natural resources, with a large and inefficient agrarian sector – in 1929, 82 per cent of the population worked on the land. The potential and realised benefit of extensive growth was enormous. Net material product grew on average by 14 per cent p.a. between 1929 and 1938, and industrial gross output by 16.4 p.a.[62] Whereas in 1928 investment accounted for 19.5 per cent of GNP, by 1930 fully 36 per cent of the nation's resources were allocated to increasing the capital stock, and though such an extraordinary ratio could not be maintained indefinitely, at no time did it fall below 25 per cent. Growth was additionally enhanced by the dynamic economies of scale available to newly industrialising countries and by the opportunities to borrow technology from more advanced nations.

The Great Patriotic War only briefly interrupted the pace of economic expansion, and during the 1950s GNP grew at an annual average rate of five per cent. Economic growth is the cumulative consequence of two basic forces; the rate at which new resource and factor inputs are mobilised and the efficiency with which they are

Table 7.4   Contributions to economic growth

	USSR	Japan	USA	NW Europe
Total factor input	70.0	39.9	58.7	35.7
Labour	25.2	13.0	33.7	17.4
Capital	44.6	26.9	25.9	18.1
Output per unit of input	30.2	60.1	41.3	64.5

Source: S. Cohn, 'The Soviet Path to Economic Growth: A Comparative Analysis', *Revenue of Income and Wealth*, 1976, p. 53.

used. Both exist in all economic systems to a greater or lesser degree but other things being equal growth which is based more on increased efficiency is less costly in material terms and more sustainable in the long run. A comparison of the Soviet growth experience with that of a group of industrialised capitalist economies shows the Soviet Union, consistent with Marxist theory, to be disproportionately dependent on increasing inputs of factors of production. Increased efficiency made and continues to make a relatively small contribution to overall economic growth.

So long as factors of production were readily and cheaply available, extensive growth was acceptable. Even when the Soviet Union grew faster than most industrialised nations, often by considerable margins, the inefficiencies inherent in extensive growth slowly but inexorably overwhelmed the benefit of youth. According to calculations based on data from Soviet handbooks, economic growth declined by an average of 0.3 per cent p.a. CIA data show a more modest rate of decline of 0.1 per cent p.a.[63] By the eleventh Five-Year Plan, growth had fallen to less than two per cent p.a., though under Gorbachev so far growth has averaged a modest 2.5 per cent p.a.[64]

The slowdown was partly a consequence of slower growth in factor inputs. In the 1950s investment increased at an annual average rate of 13 per cent p.a., occasionally reaching 20 per cent p.a. Such a pace could not be sustained and in the 1960s the long term trend fell to the more modest, but by world standards still rapid rate of 7.5 per cent p.a. Industrial investment grew even more furiously, 22 per cent on average in the 1950s, 13 per cent in the 1960s. The trend was however downwards and fell in successive plan periods to four per cent p.a.

Growth in the labour market remained buoyant throughout the period. The global data however conceal a deleterious maldistribu-

Table 7.5   Total Factor Productivity

	1960–70	1970–75	1975–80	1980–85[a]
All sectors	1.5	0.1	–0.4	–0.8
Industry	0.2	1.0	–0.7	–1.0

Source: D. Bond and H. Levine, 'The Eleventh Five Year Plan, 1981–85', in
S. Braler and T. Gustafson, *Russia at the Crossroads*, (London:
Allen and Unwin, 1982, pp. 88–9).
[a] New Leader, p. 18 (Allocations 84/5, p. 77).

tion between the economic sectors. In the dominant western regions,
the Russian Soviet Federated Socialist Republic, the Ukraine and the
Baltic states, population is barely replacing itself and labour markets
are tight. In the more agrarian Muslim provinces, the demographic
trend is more favourable. Since however Muslim workers are reluctant to migrate to take advantage of higher material rewards in the
western regions and in Siberia, the labour imbalance remains a real
constraint on economic expansion.

Lower growth is partly the inevitable consequence of economic
ageing. Cheap reserves of energy and of raw materials have been
exhausted, new wells and mines have to be sunk deeper, in more
forbidding rock structures and further away from the major centres
of production.

The single most crucial explanator of falling growth however was
declining total factor productivity, which was low at the beginning of
the period and declined steadily in almost every branch of the
economy.

This too was partly a function of age. Initially a high proportion of
gross investment was available as net addition to the capital stock,
and given also the benefits of lateness, labour productivity grew at
around five per cent p.a. Because the capital stock grew faster than
national output, capital productivity has been consistently negative
and declining. Whereas in 1970 each additional rouble of output
required an input of three roubles of capital, by 1980 the same
increase in output required six roubles of capital.[65]

Factor productivity has been squeezed by the increasing inappro-
priateness of extensive growth to modern societies where, as Gorbachev himself acknowledges, qualitative replace quantitative indices
of progress. It has also been adversely affected by inefficient investment policies forced on enterprise managers by shortage of capital,

partly because of competition from the defence industry.

The psychic, as opposed to the purely quantitative, cost of defence spending depends on the urgency with which civilian objectives requiring committed resources are sought by the leadership. So long as the extensive growth model was acceptable and consumer claims residual, the psychic burden was acceptable to the leaders if not the population at large. For Gorbachev, both the prior claim of the defence industry and the mode of allocation of which the chief beneficiary has historically been defence, are hindrances to his vision of a modern, technologically sophisticated society. To that degree the defence burden has increased and may become intolerable.

8 International Arms Trade

International trade in armaments and military equipment is an extension of east–west competition[1] and as such is a mechanism for and a consequence of the globalisation of the arms race.[2] This single central fact determines the structure of and the motivation for the international trade in armaments. Trade ratios vary from year to year, influenced by one or a small number of high value sales embedded in long term secular trends, but is always highly concentrated. At their most dominating the USA and the USSR have accounted for over 80 per cent of world trade, though the ratio has since declined. The addition of the second echelon of exporters – France, the UK and West Germany – increases the concentration ratio to a maximum of 90 per cent. However, though the arms trade can correctly be described as oligopolist[3] the market has certain characteristics, which complicate conventional oligopol analysis. Though the five biggest producers dominate, the number of countries which export some arms has since the early 1960s only twice fallen below 20. Moreover, the secular trend has been to increase the number of arms exporting countries. In the decade 1964 to 1974 the average number was 25, whereas between 1975 and 1985, the number of countries had increased to 41.[4] Of these, 14 have been identified as 'core' exporters defined as selling some armaments each year. Market performance is determined not only by industrial structure but also by the ease with which new entrants can compete for market shares. Increasing numbers suggest that entry is expensive but not prohibitive. As the total numbers of arms exporting countries increase, though each country does not export every year, the five nation concentration ratio declines, from 92 per cent in 1967 to 72 per cent in 1982. Smaller producers cannot research, develop and manufacture a comprehensive range of armaments but concentrate in areas where they have some comparative advantage, usually at the cheaper and less sophisticated end of the market, where the degree of competition is probably greater than the global data might indicate. A partial product group breakdown shown in Table 8.1 illustrates a trend similar to that in the product *sui generis*. Missile exports in particular show a high degree of monopoly.

The manner in which the basic arms trade data are collected, that is, in terms of major weapons, probably overestimates the degree of

Table 8.1   Market shares of major weapons' exporters 1985 (percentage)

	Combat Aircraft			Armoured Vehicles			Missiles			Naval Vessel		
Country	A	B	C	A	B	C	A	B	C	A	B	C
France	11	12	11	19	–	21	10	8	14	9		9
FRG	1	3	–	3	38	–	2	3	–	12		13
USSR	22	9	28	28	36	27	8	4	15	26		26
US	25	44	18	25	2	27	76	82	63	5		6
Others	26	30	25	24	20	24	3	2	5	36		34
% of Exporters	12	8	10	13	5	11	9	7	8	15	2	14

Key: A   Share of total world exports
     B   Share of exports to advanced industrial countries
     C   Share of exports to Third World countries

Source: A. Ross, 'The Political Economy of the International Arms Race: A Supply Side Market Analysis'. Paper prepared for presentation at the Annual Meeting of the International Studies Association, 14–18 April 1987, Washington DC.

concentration, in that those military categories where third and fourth level exporters are most competitive tend to be under-reported.

Market performance is influenced not only by structure and ease of entry but also by the behaviour of existing buyers and sellers, for instance the degree to which exporters compete for shares of the global market. Despite considerable customer loyalty, sometimes expensively bought, the global pattern shows a willingness by some buyers to switch from established to newer and more competitive suppliers, induced by better quality, or financial terms, or less restrictive conditions of sales. Despite the obvious advantage of buying new weapons which are compatible with existing inventories, customers are willing to buy even sophisticated equipment from more than one source. The concentration ratio of the two largest exporters has varied from 82 per cent to 54 per cent, whilst that of the next most important exporter, France, increased from a low of two per cent in 1971 to 12 per cent in 1983.

Conventional market analysis is further confused by the mixed motives of trade, which are sometimes complementary and sometimes competitive. Nations which are ultimately sovereign over export policy are motivated by an admixture of economic, political and strategic objectives, whereas the firms which manufacture and sell weapons are, in the non-socialist states at least, motivated by commercial profit. Export policy, whether a particular sales should go ahead or not, and at what terms, has some of the characteristics of bargaining between the state and the firms, and the economic benefit to society is unlikely to equate to that for the firms.[5] For the state, the type of product sold, the restrictions imposed on its use and the suitability of the recipient are not neutral parameters but determine whether the sale is acceptable or not.

The reason why, unlike civilian goods, the state and the firm have different interests and objectives, is the externalities which are embedded in weapons and military equipment.[6] For the firm, the externality is unimportant, for the state it may be decisive. The state is concerned not only with the direction of the externality but also with its weight. Lethality that is, can be positively or negatively correlated with economic benefit, and can be crucial or relatively unimportant. Although the export of arms and hence their possession by recipient countries need not in themselves lead to war, and indeed have on occasion been used as bribes to induce a more accommodating stance in regional issues,[7] since arms sales by one supplier to a client are often matched by countervailing sales to the client's regional or ideological adversary, regional and global security is more likely to be reduced than otherwise. The exporting nation, once weapons have been sold and are in the arsenals of the recipient countries, loses some control and the externality looms large. The exporter can restrict the use which the client state may make of its imported weapons, but these cannot always be enforced. It can also threaten not to re-supply if weapons are misused. But the existence of alternative suppliers, and the fact that countries have different assessments of negative externality, is seldom wholly inhibiting. Exporting countries face a problem of dynamic inconsistency,[8] that is, optimal behaviour may require the threat of embargo prior to the sale, but its encouragement if the bluff is called by the client. Given furthermore economic pressure for sale by special interest groups, and the likelihood that buyer restraint is weak,[9] the externality can reach dominating proportions.[10] Exporters have sought to exercise some restraint by not selling top of the range models or imposing constraints on weapon use which ultimately may make the sale unattractive. Furthermore, the calculus of benefits and costs can vary over time. In the short period the economic and political advantages dominate, but over the long term the disadvantages, regional or strategic imbalance, become more apparent, but since for bureaucrats the long term disadvantages emerge after they have left office, there is a tendency to discount the long term. Even if a rational calculation shows that the first best solution is not to approve, the cost of losing a market or the confidence of a customer gives a powerful impetus to the short term.[11] If over time a nation's ideological preferences change, the assessment of otherwise identical domestic and international circumstances may differ, as therefore will policy towards arms sales. This was clearly the case in the USA when, in contrast to President Carter's view that foreign arms sales should be considered an exceptional foreign policy tool, President Reagan insisted that they should be positively stimulated and used purposefully to further American objectives.[12]

A simple taxonomy identifies three types of client:

1. Countries which, formally or otherwise, are allies of the exporting nation, and where by and large the economic foreign policy and strategic objectives are mutually reinforcing. The two dominant exporters are hegemonic states. In the immediate post-war period, American exports were mainly supplied to Western Europe and Japan, designed not only to assist economic recovery, but also to promote political stability and thereby serve American strategic objectives.[13] It is therefore not surprising that arms exports were subsidised, over 90 per cent of which in the 1950s being available as grants.[14] Although the ratio changed as the Europeans became more able to pay commercial prices, by 1961 grants amounted to $1.5bn. and commercially motivated sales $630m.[15] The equipment sold to Europe was not usually front line but the weapons were nevertheless more than adequate given existing inventories. The USSR also exported equipment at highly subsidised prices to its major allies, one benefit to the hegemonic nation and its allies being the increase in the level of standardisation and inter-operability. In NATO, the recovery of the European nations and the balance of payments costs to the USA changed American policy to an emphasis on sales. In 1961 President Kennedy created the Office of Internal Logistics Negotiations, in essence an arms salesman to make exports more commercially viable, and by 1966 the ratio of grant to aid had been reversed; grants amounting to $824m. and sales $1.9bn. For exporters the combined influence of commercial profit and positive externalities tend to push sales beyond the commercially optimal.

2. The second category of countries are adversaries, where, even if trade in civilian goods is allowed, that in weapons, military related equipment or dual purpose goods is embargoed or inhibited to varying degrees, for no nation deliberately increases its adversary's military potential. The objective is straightforward, to minimise export sales.

3. The third group of countries are those which are neutral or non-aligned, and where the calculus of benefit and of the direction and dimension of externality is more complex.

Because of the array of economic political and strategic characteristics embedded in armaments, the calculation of net benefits often appear inconsistent, and outcomes depend on the relative weight of conflicting external costs and benefits.

Over the entire post-war period the dominant arms exporting nation has been the USA. Initially means (arms exports) and objectives (alliance security) were mutually congruent.[16] American exports were financed from two sources. The Military Assistance Programme (MAP), established in 1949, authorised grants, while Foreign Military Sales (FMS) was the source of the commercially motivated sales and government loans and credit. Although NATO countries and Japan decreased in relative importance, the major motivation in selling to third category nations remained political, chiefly to influence the foreign policy behaviour of the client state. Arms exports give substance to cordial relations – a symbol of support and friendship. They are also high profile conduits to foreign policy and military elites in the importing country which pay quick benefit. The 1961 Foreign Assistance Act justified arms exports as being:

(*i*) to strengthen the defence of the free world;
(*ii*) to preserve and increase American military influence;
(*iii*) to decrease the exchange cost of military troops abroad.

Although the USA did not export to its direct adversary, the ideological compatibility of the recipient nation did not assume great importance, true also of the Soviet Union. The basic characteristic was a pragmatic and therefore often short term response to opportunities as circumstances allowed. The USA was as willing to export to Marxist countries such as Somalia as those which were more obviously compatible with its capitalist ideology.[17] The USA hoped thereby to sustain the loyalty of those nations which inclined towards the American position and to entice to the American camp undecided nations, for denying leverage to the Soviet Union was quite as important to the USA. Once the initial sales have been completed, often at concessionary rates, recipient countries tend to be more dependent for spare parts, replacement of obsolescent stock or of weapons lost in war, or for personnel to service the arms and train local soldiers and officers.

Even if pragmatic concerns of foreign policy identify the direction of trade, its dimension and structural component still have to be determined. Because the objectives and the constraints are fuzzy, the basic characteristics of trade often seem *ad hoc* and inconsistent. For instance, though the USA did not re-supply Egypt's depleted stocks of armaments after the Six-Day War it did so after the Yom Kippur War.

A more fundamental problems for hegemonic states is to reconcile apparently inconsistent goals, especially if, as happens, the source nation loses control of the use which clients make of weapons. This extreme form is the American dilemma in the Middle East, where because of diverse foreign policy goals, the once symbiotic congruence between means and ends no longer exists.[18] Whereas the USA is concerned to secure Israel's security, she also seeks to minimise Soviet influence and to promote friendly relations with important strategic or oil producing states. Israeli use of American weapons in regional wars or bombing raids increases the problem of reconciling conficting objectives. American conditions of sale in response to Israeli concerns may push conservative Arab buyers not only to other capitalist sellers but, as in the case of Kuwait, to the Soviet Union.

After the initial American dominance, the mid-1950s witnessed one of the decisive turning points which have characterised the trade. In September 1955 Czechoslovakia agreed to sell $200m. worth of planes, tanks and ships to Egypt. The real supplier was of course the Soviet Union, and the agreement with Egypt represented its first outside the Soviet bloc. The Egyptian agreement was swiftly followed by similar deals with Syria, Afghanistan, Yemen, Iraq and others. The Soviet decision to export arms to non-Warsaw Pact countries was important not only in its own right but, in conjunction with change in the international political system, increased the salience of the international arms trade.

Historically Russia, as an agrarian economy, had limited political and economic links with other agrarian states, and less developed countries played a minor part in Stalin's Manichean view of systemic confrontation. Only with his death did the Third World assume prominence in Soviet foreign policy. The attainment by the Soviet

Union of the hydrogen bomb and increasingly its means of delivery, created a position of internal deterrence in Europe which reduced the likelihood of direct confrontation there. The Third World offered an arena where the Soviet challenge to American hegemony was less risky and more likely to bear fruit.[19] Indian independence proved a catalyst for decolonisation in Africa and Asia. Between 1949 and 1957 the number of independent countries increased from 50 to 120. Decolonisation not only increased the number of potential buyers but also created a political environment which transformed them into active customers. The withdrawal of the metropolitan powers created a power vacuum in previously stable geographical areas. Borders between newly independent countries were often ill- and arbitrarily drawn, and arms were essential when claims which were resisted were pushed for disputed territories. Sometimes tribal loyalties within states caused incipient or actual civil war, and central governments required arms to put down local insurrections. The purchase of arms by one country almost inevitably boosted a regional arms race and hence exports. Modern armaments also symbolise modernisation and prestige for nations often lacked a historical legacy of legitimacy.

The newly independent states were often hostile to the system of political, and later economic, imperialism which had enslaved them and by association to the capitalist nations in whose interests the imperialistic system functioned. Radical leaders such as Nkrumah, Sukarno and Nasser articulated a hostility to the exploitative system and to many of its operational characteristics. Socialism offered an alternative blueprint where centralised control over economic resources which could be deployed in desired directions to meet pre-determined developmental objectives contrasted with the arbitrary outcomes of markets. The Soviet Union offered not only a model which had successfully managed the transition to powerful industrial statehood,[20] but was moreover in the 1950s and 1960s outgrowing most of the capitalist nations. The Soviet Union was also, in rhetoric at least, a passionate supporter of decolonisation and, hence, a natural political ally of new states. As far as arms were concerned, it also offered more practical benefits of low prices, favourable conditions of sale, and a range of weapons well suited to Third World armies, although traditional ties between the metropolitan and the newly independent countries sustained a profitable commercial nexus.

Once Soviet leaders identified the Third World as an area where they might with advantage challenge American hegemony, they

Table 8.2   Military and Economic Aid 1955–1960 ($m.)

	Military Aid	Economic Aid
Middle East	1437	1217
South Asia	1695	180
Africa	735	33
East Asia	404	1136
Latin America	30	–
Total	4291	2566

Source: Gu Guan-Fu, 'Soviet Aid to the Third World', *Soviet Studies*, vol. XXXV, no. 1, 1983, p. 74.

quickly and effectively moved to maximise the Soviet advantage.

Despite their unrivalled experience with central planning, the practical guidance which Soviet planners could offer newly independent Third World countries was limited, and Soviet enthusiasm for economic aid, which was often difficult to administer and bore fruit only in the long run, quickly waned. Military assistance, export of arms and equipment, technical and military advisers, training Third World officers in Moscow, and so on, offered opportunities for more immediate return and quickly became the major Soviet foreign policy instrument in Asia and Africa, though exports remained relatively modest.

The Soviet Union's nuclear strategic doctrine made obsolete in the mid- to late 1950s a large proportion of its weapons inventory, which was, however, appropriate to Third World countries and which were available for immediate despatch to customers. Furthermore, when the USSR exported weapons from current production, the existing inventory and new stock benefitted from Soviet preference for simple, sturdy weapons with a high degree of commonality. When an arms agreement stipulated weapons from current production, the marginal cost to the Soviet Union was often low. It was in any case producing large quantities for its own forces and those of its Warsaw Pact allies, and the additional cost of extending the production line to meet a Third World order was small. This was especially so given the surge capacity which was habitually built into Soviet plant. So effective were Soviet production and delivery schedules that the time between agreement of sales and delivery was routinely about half of that taken by American firms.[21] Soviet weapons were also competitive in terms of price and conditions of sale. Soviet prices were usually below Western prices for equivalent equipment, and credit was available on generous terms, usually at two per cent interest, the principal repayable over ten years or longer, and with a grace period of one to three years.[22] If, even so, its clients were unable to repay, the Soviet Union was usually prepared to accept repayment in local soft currencies, or in raw materials which could be re-sold on international markets. From the outset the Soviet Union showed a remarkable adroitness in selling armaments such that whereas pre-war it accounted for only six per cent or so of world exports, by 1970 the ratio had increased to 30 per cent. In civilian manufactured equipment the Soviet share of the market does not exceed two per cent. By the beginning of the 1970s arms exports to the Third World accounted for 75 per cent of total sales, and had become its primary instrument of foreign policy.[23]

The motivation, as for the USA, was primarily political and strategic,[24] to obtain access to political elites and exert leverage on the foreign policy decisions of the recipient nation, to induce neutral states not to lean towards the West, and after the break with China, to offset its influence in the Third World. Arms sales were also exchanged for military bases and landing rights, for example South Yemen, Somalia, Syria and North Vietnam.[25] The Soviet Union, like the USA, opportunistically responded to circumstances as and when they arose. It sold arms to conservative states, ideologically opposed to the socialist principles which it espoused, some of which even waged war on local communist parties, for example, Pakistan, Iran, Egypt and Guinea.[26]

By the early 1970s the USA and USSR together accounted for 80 per cent of world trade in armaments in which the Third World had become the largest and fastest market, equivalent in 1969 to $6.2bn.

The Soviet Union was not the only country to take advantage of the growth of world trade. A second echelon of producers, France, the UK and later West Germany, established the basis for arms industries which were later to challenge the duopoly of the two superpowers, and in so doing increased the degree of commercialisation.

Growth and change in the volume and structure of the arms trade in the 1970s were enormously enhanced by the tenfold increase in oil prices in 1973–4, and again in 1979. In 1970 Third World imports amounted to $11bn. By 1980 they had increased to $20bn.

In 1968 oil producers as a group accounted for only 12 per cent of

Third World imports, though the ratio is deflated by the exceptional rate of American deliveries to South Asia during the Vietnam war. By 1975 the ratio had increased to a remarkable 39 per cent. Not only did the oil rich nations themselves buy arms, they also lavished aid on poor belligerent allies. For instance in 1974 Saudi Arabia, Abu Dhabi, Qatar and Libya pledged $2.3bn. for four years to the front line states Egypt, Syria and Jordan.[27] The USA similarly supported its ally Israel. Petrodollars which could not be absorbed by the oil producers, were deposited with Western commercial banks which in turn lent to poorer Third World countries, much of which was spent on armaments. By the end of the decade 80 per cent of Soviet and 60 per cent of American exports were delivered to the Middle East. Prior to 1974 exports to the Third World were financed largely from grants and were highly subsidised. The two major exporters could therefore exercise a high degree of product control over their clients. They not only regulated the volume of trade but also controlled the level of technology embodied in exports. Weapons exported to the Third World were usually old and, for the two powers, obsolete. Where sales were made from current production, less advanced models were usually delivered.

However, nations which were able and willing to pay cash could not be fobbed off with second rate products. For oil-countries or aid recipients only the most advanced weapons were acceptable. The spread of high technology throughout the Third World equalised military technology between countries at different levels of economic development to a far greater degree than in the civilian sectors.

In 1964 nine less developed countries possessed supersonic aircraft, and eight SAM missiles. By 1974 the numbers had increased to 41 and 32 respectively.[28] Arab customers were sold front line models from current production often before they were available to the armed forces of the manufacturing country. The Soviet Union sold MIG 29 to India, the UK sold Chobham protected tanks to Iran, and France the Crotale SAM missile.

Growth in the volume of trade and in the diffusion of technology coincided with the increasing importance of a new echelon of arms producers and suppliers less concerned with the externality dimension of exports, and in consequence more amenable to customer demands. The second and, eventually, third rank producers increased the degree of commercialisation, weakened customer loyalty and thereby the control which the USA and the USSR had traditionally exercised.

For the second echelon of arms producers, initially the UK and France, but later West Germany, Italy and Spain, economic considerations were paramount.[29] In France and the UK the economic factors followed naturally from a prior determination that their political and strategic independence required a comprehensive indigenous R and D and production capacity from light arms to nuclear weapons and delivery systems. For the other countries the motivation was more essentially economic.

Sophisticated weapons systems, which require high prior expenditures on R and D, are characterised by high learning curve economies. For the second echelon countries the domestic market is too small to reap the full benefits of scale. Exports spread R and D costs and increase production beyond levels justified by domestic demand and therefore reduce the unit cost to the nation and keep a warm mobilisaton base which might be required for surge production.

For countries such as France and the UK, domestic procurement at current levels is almost certainly not sustainable without a commitment to exports. France exports around 40 per cent of total domestic production, and the UK 35 per cent.[30] For particular industries at times the degree of export dependence is even greater. Fifty per cent of French aero engines and 60 per cent of electronics output is exported and for firms such as Dassault and British Aerospace the ratio is 70 per cent.[31] Without exports these key European defence contractors could not survive. With high concentration in the second and third echelon countries, failure of a single firm might signal the end of the industry and therefore of a domestic capacity. The distinction sometimes made between local and national objectives all but disappears.

In the USA a Congressional Budget Office Study calculated savings of $560m. on an $8bn. FMS programme equal to a half of one per cent of the defence expenditure. For France the savings from lower unit costs amounted to six-tenths of one per cent.[32]

Defence has been perceived as a potent carrier of new technology, and medium sized industrial nations such as Italy and Spain, consciously supported and promoted production and by extension exports as part of a long term strategy of modernisation.[33] By virtue of steady expansion the sector in many countries is a not inconsiderable employer. Arms sales directly or indirectly create about 277 000 jobs in the USA, 70 000 in the UK, 60 000–70 000 in West Germany and 130 000–140 000 in France most of which because of high R and D embodiments are highly skilled.

Exports also directly improve the balance of payments, which for many nations in the 1970s was of considerable importance. Although it is economically specious to match one category of exports to another category of imports, many nations sought for a while to directly compensate for high oil costs by stimulating arms sales.

Nor, despite the traditional primacy of political motives, were commercial motives wholly absent in the two superpowers. Apart from a brief hiatus when President Carter sought to transform arms sales into an exceptional foreign policy instrument, when many profitable transactions were foregone, commercial motives became more salient. They were never important enough to dominate policy however.

In the USSR too, the economic motivation did not dominate, but did increase in relative importance. Soviet conditions of sales hardened and by 1980 over 40 per cent of agreements were invoiced in hard currency or commodities such as oil amounting to $4.2bn., increasing to $6.1bn. in 1982 before falling back to $4.3bn. in 1985.[34] Even poor countries such as Zambia were expected to pay in hard currencies over a shorter period of time, though favoured customers such as India could depend on heavy subsidies. In 1975, hard currency payments amounted to $1.5bn. Despite the windfall benefit to Soviet energy exports after 1974, the balance of payments worsened. Exports of civilian manufactured goods were not competitive on world markets, and Soviet officials pursued a conservative borrowing strategy. Much potential oil exports were committed to Eastern Europe at subsidised prices. Imports of food sometimes amounted to $9bn. per year, and of industrial and high-tech goods a further $14 bn. Armaments were one of the few manufacturing sectors which were competitive on world markets. By 1980 the Soviet Union accounted for 37 per cent of world trade which with energy and gold, was the most important earner of foreign exchange.

Despite the contribution of the trade to the balance of payments and to economic activity, the net benefit to the state may be low, even negative.[35] The economic interest of the state and the commercial interest of the firm may diverge sharply. For the firms, sales increase profits and are thereby beneficial. For the nation, or at least the taxpayer, this need not necessarily be so. Because of high overheads, average costs usually exceed price so that without public subsidy exports would not be profitable. R and D costs paid by the state, export finance, concessional aid and other similar items borne by the state, are often essential pre-requisites for accounting profits.

The secrecy which habitually characterises the terms of agreement between buyers and sellers precludes precise calculation of net gain. For countries with large domestic production capacity the leakage into imports is minimised. For the largest western producers the ratio of arms to total exports ranged from 1.5 per cent to three to four per cent for the UK, 1.7 per cent to four to five per cent for France, and 4.5 per cent to 4.7 per cent for the USA. For the Soviet Union the ratio was a much higher ten per cent or so.[36] However, civilian exports 'crowded out' reduce the net benefit. When, as often happens, the recipients subsequently fail to repay the loan, the benefit to the state is even less. In one two-year period, 1982–84, four of eleven American clients were late by more than 50 per cent, and from one group of African countries it did not receive repayment of 57 per cent to 99 per cent of its original loan.[37]

The economic incentive for industries and corporations creates a powerful arms lobby which is concerned to maximise the local, rather than the national interest, of such weight as to create an almost autonomous dynamic for sales.

Despite the complex calculation of real net cost, more nations were induced to enter the export market in the 1980s, many from the Third World. The two-nation concentration ratio naturally declined from its peak to 62 per cent in 1984. The market changed from an effective duopoly to an oligopoly to a polyopoly. The increase in the number of sellers coincided with a deceleration of growth of deliveries and agreements. Third World imports increased by 60 per cent from 1965 to 1969, 230 per cent 1975–79 and by only four to five per cent 1980–85.[38]

One explanation was the completion of procurement cycles by some major buyers such as Libya. The major explanation is however economic:[39] the fall in the price of oil exports for some countries, the increase in arms related external debt in others.[40]

The generally greater salience of economic motives and the importance of non-hegemonic states where economic motivation always had been higher loosened the externality constraints on conditions of sale. Increasingly economic prevailed over diplomatic considerations. When Congress imposed unacceptable conditions on the sale of F-15 fighter planes to Saudi Arabia, it easily switched to buy Tornadoes from the more accommodating British. Not only were the lower echelon countries prepared to waive unwelcome restrictions, but other things being equal, were in any case more favoured by many buyers, lacking the edge of superpower confrontation which often accompanied purchases from the USA or the USSR.

For many customers not engaged in hot conflicts, large item procurements declined in relative importance as economic stringency forced a more careful matching of demands to resources. Fewer agreements included large aircraft and missile sales and more included ammunition, infantry, electronic and communication equipment.[41]

In the long run more significant was a growing insistence by buyers on importing technology and arms manufacturing equipment in addition to armaments themselves. Historically the USA had been more accommodating over the transfer of technology than the USSR which, with the exception of the agreement which allowed India to manufacture the MIG 21 under licence, had resisted diffusing its technology abroad.

The smaller exporters were less inhibited than either of the two superpowers. France had seldom expressed concern about the spread of weapons-making technology and when later Italy and West Germany traded at significant levels, technology exports were a deliberate strand of the competition against the more established sellers. Indeed, one explanation for the Soviet Union's recent relatively poor performance may be its conservative refusal to export its technology.[42] Demands from buyers for more technology were often formulated as offset agreements, defined as any arrangement whereby the exporting country shares production of a system or purchases items from sources within the foreign country to offset an established percentage of the cost of procurement and can include co-production, licensed production, subcontracting overseas investment, technology transfer and counter trade. The aim usually is to decrease the currency necessary to buy a military item, or to increase the revenue to pay for it. The evidence, suggests that for the USA offsets may account for up to 33 per cent of total trade.[43]

The incentives, of different intensities, which stimulate nations to export weapons, the technology for their manufacture and related equipment to allies and to third countries clearly does not extend to their adversaries. Nations do not consciously augment the military capability of enemies, and embargo rather than encourage such trade. The principle is easily established. The degree and the manner of embargo is not. This often arises from confusion over objectives. Weapons and related critical inputs create no problems of principle which do exist however for exports which increase the adversary's long or medium term economic, but not its immediate military, capability.

Military power is ultimately founded on economic might, and policy-makers face a continuum along which the optimal trade-off between welfare – which requires trade stimulation – and security, which requires its restraint, must be determined.[44] A simple taxonomy identifies three categories of potential benefit to an adversary importer:[45]

(i) direct near term military;
(ii) indirect long term military;
(iii) long term economic.

Failure to distinguish between the military and the economic and the short and the long terms confuses means and ends, and creates inconsistent and poorly executed policies which reduce the realisation of the full potential benefits of embargo.

There is in most countries and alliances consensus that exports of weapons and military technology that yield short term military benefit to the adversary must be prohibited. The greater the economic as opposed to military benefit, and the longer the period before it becomes effective, the less secure is the consensus. If furthermore the embargo is collectively applied by a group of allied nations, consensus is more easily achieved the narrower the list of embargoed goods. International trade is a powerful mechanism for increasing income and wealth and its deliberate impedance is unlikely to be tolerated unless the security benefits are clear and large. Economic communities which benefit from trade, and therefore lose by its impedance, form usually powerful political groups to resist a reduction in wages or profit unless the political circumstances dictate otherwise.

In the 1930s, the Soviet Union, as the technological follower, financed an extensive programme, both legal and clandestine, to import weapons and weapon-making technology from most of the advanced industrial nations, including the USA. After receipt, however, Soviet designers and technicians usually modified the imported equipment and blueprints to the more rugged demands of the Red Army. Despite claims that Soviet military technology was almost exclusively capitalist in origin recent assessments conclude that foreign technology made an important, though not decisive, contribution to the modernisation of the Soviet armed forces in the 1930s.[46]

In the post-war period, both sides embargoed trade in weapons and related technology. As the technological follower, with a pattern of sectoral allocations other than its large defence sector more appropriate to a less developed economy, the Soviet Union had, economically, more to gain from bilateral trade which might ease the chronically acute trade-off between defence, consumption and investment, and more to lose from its curtailment. However since the mid-1930s the Soviet Union had sought self-reliance where possible and was unwilling to become dependent on imports crucial to its security from uncertain and hostile capitalist sources.[47] The priority which security goods were customarily accorded in the USSR made embargo a simple issue of principle. Since foreign trade is centrally controlled, decisions on whether to allow or embargo trade in a specific category or with a particular country can easily be sanctioned through institutionalised political/bureaucratic channels.

For the USA, however, the degree to which goods should be embargoed is far from clear. As a more powerful technological and economic leader, it had little expectation of becoming dependant on the USSR for military or civilian goods. The point at issue thus always was where along the continuum should be the break between embargoed and non-embargoed goods. Even though, because of its size, international trade was relatively less important compared to European economies, there existed as in all capitalist countries powerful financial and commercial pressures to expand to international markets enshrined in the intellectual and political orthodoxy of liberalism. For the USA, therefore, the curtailment of international trade is a deliberate political decision which runs counter to a broad consensual orthodoxy and to the material interests of powerful economic groups. The decision whether to pursue narrowly military or broadly economic objectives is essentially political and lacks objective guidelines. Even if the objective is narrowly conceived as one of military impedance, the means by which the objective can be obtained range from narrow to broad. In a constrained economy such as the Soviet Union, any commodity which eases the civilian–military trade-off, whether it is itself military or not, increases the potential defence capability. It is not necessarily the innate characteristic of the commodity which determines whether it should be embargoed or not, but its consequence on military–economic choices in the importing country. In the initial post-war years the USA pursued a broad policy of economic warfare, 'to inflict the greatest economic injury to the USSR and its allies'[48] and again in the 1980s the USA sought the broad objective, to control exports of equipment, technology, licences and so on, which contribute directly and indirectly to the military–economic potential of the Soviet Union.

In the late 1940s the USA undertook to organise an alliance-wide system of strategic trade and technology control against the USSR. In 1947 the National Security Council determined that shipments of materials and equipment which contributed to Soviet military potential should be terminated. In 1949 the previously *ad hoc* controls on embargo were formalised in the Export Control Act, which prohibited the export to communist states of equipment and technology which increased their military and economic potential, and the USA began constructing its economic warfare apparatus against the USSR.[49]

The USA also took the lead in establishing the multilateral Paris-based Co-ordinating Committee for Multilateral Export Controls (COCOM) in 1950. American officials established an extensive list of goods and technology which required formal consideration and decision on whether they could or could not be exported to the USSR. Whereas the Americans defined their security interests widely to include economic impediment, the European definition of national security was narrower and they sought a more liberal interpretation of the embargo.[50] Since membership of COCOM was voluntary, adherence to its guidelines was based on a consensus of different national objectives, and because of its broader strategy of impedance the USA maintained its own more extensive National Commodity Control list of prohibited and controlled exports. Periodically, American officials sought to broaden the economic dimension of embargo, most particularly when it tried with little success to prohibit the export of oil pipes in the early 1960s. Gradually the economic dimension became less pronounced. European pressure for a more liberal interpretation of COCOM guidelines coincided with high Soviet economic growth which made a policy of economic damage appear less fruitful. Eventually, economic warfare coexisted uneasily with a general improvement in American Soviet relations, and in 1969 the USA relaxed its restrictions to embargo only those goods which increased the military potential of the USSR.[51] This change represented *inter alia* a new direction in policy. Instead of being a tool for impediment, trade could more flexibly be manipulated to put leverage on Soviet behaviour by linking it to other issue areas. President Kennedy had previously urged that American economic superiority should be used constructively to modify Soviet behaviour. President Carter also argued that the USA should use its economic strength and technological superiority positively to encourage co-operation with the USSR,[52] and Henry Kissinger undermined the validity of a broad conception of economic warfare in disallowing a necessary relationship between military and economic strength.[53] Leverage implied that trade could be increased or decreased as circumstances warranted, and provided in the 1970s a powerful rationale for increased exports of manufactured goods, technology, food and investment to the USSR.

Soviet behaviour was not influenced as predicted. Behaviour unacceptable, to the USA – domestically in the trial of the two dissidents Shcharansky and Ginsberg in 1978, internationally the invasion of Afghanistan in 1979, and covert control in Poland coincided with the renewal of a radical conservative ideology which *inter alia* widened again the purpose, and hence the range, of embargo. The more aggressive policy was most forcefully embodied in restriction on pipes and related equipment for the enormous Soviet investment in the Orenberg gas fields, as well as a more restrictive interpretation of militarily useful exports.

The Reagan administration rejected the until then dominant view that the USSR could be induced to co-operate with the West by a judicious mixture of economic sanctions and reward. Administration spokesmen denied that American economic policy directly influenced Soviet foreign policy. Only by challenging at its very core the domestic trade-off between civil and military allocations could Soviet decisions be influenced. For the USA therefore, the most effective trade strategy was one which forced the Soviet Union 'to bear the brunt of its economic shortcomings'.[54] According to the administration American trade policies in the 1970s were not only ineffective, but by enabling the Soviet Union to make up its technological lag had weakened American security. Since about 1970 or so the USSR had stepped up its legal and clandestine programme to acquire military related technology from the West.[55] Using the offices of the Soviet State Committee for Science and Technology and the rather different skills of the KGB and the GRU, the Soviet Union had established a number of collecting agencies to consolidate information obtained from legal imports of goods and licences, attendance at international scientific conferences, semi-illegal dummy corporations in the USA and elsewhere, and technology collecting officers under the guise of diplomats and newspapermen and wholly clandestine industrial espionage. So successful was the Soviet effort that some senior American intelligence officials refer to a 'hemorrhage'[56] of American technology to the Soviet military. A CIA report claimed that the technology gap had, and continued to be, eroded to such a degree as to pose a significant threat to America's security interests.[57] In key sectors such

Table 8.3 Selected Soviet and East European legal and illegal acquisitions from the West affecting key areas of Soviet military technology

Key Technology Area	Notable Success
Computers	Purchases and acquisitions of complete systems designs, concepts, hardware and software, including a wide variety of Western general purpose computers and minicomputers, for military applications.
Microelectronics	Complete industrial processes and semi-conductor manufacturing equipment capable of meeting all Soviet military requirements, if acquisitions were combined.
Signal processing	Acquisitions of processing equipment and know-how
Manufacturing	Acquisitions of automated and precision manufacturing equipment for electronics, materials, and optical and future laser weapons technology; acquisition of information on manufacturing technology related to weapons, ammunition, and air-craft parts including turbine blades, computers, and electronic components; acquisition of machine tools for cutting large gears for ship propulsion systems.
Communications	Acquisitions of low-power, low-noise, high-sensitivity receivers.
Lasers	Acquisitions of optical, pulsed power source, and other laser-related components, including special optical mirrors and mirror technology suitable for future laser weapons.
Guidance and navigation	Acquisitions of marine and other navigation receivers, advanced inertial-guidance components, including miniature and laser gyros; acquisitions of missile guidance subsystems; acquisitions of precision machinery for ball bearing production for missile and other applications; acquisition of missile test range instrumentation systems and documentation and precision cinetheodolites for collecting data critical to post-flight ballistic missile analysis.
Structural materials	Purchases and acquisitions of Western titanium alloys, welding equipment, and furnaces for producing titanium plate of large size applicable to submarine construction.

Table 8.3 *continued*

Propulsion	Missile technology; some ground propulsion technology (diesels, turbines and rotaries); purchases and acquisitions of advanced jet engine fabrication technology and jet engine design information.
Acoustical sensors	Acquisitions of underwater navigation and direction-finding equipment
Electro-optical Sensors	Acquisition of information on satellite technology, laser rangefinders, and under-water low-light-level television cameras and systems for remote operation.
Radars	Acquisitions and exploitations of air defense radars and antenna designs for missile systems.

Source: CIA, 'Soviet Acquisition of Western Technology', in G. Bertsh and J. McIntyre (eds), *National Security and Technology Transfer, The Strategic Dimension of East-West Trade* Boulder: Westview Press, 1983, pp. 100–1.

as microelectronics, Western technology imports had been crucial, but Soviet acquisition had been general and widespread.

According to the CIA, acquisition of Western technology has saved the Soviets hundreds of millions of dollars each year, allowed them to modernise the economy, to increase the performance characteristics of many weapons systems, and increased costs in the West to counter the enhanced Soviet weapons.[58]

The most publicised example of Soviet benefit from the legitimate purchase of Western technology is that of 164 bearing grinders from the Bryant Grinder Company. For over a decade the Soviet Union had sought to buy the American grinders, capable at that time of greater precision than those produced domestically. With the easing of restrictions in 1969, the sale was eventually sanctioned in 1972. Within a few years of purchase the Soviet Union began deploying a new generation of ICBMs, up to ten times more accurate than their predecessors, and for the first time capable of carrying multiple warheads. American officials have implied that the imported grinders alone could have provided the precision inertial navigation system which enabled the ICBM to be MIRVed.[59] American spokesmen also claim that the ground control system incorporated in the MIG 25 is so much more advanced than the plane's other avionics that it could only have been developed from illegally obtained Western technology.[60] In fact, the Bryant grinders probably arrived too late to decisively influence the Soviet MIRVing programme, and others of equivalent quality were in any case obtainable from Japan and other Western countries.[61]

American intelligence sources emphasise the adverse consequences of illegal as well as legally obtained technology. Admiral Inman, one time Deputy Director of the CIA, has claimed that about 70 per cent of Soviet acquisitions of militarily useful technologies have been obtained by intelligence officers.[62] Western sources refer to a systematically organised effort under the aegis of the KGB to subvert the Export Administration Act. The existence of profit-seeking firms in the USA and elsewhere wanting to benefit from the high prices paid for illegally acquired technology and equipment – reportedly up to three times market rates – offer one source of illegal transfers. Dummy Soviet corporations in the USA, the semi-legal transfer of equipment nominally destined for third European countries, complacent governments which often turn a blind eye to sales and agreements which in the USA would be prohibited are others. While there clearly does exist a programme of covert activities, its benefit to the Soviet Union is difficult to evaluate. Given an effective policy of legal embargo of militarily sensitive equipment, it is almost inevitable as a matter of arithmetic that the majority of militarily significant technology will be obtained covertly. On the whole the quality of the covert information is of low grade, usually from unclassified sources. The Department of Defense concedes, unlike the CIA, that the majority of Soviet acquisitions have been obtained legally.[63] Illegal acquisitions are by their very nature episodic and uncertain, and are not likely to be a satisfactory source of information for such a continuously dynamic and on-going activity.

More problematic for deciding the extent of embargo is the growing importance, both quantitatively and qualitatively, of dual use technologies. Given the historic dominance of military R and D it was, despite overlap at margins, not difficult to identify technologies which originated in, and were mainly useful for, defence. Increasing military penetration of science blurred the once easy distinction between civilian and military significant technologies. Too narrow a definition of military useful technologies might allow the export of equipment which could be justified by the Soviets for civilian purposes, but which could be transferred for military purposes. Too broad a definition could adversely and unfairly affect the legitimate economic interest of American capital and labour, and might lead to disagreement with Japan and Western Europe, who conventionally took a less restrictive view of embargo.

Dual use technologies made acute the viewpoint that one-off acquisition of machinery or equipment offered less value to Soviet military planners than the intellectual capital embodied in its origin. The Bucy Committee, established to identify policy guidelines to control and regulate the transfer of potentially sensitive technology, recommended that the appropriate authority should set in motion a programme to draw up a list of militarily crucial basic technologies which should be controlled,[64] a shift from hardware to know-how, irrespective of sector of origin. In 1979 the Export Administration Act, reflecting an already more restrictive policy, required the government to draw up such a list.

The incoming Reagan administration inherited what it considered a critical and deteriorating problem of technology erosion, and moved to reverse a 30-year or so trend of liberal trade with the USSR. It sought to restrict the flow of militarily significant technology and to licence exports more in accord with what it regarded as America's security rather than economic interests. It tightened the list of embargoed goods and increased surveillance over domestic evasions. It established a Military Technology Critical List; and though it has refused to disclose the full range of products which are embargoed on the grounds that an open list might itself constitute a security problem, the embargo has been widened. By 1987 up to 40 per cent of all US manufactured goods to the USSR required some form of export control licence.[65]

Historically the USA had emphasised the security aspects of East–West trade more than Europe, and its indigenous list of embargoed goods had consistently been more extensive than that of COCOM. Furthermore, better East–West relations, especially during the detente years, dampened European enthusiasm for strict interpretation. The Reagan administration was especially distressed by what it regarded as a too complaisant attitude towards the security aspects of East–West trade, and as well as tightening its own lists, sought more co-operation from its major allies. At the economic summits of 1981 and 1983, the leaders of the industrial nations agreed that 'economic relations with the East should be compatible with the security interests of the alliance',[66] but the consensus which by and large existed over narrowly defined security goods could not be sustained for economic goods and technology, and the allies' response was unenthusiastic and tepid.

The Americans sought also to make COCOM more effective by upgrading its status, increasing the element of compulsion in an organisation which still works through national discretion and consensus, by increasing the size of the staff, by regular review, and also by increasing the military component in the decision process. Most of the officials who investigated the provenance of controlled items, were historically drawn from foreign or finance offices, departments which organisationally were induced to expand trade. In 1985, the Americans succeeded in creating a sub-committee of military experts (STEM) which advised on the military implications of trade and which would in all probability advocate a more restrictive policy than the civilian members. It also sought to widen the COCOM list to include a Military Critical List which would automatically enlarge the range of embargoed goods to include not only obvious categories such as computers, electronic equipment, semi-conductors, but also chemicals, metallurgy, heavy vehicles, etc. The more vigorous prosecution of a wider definition of embargoed goods than was generally accepted in Europe and Japan, strained the alliance to a degree which many believed excessive in terms of the benefit achieved by the COCOM embargo.

Despite the largely unsubstantiated claims of military benefit, the economic contribution of Western machinery and technology most likely to fit into the dual use category is unlikely to have been decisive. Even at the height of detente, imports of machinery and equipment at no time exceeded six per cent or so of total investment and were usually much lower. Exports of Western technology to the Soviet Union seldom exceeded four per cent of the total. Aggregate data are incomplete in themselves however, for if imports are concentrated in key sectors, where Soviet lag is particularly acute or where bottlenecks are severe, the contribution of marginal quantities of Western machinery could be disproportionally beneficial.

Trade embodied in goods and equipment does not exhaust the benefits of international exchange. That in licences and other forms of software may be more important in high-tech sectors. Soviet imports of licences in general have been of limited significance and, unusually, the Soviets have a surplus with the capitalist world.

Because of the higher level of achieved technology, Western equipment, though quantitatively modest, may make a greater contribution to economic progress than an equivalent amount of Soviet made equipment. The evidence, as with so much else, is ambiguous. Some investigations conclude that the marginal productivity of Western technology is up to 14 times as high as the indigenous stock[67] and as a consequence economic growth has been up to one per cent higher than it would otherwise have been. Other investigators, using different data and models, conclude that the productivity of Western capital is negligibly different to that of domestic capital.[68]

Aggregate data from mainly civilian branches do not indicate benefit to the military–industrial sector. Soviet military technical skills are high and systemic barriers to effective innovation reduced. Thus Soviet scientists and technologists in the defence sector have probably more effectively Sovietised Western imports than is normally the case in the civilian branches.

Nevertheless, outside the more alarmist sections of Western defence communities there is a general opinion that the scale and significance of the military benefit to the Soviet Union has been overstated,[69] almost inevitably so if the embargo is effective. Single items of acquisition on an irregular and unpredictable basis are unlikely to be critical to a sector so crucial and well-funded and capable of effective indigenous innovation. Given the Soviet strategy of stable design teams working on evolutionary principles of weapons development, the importance of the single breakthrough can easily be exaggerated. According to the Office of Technology Assessment, the Soviet Union has obtained no technology from the West which it could not have developed itself given adequate initiative and resources, and the Soviets have often surprised the West by the speed with which they have been able to close specific gaps opened up by Western advance. For the Soviet Union, the major problem is not the inability to produce one-off prototypes of the highest quality, but the more complicated one of diffusion throughout the economic system;[70] a problem which single copies of Western models, whether obtained legally or covertly, does little to resolve.

9 The Arms Race in the 1980s

From 1980 the armaments performance of the USA and the USSR, as measured by expenditures, diverged to a degree seldom observed in the post-war period. Although in the broadest sense the armaments policies of one country are dominated by that of the adversary[1] the departure – first established in each country in the final years of the previous decade – from long term trends, renders inadequate simple action–reaction and bureaucratic models of the arms race. In President Reagan's first administration, military expenditure grew at an annual nominal rate of 14 per cent, in real terms 8 real terms p.a. By the end of his second administration, however, real growth was negative. In the Soviet Union expenditures declined from a long term trend of four to five p.a. to two per cent p.a. to the middle of the decade and perhaps beyond.[2]

In the USA the extraordinary growth in military spending from 1980 to 1985 was at one level simply another up phase in a long established, but irregular, cycle of expansion and relative decline.[3] Samuel Huntington has charted three cycles where exceptionally high growth stimulated by an external trigger which mobilises public support is sustainable only for a relatively brief period of time, after which budgetary and macroeconomic constraints force retrenchment to lower rates, a cycle which reflects a basic societal inability to determine upon and sustain either confrontation or detente as the proper policy towards the USSR.[4] Over the long term, the USA has been unable to reconcile its commitments with the resources it is politically prepared to release from civilian consumption and investment. The expansion of 1981 and 1982 replicated in part therefore those of 1948–9 and 1967–8, but even at a descriptive level differs from its predecessors. The Reagan up phase, a continuation of President Carter's policy to increase the rate of expansion, took far longer to attain maximum momentum partly due to the lack of a single galvanising external trigger. The Soviet invasion of Afghanistan though it offered no direct threat to American security, eventually did consolidate a growing but until then unfocussed resentment of Soviet policy. Although the pattern recurs irregularly throughout the period, it is not endogenous in the sense of possessing within itself the seeds of automatic renewal and decay. The morphology of growth, the timing, the pace and the duration of expansion depends on exogenous factors such as the underlying state of international relations and on the political–ideological dynamic in the USA. What decisively distinguished the up phase in the 1980s was the visceral anti-communism which President Reagan brought to bear on international affairs which in a few years re-wrote the context of the defence debate.[5]

President Reagan – at least in his earlier manifestation – and many of his most influential advisers, held an 'essentialist' view of the USSR[6] according to which the Soviet Union is always and irredeemably evil.[7] Since foreign policy originates in the essence of the domestic system,[8] it necessarily follows that the USSR is the focus of evil in the world and according to the essentialist Reagan world view underlies all the unrest that is going on.[9] Marxist ideology melded with Russian geopolitical concerns created an expansionary dynamic made aggressive by the failure of Marxist states, as exemplified by the Soviet Union, to meet the legitimate political and welfare needs of its citizens. The Soviet Union was imbued with an aggressive lust for domination, its objective being nothing less than dominance or hegemonic control of the great Eurasian land mass. With such an adversary international affairs was reduced to a Manichean struggle between two contending systems of good and evil in a bipolar world where the essentially zero-sum pay-off structure[10] meant an advantage to one side necessarily imposed a cost on its adversary. Foreign policy was simplified to a systemic conflict between contending systems,[11] which was as real and immediate as it had been in the late 1940s. The one transcendent issue was American–Soviet relations, but, in contrast to the preceeding administrations, that of President Reagan concluded that the Soviet Union had no real interest in a stable and managed international system which could bring about a new structure of peace in the world. The USA had the right and the duty to meet and overcome the Soviet hegemonic challenge by means of an abrasive, confrontationist stance.[12]

To assume, as had previous administrations, that Soviet foreign policy was responsive to chastisement for bad, and reward for good behaviour was not only a delusion doomed to inevitable failure, but dangerous in that it lowered Western vigilance and hence its defence of essential freedoms, a truism which to President Reagan's conservative supporters was amply proved by detente. A policy of influencing Soviet calculation of the costs and benefits of alternative foreign policies had to be thrown over for one which directly attacked Soviet expansionism at its domestic source. This could be successful only if the USA deployed the most powerful resources in its confrontation with the USSR. At the core of President Reagan's policy therefore was the restoration of American primacy in East–West affairs. The Soviet Union's only source of superpower status was the military instrument. This is where the American challenge had to be targeted. Soviet foreign policy could be changed only by influencing at its domestic core the calculation of Soviet rulers, in particular by making clear to the military–industrial complex the economic cost of military competition with the USA and the unlikelihood of successfully prevailing in the bilateral arms race. Of necessity rather than choice the Soviet leaders would be forced to adopt a more accommodating stance in international affairs. The proper response to Soviet expansionism was military might,[13] which became the cornerstone of American foreign policy. Negotiations had no place in the tough stance, not only because the Soviets could not be trusted to keep their word,[14] but also because negotiation from a position of weakness was incompatible with confrontation. Negotiations, it was also rationalised, could be perceived by the Soviet Union as a sign of weakness and therefore encourage mischievous behaviour.[15] It is no surprise that the major institutional driving force behind the essentialist view was the Department of Defense[16] which organisationally and materially had most to benefit from a confrontational, military-dominated foreign policy.

The task of confronting the evil empire was more urgent and taxing because of what President Reagan argued had been the pusillanimous policies of his predecessors. Having conceded strategic parity to the Soviet Union and therefore the ability to negotiate from strength, they had so neglected American defences as, according to the President, to leave it more vulnerable than at any time since Pearl Harbor.[17] As a consequence, the USA was incapable of defending itself. Not only had the Soviet Union out-produced the USA, as had traditionally been the case, but by virtue of a determined policy of modernisation, had eroded America's traditional qualitative superiority, and had therefore opened an American window of vulnerability.

Higher military spending was, according to President Reagan, an effective response by the USA because capitalism was inherently more dynamic than the systemically inefficient socialism. Soviet economic growth was sustainable at impressive rates for a short period of time only, so long as the enabling benefits of youth and lateness were easily available. Poor Soviet management had compounded the inherent system inefficiencies of the command economy, and by 1980 the Soviet performance was poor and getting worse. An economically powerful USA could exploit this fundamental weakness by increasing the economic cost of the arms race, and making clear to the Soviet leaders the enduring and increasing burden of welfare, growth and technological progress foregone. Although not articulated into a coherent doctrine, William Clarke, President Reagan's National Security adviser, made the case in 1982 that the USA must force the USSR 'to bear the brunt of its economic shortcomings',[18] and a 1987–88 Fiscal Year Defense Guidance document leaked to the press in 1982 argued that 'the USA should develop weapons that are difficult for the Soviets to counter, impose disproportionate costs, open up new areas of military competition and obsolesce previous Soviet investment'.[19] A more accommodating Soviet Union would result not from transient calculation of the costs and benefits of this or that foreign policy, but from a single organic calculation of the costs of militarisation. The apocalyptic maximalist strand of conservative American thinking perceived the Soviet economy as so wracked by economic inefficiency and social ennui that a spending race, by divesting resources from essential tasks of modernisation and domestic reconstruction would bankrupt the economy, and, in President Reagan's own words, consign Marxism–Leninism to the 'ash heap of history'.[20]

Such a policy was predicated on a powerful American economy where the economic costs of arms competition would not prove prohibitive. President Reagan's predecessors, it was alleged, had not only conceded military supremacy but because of a commitment to inappropriate welfarist policies had allowed the USA to slip from hegemonic dominance of the international economy. President Reagan rejected theories of hegemonic decline, claiming that America's decline was policy induced[21] and therefore reversible. Higher military spending would not only secure America's security but would also restore supremacy in the capitalist political economy, for the *Pax Americana* had always been based on economic and military power.[22] Reaganomics, by releasing the supply side potential of the American economy, was a crucial adjunct to foreign and defence policies. It accommodated the primary objective of higher military spending

Table 9.1   Annual real growth in defence spending authority (percentage)

	1981	1982	1983	1984	1985	1986	1987
Military personnel	2	2	2	2	1	2	1
Operation and maintenance	9	6	5	5	6	–3	2
Procurement	25	25	17	3	6	–4	–8
RDT and E	13	14	10	14	10	7	4

Source: D. Sorenson, 'Declining Defence Budgets and the future of the US Defence Industry', *Defence Analysis*, vol. 4, 1988.

which both symbolised and implemented the new security policy,[23] and would allow the USA to bypass the classic choice between guns, butter and growth.[24]

Higher military spending showed resolve and lower spending weakness. The administration did not therefore need to specify what the money was to be spent on – only that it intended to spend a lot.[25] Within ten days of taking office, President Reagan added $32bn. to an already rapidly expanding defence budget. In 1981 and 1982 military expenditure increased at a real rate of 12 per cent p.a. – which could not be sustained, however. Between 1980 and 1985 defence spending growth averaged 8.0 per cent in real terms, 14.3 per cent nominally, an increase excluding inflation of $330bn.

Although the additional spending was poorly related to strategic precepts,[26] American policy was best served by concentrating the additional resources in military investment where American comparative advantage was greatest. Investment in procurement and R and D was in any case urgent in view of the extensive programme of military modernisation undertaken by the Soviet Union in the 1970s and neglect by the USA. Some of the additional $330bn. paid for higher salaries and associated manpower costs. Most of the initial increase was spent on procurement and R and D.

The ratio of investment to operations and support increased from 0.53 in 1977–80 to 0.83 in 1981–85[27] and in five years military procurement doubled, increasing the weapons manpower ratio.

	1976	1980	1985
Procurement	22	24	35
Manpower	26	21	18

Military R and D claimed increasing ratios of total science spending. By 1987 the Pentagon's share of government sponsored R and D had

Table 9.2   Federal R and D expenditure ($bn.)

	1980	1981	1982	1983	1984	% increase
Total R and D	39.0	39.2	39.6	40.4	45.7	17
National Defence	19.4	21.7	24.2	26.2	32.0	65
All other	19.6	17.5	15.4	14.2	13.7	30

Source: F. Long, 'The Federal R and D Budget: Guns versus Butter',
    Science, 16 March 1984, vol. 223, no. 4641, p. 1133.

increased to 73 per cent, compared with 50 per cent in 1981[28] the
focus of which since 1983 has been the President's much vaunted and
criticised Strategic Defense Initiative.

The origin of SDI was President Reagan's vision of a protective
shield which would banish forever American dependence on nuclear
weapons and hence on mutually assured deterrence. Although the
original concept of complete protection has been modified to one of
enhancing rather than eliminating deterrence, the economic component remains enormous. Since 1984, $4bn. has been spent on R
and D, and a further $39bn. is to be spent by 1992.[29] The final figure
is difficult to estimate. Officials of the SDI office forecast total
spending of the order of $500bn. One independent source predicts
total investment plus ten year operating costs of the full system in
2012 to be around $770bn. in 1985 prices[30] which in peak years will
amount to $44bn. p.a. A further estimate by J. Schlessinger and H.
Brown projects the final figure at over $1 trillion.[31] The uncertainty is
explained not only by the inherent problems of projecting into the
future outcomes and hence costs of research and development at the
forefront of technology, but also by uncertainty over the Soviet
response to the strategic challenge. Although scientists disagree over
the technical feasibility of the original concept, Pentagon sources
concede that there is 'no way that an enemy cannot overwhelm your
defence if he wants to badly enough'.[32] The cost to the USA therefore depends in part on what will be the Soviet response, and how
well it will be funded. The Soviets have various options,[33] but if SDI
goes beyond the research phase in the USA there can be no doubt
but that it will provide a powerful impetus to the arms race.[34]

Given the political economy of the military market place, the SDI
programme has already taken on an expansionary dynamic of its
own. As the largest and fastest growing single military project ever
conceived, the economic rewards to defence contractors are enor-

mous and as other procurement programmes contract in response to declining military expenditures, SDI may generate an unstoppable economic, scientific and bureaucratic momentum. To forestall backsliding by succeeding administrations less committed to the vision of ballistic defence, the SDI Office has accelerated deployment of R and D programmes and the SDI budget is heavily geared towards engineering rather than experimental research.

Department of Defense experts believe the USA to be ahead of the USSR in virtually every technology that is likely to be militarily important in the next ten years, in conventional strategic defence by as much as ten years.[35] According to the CIA, the Soviet Union offers no unacceptable threat to the security of the USA.[36] That is, there is no great strategic justification to proceed so rapidly with such a large programme with so many unresolved uncertainties, which is almost certain to boost the arms race. The rationale may have to be sought elsewhere, to increase the economic cost of competition for the USSR[37] as to finally push it over the brink into bankruptcy, the maximalist and almost certainly vain hope, or to a more conciliatory foreign policy, the minimalist position.

The Reagan administration made a virtue of not precisely articulating its strategic assumptions, but enough information has emerged from occasional official documents, advisers, leaks to the press and procurement programmes to reveal significant departure from the strategic doctrines which have guided previous administrations. In essence deterrence had been downgraded for a more positive warfighting strategy without which much of the important procurement programmes would have been unnecessary.[38] In 1982 an internal defence document revealed the Department to be considering as a possible option a six-month war, in the event of which the USA would have to be in a position to prevail. Counterforce escalation dominance inevitably requires a more demanding range of missions and no obvious ceiling to expenditures.[39]

A legitimate question, asked by many critics of the Reagan programme, not all inherently hostile, is whether the enormous expenditures have brought about a corresponding improvement in America's security, or conversely, whether the attained level of security could have been obtained cheaper. Military–economic efficiency has two characteristics. Managerial efficiency relates the value of inputs to outputs, economic resources to specific objectives. Geopolitical efficiency is the appropriateness or otherwise of the objectives.[40]

Many observers outside the administration aver it consistently and perhaps wilfully exaggerated the scale and effectiveness of the Soviet build-up during the 1970s,[41] and hence the appropriate scale of military response. Given the salience of Soviet action to American expenditures, exaggeration is a chronic source of escalation in the arms race dynamic. (There is every reason to assume that Soviet generals and leaders behave similarly.) The public rhetoric necessary to justify high and growing expenditures is often contradicted by more technical assessment from within the defence community. The CIA conclusion that there is no realistic possibility that the Soviets will be able in the 1990s to deploy a system that could pose a significant threat to American nuclear submarines on patrol,[42] the third leg of the American triad, is echoed in the Sowcroft Commission, established by President Reagan, which questioned that the USA ever faced a window of vulnerability. Indeed by 1982 the rhetoric of the window of vulnerability which a few years previously had been so potent had largely disappeared from President Reagan's speeches and those of his advisers.[43] Nor did the disproportionate spending on R and D and procurement, the beneficial effect of which would be available only in the long run, meet the immediate problem of the window of vulnerability even if it did exist in the form and to the degree initially argued by the President.

Despite widespread doubts about the feasibility of SDI even in its modified form, deployment will almost inevitably provoke a Soviet response, much as they might prefer to avoid the challenge and boost the arms race once again. Counterforce superiority if and to the degree it is sought, also stimulates the arms race if for no other reason that conventional wisdom requires offensive to exceed defensive forces by a margin of at least three to one, and probably more.

Inefficiency in managing the large military expansion is revealed by a failure to match commitments to resources.[44] After the initial increase, popular support for more growth at the same rate declined, as historically has always been the case, and concerns with the economic consequences of an overheated economy, took higher priority in Congress. Disparate trends in commitments and resources imply that by the 1990s inputs will be inadequate to meet America's strategic objectives, a further failure to bring into some rational relationship military needs and economic means.[45] To the degree that the resource gap is financed by external borrowing, the burden was transferred temporarily to other countries, especially Japan, which though in the main politically stable does undermine American hegemony.

Despite the enormous expenditure, the American force structure remained essentially unchanged from 1980, though the distribution of expenditure clearly changed. Readiness as a proportion of the budget fell from 60 per cent in 1981 to 53 per cent in 1987.[46]

President Reagan inherited an inefficient defence economy, and microeconomic evidence of managerial inefficiency is a deep-rooted problem. Indeed, during his term of office genuine reforms in budgeting and procurement were imposed on the Pentagon. However, the excessive pace of the initial expansion when in 'a carnival of indiscriminate military spending',[47] programmes of doubtful urgency and questionable priority were funded with little regard to overall central strategy aggravated the chronic tendency to inefficiency. No effort was made to alter the structure of the market, to make it more competitive, most contracts still being negotiated on a single source basis. Prices maintained their inexorable increase. In 1983 the F-16 fighter cost $16m. In two years the price had increased to $24m. In four years the price, excluding inflation, increased 50 per cent.[48] Cost overruns of up to 67 per cent were recorded on some planes but were endemic throughout the services. As costs increased numbers procured fell[49] without necessarily increasing security. Critics of the Reagan defence build-up argue that the same level of security could have been obtained with savings of $22bn. in 1988 and $25bn. in 1989.[50] Although such simulations are clearly judgemental, there is a widespread conclusion that in the final analysis America did not get value for money.[51]

Exceptional growth has not been sustainable for more than a few years, and so it proved even for so committed as ideologist as President Reagan. By 1987 growth in real terms was negative. Slowdown coincided with what was, on the whole, a softening of the anti-Soviet rhetoric, and a broadening of the foreign policy perspective. The single issue of American–Soviet confrontation though never less than dominant was given over to a more broad concern with traditional diplomacy. America's allies brought a less confrontationist focus to East–West affairs in particular and to international political issues in general. The essentialist perspective was gradually eroded in favour of a view of East–West affairs which, whilst still perceiving Soviet objectives as adversarial, conceded that bilateral negotiations from strength could influence the conduct of Soviet policy. International and domestic Soviet trends were favourable to American interests, and after the enormous expansion, the USA was in just such a position of strength. Even during the most intense period of the second Cold War, some communication between the two countries had been maintained,[52] and resumption of arms control negotiations led to the series of summit meetings between President Reagan and Mr Gorbachev, and to the INF Treaty, and for President Reagan a remarkable transformation from his initially essentialist stance on East–West relations.

Despite the importance of external influences on American defence expenditures, the primary explanation for slow and eventually negative growth was economic[53], forced upon an often reluctant President by a Congress increasingly concerned with the domestic economic consequences of over-extension.

East–West confrontation was predicated on a position of hegemony in the international economy which had also been dissipated by the excessively welfarist policies of previous administrations. Government, according to President Reagan, was the problem not the answer, a problem which he promised to take off the backs of the American people, by deregulation, by stimulating private enterprise, and most spectacularly by reducing taxation, which according to supply side theorists would so stimulate economic activity as to reduce and even eliminate the federal budget deficit. In only three years he cut many taxes by up to 30 per cent across the board. Following a short and very severe depression, the impact of fiscal policy on the real economy was positive, due ironically enough to what has been described as the greatest experiment in Keynesian reflation in history.[54] Lower taxes and higher defence spending could not be simultaneously achieved with domestic and external balance however. The budget deficit which rose to a maximum figure of $221bn. in 1986 and the current account deficit to $160bn. in 1986 were major provocations to Congressional revolt against the high rate of increase of defence spending. In 1986 real defence spending declined by 4.7 per cent, and again by 3.5 per cent in 1987.

Military related R and D, procurement and deficits had an impact on the American and also the international economy. Econometric investigations that economic growth would be stimulated were borne out, the economy growing at over 3.8 per cent from 1983 onward, creating 12 million new jobs, most of which however were in service occupations and often poorly paid.[55] Unlike previous cycles, inflation was kept well in check due to the restrictionary monetary policies of the Federal Reserve Board and deregulation of labour and other markets. Real interest rates increased to over 18 per cent,[56] which in 1983 alone cost an additional $96bn.[57] Servicing the national debt increased from 8.9 per cent to 14.6 per cent of the budget. High interest rates not only dampened down inflationary pressures, but provided the essential mechanism to finance the deficit by stimulating capital imports from Europe, and especially Japan. In 1985 the USA became for the first time since 1914 a net importer, and on such a scale – up to $100m. per annum – as to push it with extraordinary rapidity to the position of being the most indebted country in the world, over $400bn. in 1987 and increasing. The debts are overwhelmingly the result of President Reagan's economic policies, at the heart of which was defence.[58]

Increased spending on defence could not be reconciled with lower taxes without sacrificing public spending elsewhere, the brunt of which was borne by welfare. Cuts in welfare were not wholly due to the exigencies of budgetary constraint, but also reflected President Reagan's conservative ideological preferences. Entitlements precluded an even and equal spread of burden, which was concentrated on the unprotected 30 per cent or so of the federal budget which declined by 30 per cent from 1980 to 1985. For the first time in decades guns v. butter once more emerged as a politically salient issue.[59]

Between 1980 and 1985 the distribution of the federal budget reflected these changed priorities:

	1980	1985
Defence	23	27.8
Income Security	15.0	13.2
Health	4.0	3.6

In real terms, non-defence spending declined by two per cent p.a., which inevitably fell most heavily on poor Americans.

Military R and D and procurement, which so dominated the Reagan military expansion, almost certainly crowded out civilian investment,[60] especially in high technology sectors, increasing import penetration in such goods as machine tools. Nor were the spill-in benefits of military R and D so readily available. In 1985 the President's Commission on International Competitiveness reported that increasing specialisation reduced its commercial value to the civilian sector. The Department of Defense had indeed become a net consumer of civilian technology.[61] In the long run a powerful military rests on a secure economic foundation, but some of the economic consequences of President Reagan's military programme undermine the very bedrock on which American security must ultimately rest.

The latest phase of the defence spending cycle illustrates in acute form America's difficulty in reconciling resources and commitments, according to which the USA is not rich enough, smart enough or dedicated enough,[62] and sustained defence spending on the scale of the early 1980s merely intensifies the contradictions of hegemonic decline.

Economic crisis in the USA, which may follow from current spending trends[63] is, according to Mr Gorbachev, already a reality in the Soviet Union, where defence expenditures account for between 15 per cent and 17 per cent GNP.

Unlike the USA, military allocations in the Soviet Union have shown a remarkably stable trend sustained by the follow-on momentum of a powerfully entrenched political and bureaucratic constituency. Defence expenditures have grown regularly, but not spectacularly, at around four to five per cent p.a. In 1983, the CIA revised downward its estimates of defence expenditure growth from around 1976 or so to two per cent p.a., measured in constant dollars.[64] Although a short downturn was not unanticipated following a long period of procurement and modernisation, lower growth has been sustained beyond the few years customary in the periodic and mild Soviet downturns. Procurement, which accounts for 25 per cent of total expenditures and which had fed the previous expansion, fell to an almost static trend[65] and was the most decisive single influence on the global figure. The CIA and the Pentagon's Defense Intelligence Agency agree on the basic trend from 1976 to around 1982 and on the key explanation. The two agencies differ on growth beyond 1982 and why procurement fell to a static trend. The CIA argues that procurement has remained essentially flat into the final years of the decade, whereas the DIA argues that following improved economic performance from 1983 onwards, procurement has increased at around three to four per cent p.a.[66]

Part of the difference derives from the different methods used by the two agencies to estimate Soviet expenditures. The CIA estimate total procurement in constant dollars, whereas the DIA, which admits to a wide margin of error, estimates in current dollars only about 70 per cent of the CIA range of weapons.[67] Price changes, even in a command economy, affect the estimates. The CIA, in the face of criticism that its 1970 base year had become increasingly untenable, in 1985 updated its base to 1982 prices. Because end year prices tend to exceed those in the base period, the recalculation alone increased the estimated level of military expenditures, and as a consequence

Table 9.3   Dollar cost of USA and USSR defence expenditures ($bn. 1984)

	1970	71	72	73	74	75	76	77	78	79	80	81	82	83	84	85
USSR	180	185	190	195	200	210	212	215	220	225	225	230	230	235	240	245
USA	200	185	160	155	150	148	145	150	151	160	168	175	190	212	224	245

Source: *Allocations of Economic Resources in the Soviet Union and China, 1985*. A Compendium of Papers submitted to the Joint Economic Committee, Washington DC, 1986, p. 156.

the defence quotient. Defence increased from 12–14 per cent of GNP to 15–17 per cent in 1985,[68] around 33 per cent due to price changes, inflation being higher in the military than in the civilian sector. However, precisely the same index number phenomenon marginally reduces the growth of military expenditures. A comparison of Soviet and American data measured in constant prices illustrates the contrasting trends in the two nations and also, because of the extraordinary recent growth in the USA that, as estimated by the CIA in American dollars, for the first time since 1970 American defence expenditures equal those in the Soviet Union.

General Vitaly Shabanov, the principal Deputy Minister of Defence for armaments, described as the Soviet Union's top weapons procurement officer, announced in July 1988 that the country's military budget had recently declined and probably would decline for some years to come.[69] However, since the Soviet definition of the defence budget is incomplete, it is difficult to evaluate the significance of the statement, as is more recent statements by Mr Gorbachev and others.

According to the DIA, the major explanation for the albeit temporary static trend in procurement has been exceptional difficulties in incorporating advanced technologies into new weapons systems. The conservative and evolutionary Soviet style could not easily adjust to the growing qualitative demands of multi-purpose weapons systems and as a consequence procurement programmes were stretched, and deployment of new models postponed.[70] Costs in successive models of some weapons have increased by almost 300 per cent, and as with the USA when prices increase numbers bought decrease[71] – (claims of technological backwardness sit uneasily with others emanating from the same source that the Soviet Union posed a mounting and critical technological challenge to the USA).

The deceleration of military spending growth coincided with a significant worsening of both macroeconomic and microeconomic performance during the eighth Five-Year Plan. Economic growth, which had declined in virtually every five-year plan period since the early 1960s, fell in 1979 to only 1.6 per cent. Growth in total factor productivity declined to -0.8 per cent p.a.,[72] and bottlenecks in key industrial sectors resulted in an economic performance of crisis proportions. Given the economic context it is well nigh inconceivable that the static trend in procurement and the decline in overall growth were organically unrelated. The slowdown was due as much to leadership decision as to short term constraints.[73] As early as 1976 Brezhnev informed the high command that the Party was prepared to allocate to the defence sector 'as much as it needed' to rebuff the enemy, and in a speech to the high command and to leading officials of the Ministry of Defence in 1982, Brezhnev repeated the claim,[74] reaffirming that the Party remained the final arbiter of resources and that in view of the importance given to consumer welfare and security no more than was absolutely necessary could be given to military spending. The armed forces should look to improved efficiency, better training, leadership, and other factors rather than simply expect the state always to provide more resources.[75]

The military high command chiefly in the person of Marshal N. Ogarkov, Chief of the General Staff, countered by arguing that more not less resources should be allocated for defence even at the expense of social progress,[76] and in one of his pamphlets reminded his readers of the consequences to the Soviet Union of failing to provide adequately in the 1930s.[77] With the attainment of strategic parity in the 1970s and a guaranteed second-strike capability by either side, Brezhnev, despite his strong links with the military industrial complex, sought to cap the ever increasing demands of the military. Only those seeking suicide, he announced, would start a nuclear war with the expectation of winning.[78] Since the USSR rejected this objective it had no need of strategic superiority. Nor, Brezhnev added, would it be the first to use nuclear weapons. Brezhnev, despite conservative criticism, committed the country to a dual track approach to national security based on the utility of continuous expansion of Soviet military might and diplomatic negotiation with the West.[79] The military, mainly in the person of Marshal Ogarkov, opposed the wholehearted conversion to Western doctrine. While accepting no first strike, the USSR should prepare for a war-winning strategy even if that meant a protracted nuclear war, which of course could only be based on strategic superiority. Even when, presumably in the light of internal political pressure, Ogarkov appeared to compromise on whether the Soviet Union could win a nuclear war, he maintained that it should sustain its war-fighting strategy which *inter alia* justified limitless spending on weapons.[80] The outcome of a debate between the military in the person of Ogarkov and the civilian authorities, in the form of the civilian Minister of Defence Ustinov, over nuclear doctrine would profoundly influence Soviet defence posture, the appropriate level of defence spending and hence the morphology of the arms race to the end of the century. Ogarkov gradually, and it must be presumed, reluctantly, modified his belligerent stance, though it remains unclear whether he totally recanted. In 1984, presumably because of his criticism of the Party line, he was demoted from Chief of the General Staff to command the Soviet forces in the European theatre.

Ogarkov's demands for more resources were not determined exclusively by his views on war fighting and war winning. They also related to the changing technology of war. Brezhnev had redressed Khrushchev's predilection for an unbalanced nuclear posture, but at both strategic and theatre level the Soviet Union deployed a formidable nuclear armoury. Given the second-strike capacity enjoyed by either side, however, the usefulness of nuclear weapons has been questioned by some military experts in the Soviet Union.[81] Conventional, so-called 'smart weapons', those with high yields which could be terminally guided with virtually no error, were on the other hand increasingly vital to Soviet security. Smart Western weapons which could locate Soviet submarines, decript Soviet codes and handle fast moving battle scenes held out the eventual possibility of stymieing Soviet forces relegating nuclear strategy to a secondary role and shifting the arms race into areas where the Soviet Union was least able to compete.[82] Indeed, so efficient and destructive could conventional weapons be expected to become, that Ogarkov and others contemplated the possibility of a war in Europe which would remain wholly conventional. The Soviet Union had no alternative but to massively improve R and D in and procurement of smart conventional weapons. This posed a unique challenge to the Soviet military–technological community, which would require it to throw over the habits of technological followership developed over half a century and compete with the technologically most dynamic military nation in the world over the entire range of militarily significant technologies. It would also inevitably be expensive. The Soviet Union simply could not sustain a war-fighting strategy and invest in a range of new conventional weapons without allocating far more money to defence than the political leadership was currently prepared to contemplate.

Although Ogarkov was publicly outspoken in his demand for more resources, his views were shared by other officers[83] and even after his demotion and partial recantation the resource implications of a greater reliance on conventional weapons remains valid. The debate between the 'diplomatists' faction in the Soviet political hierarchy which favours greater genuine co-operation with, and involvement in, the international community and the 'unilateralists' who favour the traditional path to strategic superiority based on a conservative interpretation of the correlation of forces[84] did not become acute until Mr Gorbachev was elected General Secretary of the Communist Party in 1985. Despite a partial recovery from the nadir of 1979–81 the economy remains in the grip of a systemic crisis. Over the long term, growth has declined at between 0.1 per cent and 0.3 per cent p.a.,[85] though the economy has grown at a modest 2.5 per cent p.a. during Mr Gorbachev's period in office. Capital and labour inputs are increasingly tight and total factor productivity has been negative throughout most of the post-war periods. Living standards grow at best modestly. Gorbachev's diagnosis of crisis begins and ends with the economy, though economic reconstruction to the degree and at the pace which he deems essential cannot be achieved without a concomitant process of political renewal.

The draft plan for 1985–1990 and longer term perspective plans have established an ambitious programme of growth and modernisation. During the twelfth Five-Year Plan, GNP is postulated to grow at four per cent p.a. (double that achieved on average in 1976–85) which, to be successfully implemented, would reverse a 20-year downward trend. In the 1990s GNP is to grow at an even higher rate, five per cent p.a.[86] Industrial growth is to increase at twice, and agriculture at three times the previous decade. The acceleration is to be brought about partly by improving the efficiency of the labour market, which was in part a continuation of the strict discipline campaign initiated by Andropov, but pushed much further. Those who failed their economic responsibilities had to be punished, and within a few years the Chairman of the Council of Ministers and five deputy chairmen, plus 25 of the country's economic ministers and state committee chairmen had been sacked, some replaced by managers brought in from the defence industry. There is no doubt that within its own terms the discipline campaign had been successful.[87] *Perestroika* more positively requires workers and managers to be more responsible for their economic welfare, linked to a restructuring of the economic mechanism.

Personal *perestroika* was predicted on a deep and sustained intensification of production in all economic spheres. Despite massive investment since the first Five-Year Plan, the nation's capital in the 1980s was old and inefficient. On average over half of the machine inventory was 20 years old.[88] By 1990 fully one-third of the capital stock and half of the nation's machinery is planned to be new, to be achieved by concentrating on capital reconstruction. Industrial modernisation on such a scale requires an increase in the growth of machinery production to bring the percentage of modern quality machinery in the nation's inventory to 90 per cent compared with the current ratio of 20 per cent. Modernisation of machinery has been identified by Gorbachev as a vital and urgent task,[89] yet overall investment is planned to grow by only 3.5 per cent to four per cent p.a. Not only is overall growth low, but major programmes in energy and agriculture have pre-empted a high proportion of total investment. Nevertheless machinery, and in particular the crucial machine tools branch, is planned to increase by seven to eight per cent p.a., so that by 1990 capital investment in machinery will increase by 80 per cent.[90] In fact performance in the machinery sector has been disappointing, growing on average at only two-thirds of the planned rate.[91] The failure to achieve the growth targets makes acute the key issue of civil–military resource competition. The machinery sector supplies both military and civilian producers. On average around 25–30 per cent of its output is delivered to the military, a ratio which on occasion may have reached 60 per cent. Slow growth in this sector intensifies competition between claimants and makes leadership political choices more confrontational.

Gorbachev's objective was more than shifting upwards a few performance indicators. It was nothing less than the complete transformation of the technological base of Soviet economic society, the sole means, according to Mr Gorbachev, by which the Soviet Union could sustain its hard-won status as a superpower.[92] Failure to reverse the systemic and policy induced technological lag would demolish his plans for economic growth and long term improvement in welfare, and further destroy the legitimacy of the Party. The Soviet Union would offer an even less attractive model to Third World countries and be unable to assist at other than mundane levels. In civilian terms, the Soviet Union would be left behind by the revolution in micro circuitry electronics, computer aided design and manufacturing, ceramics, fibre optics, lasers and robotics, with which the Americans, Japanese, Europeans, let alone smaller industrial nations, were transforming their industrial societies. Finally, failure to devise and diffuse military technology would compromise the very security of the state. Technology is the fulcrum upon which all else revolves. Gorbachev, in short, is a technological determinist.[93]

The Soviet Union graduates each year more scientists, engineers and technologists than the USA, but a lower percentage of highly skilled and trained graduates, those most likely to influence the pace and direction of fundamental innovation. To aggravate the proportionate imbalance, a disproportionate ratio of top scientists are directed each year into military related research and development. Although the military has been the technologically most dynamic sector,[94] the secrecy which habitually characterises it and the lack of commercial pay-off has inhibited spill-in of its expertise to the civilian economy.

The Soviet dilemma over the allocation of economic and technological resources between the military and civilian claimants is real and immediate. The Party has successfully identified itself with the goals of national defence and power[95] and will not willingly concede the high ground. Given the enhanced pace of the product cycle and hence the rate at which new or improved weapons are deployed in the military arsenals, the resources implications of smart conventional weapons and the challenge posed by SDI, the military cannot easily contemplate lower spending on defence, and has made clear its fears that failure to invest in forced modernisation will leave it behind in the technological arms race.[96] Each upward spiral in technology which places emphasis on quality diminishes the Soviet quantitative advantage,[97] and is more costly to counter. Moreover, as the one sector which has shown it can use resources effectively, it might be efficient for Soviet leaders to concentrate scarce technological resources on the military economy and improve mechanisms of transfer to the civilian branches.

Soviet leaders have always understood a powerful economic base to be a pre-requisite for military might, but in modern societies the quantitative criteria at which the Soviet Union often excelled no longer suffices. Economic progress demands a more innovative response to new technological challenges and opportunities, which in the Soviet Union is vitiated by the organisational structure and reward mechanism. The Soviet Union will not meet Gorbachev's objective to project it to the front rank of technological powers without reform of organisation and incentive structure. These alone will not be enough, however. There must also be investment in civilian hardware and software in precisely those branches which are competitive with the military sector.

The urgency to modernise Soviet society is greater in view of the greater salience of non-military factors to the world correlation of forces which have been so influential for the conduct of Soviet affairs. When the correlation could, from the Soviet point of view, be easily measured in military terms, lagging economic and technological performance was explicable as a necessary sacrifice to military parity. With the decline in the military instrument and the increased and increasing salience of economic issues,[98] traditional trade-offs are less useful. Economic well-being at home and a reversal of what Western-ers claim to be the ennui which afflicts large segments of Soviet society, the public face of socialism as a more progressive and effective model for Eastern Europe and the Third World, and above all technological progress, are crucial aspects of a more embracing conception of means and ends of Soviet policy and security. World trends in the correlation of forces are increasingly disadvantageous. The Soviet dilemma spans the choices between civilian and military and the short and the long term; a dilemma which is less easily reconciled in a low growth society. Though growth and factor pro-ductivity have recovered from 1979–81, the recovery has been modest, and partly due to temporary factors. GNP increased at 2.5 per cent p.a. between 1981 and 1985 and factor productivity fell at 0.8 per cent, an improvement on the minus 1.3 per cent p.a. in the previous plan period. Investment in mid-decade grew at between 1.5 per cent and 2.5 per cent, but for 1986 was planned to increase by 7.5 per cent, and, significantly, that in civilian machinery by 30 per cent[99] reflecting not only its key role in Soviet modernisation, but also its failure to meet the growth targets in the eleventh Five-Year Plan.

Although overall military expenditure has grown at a modest pace, military R and D has been sustained at the long term norm of four to five per cent p.a.,[100] and according to the CIA was by 1985 estimated with, an admitted wide margin of error to total about R27bn. (equiv-alent to $35bn.), compared with $28bn. for the USA. An alternative estimate derived from Soviet handbooks gives a most plausible range of R8.7–9.9bn. in 1984.[101]

Although Gorbachev lacks Brezhnev's close links with the mili-tary-industrial complex, he is not overtly hostile and has promoted many of its managers to revitalise the civilian economy. But it is probable that at a secret meeting in Minsk in July 1985 he told senior officers that the defence budget would be cut and that the military would have to do more with less resources. The programme accepted at the 27th CPSU Congress stated that the Party would make 'every effort to ensure' that the military had the resources it needs,[102] a form of words which compares unfavourably with the Brezhnev guarantee that the Party would 'ensure' that enough resources would be available. Given the enormous scale of defence activities there is every possibility that *perestroika* will release resources currently ill- or under-utilised.[103] A policy stance which accepts Ogarkov's interpretation of East–West affairs and continues to allocate a disproportionate ratio of the nation's high-tech and high skill resources to the military inevitably enhances the already powerful autarchic forces in the Soviet Union. If in response to an awareness of the greater complexity of domestic and international politics, the civilian claimants successfully appropriate a greater share of resources, the impetus to a deeper involvement in the international economy becomes almost irresistible.

Even before Gorbachev came to power the diplomatist faction in the Kremlin, which advocated amongst other things a more genuine, reciprocal approach to arms control, appeared to be in the ascendancy. Since he took office, Gorbachev has strengthened this group at the expense of the atavistic forces in society which sustained conservative policies in the Soviet Union.[104]

Gorbachev's New Thinking accepts the political view that a nuclear war is unwinnable. The Soviet military perspective therefore should be a reasonable sufficiency. Anything in excess not only does not increase Soviet security, but by exacerbating psychological tension and provoking a response by the USA might reduce security in the USSR and in the world as a whole. In an interdependent global society, the Soviet Union cannot isolate itself from the world, and whatever increases international tension diminishes Soviet security. Furthermore, in a departure from conventional doctrine, Soviet military activity, by provoking an inevitable response from the USA, endogenously sustains the action–reaction dynamic of the arms race,[105] which is not therefore exclusively due to militaristic imperialism in the capitalist states. Military strength alone cannot guarantee the security of the USSR or the USA, which are interdependent and mutually interactive. Security can no longer be measured by military might alone, but by a complex amalgam of military, economic, diplomatic and even humanitarian variables, which organically bind the

USSR to the international community of nations. The wider conception of security logically requires a cap on military spending. Mutual
military interdependence in the era of nuclear stalemate requires the
downgrading of the international class struggle as the crucial element
in international politics,[106] as both sides seek new forms of relationships between the different systems and states. The Soviet Union can
no longer isolate itself from a deeper involvement in international
affairs reflected in its non-participation in many of the leading international financial and trade organisations, the non-convertibility of
the rouble and its disproportionately small share of world trade in
manufactured goods.

Gorbachev's world view is incompatible with Cold War rhetoric
and expenditure patterns and as the first step he argues that military
forces should be limited to those compatible with reasonable
sufficiency,[107] consistent with a diplomacy of decline.[108] In an era of
limits, traditional Soviet foreign policy has ill-served the Soviet
Union's fundamental interests. Despite being essentially adversarial,
many civilian specialists argue that the threat of invasion from the
West is outmoded.[109] There is therefore less need to devote so many
resources at such cost to East–West competition. To this purpose
Edward Shevardnadze has argued that 'the main thing is that the
country not bear additional expenses in connection with the need to
maintain its defence capability'.[110] In his speech to the United Nations
in November 1988, Gorbachev promised a total cut of 500 000 men
from the armed forces, 240 000 of whom will be withdrawn from the
European front. Soviet forces will also be reduced by 200 000 men
from the eastern part of the country, and 7.5 per cent of Soviet troops
in Mongolia. In addition, 10 000 tanks, 8500 artillery systems and 800
combat aircraft will be withdrawn, some of the most modern models.
Six tank divisions in all will be removed from Eastern Europe.
Assault landing, river crossing and other special units will be withdrawn from the GDR, Czechoslovakia and Hungary, and the remaining division will be reorganised on a more defensive alignment.
This unilateral move has been followed by similar statements of
contraction in most of the Warsaw Pact countries.

Gorbachev's analysis of systemic crisis and the appropriate response to it is more advanced than the Party in general, and he
seldom speaks of restructuring without also referring to the opposition his ideas provoke at all levels of society. However much Gorbachev might genuinely plan to hold down military spending and
dampen the arms race, his ability to transfer his views into effective

policy depends on political alignments in the Soviet Union, on how far traditional forces are willing to forego their special claims on the nation's resources. Despite the slower growth in expenditure, strategic forces continue to be modernised. A decisive shift to conventional technology along the lines advocated by Ogarkov or deployment of SDI in the USA might push forward the arms race irrespective of leadership preferences. Nevertheless, despite criticisms of the prevailing trends in military doctrine and in civil–military relations which occasionally appear in the specialist military press, defence chiefs by and large concur with the main thrust of Gorbachev's modernisation. Many officers acknowledge that long term military strength must be based on a more innovative economy, and that the two sectors must be more thoroughly integrated, bonded by a common technology. The Soviet Union is ill-equipped to compete with the technological dynamism of the USA and will be unable to take full advantage of emergent military technology without a more secure civilian base. In the long run the military may be the greatest beneficiary of restructuring and reforms, but in the short term must accept a curtailment of its traditional claim of automatic priority. In December 1988 Marshal Akromeyev resigned as Chief of the General Staff, on the day that Mr Gorbachev announced to the United Nations that he was planning unilaterally to withdraw troops and equipment from Eastern Europe and China and to deploy those remaining into more defensive arrangements. Although the ostensible reason for his resignation was ill-health, it may perhaps be a public consequence of an internal battle for economic resources, which the armed forces, temporarily at least, have lost. His replacement, General Moisezev, is a young (50 years old) and comparatively little known officer, which sustains the belief that Mr Gorbachev is in effective control of the military high command.[111]

A new generation of technologists and managers who lack the close links to the military–industrial complex of its predecessors must be placated and rewarded if modernisation is to be supported at the crucial middle level.[112] Civilian arms control experts independent of and not wholly sympathetic to traditional military concerns have breached the armed forces monopoly on military information. Although weight of numbers, skills and organisation still remains with the defence chiefs, the political leaders do have access to an alternative, and presumably less militaristic view. The conservative elements in the military-industrial complex for the moment at least are on the descendancy, but even in systemic crisis the Party is not likely to so starve the military of resources as to provoke a Bonapartiste reaction. Mr Gorbachev's position is not, however, politically unassailable. Despite reasonable economic growth, many observers both in the West and in the Soviet Union are gloomy about the state of the economy and its medium term prospects.[113] Western economists identify various potential growth scenarios from very poor to very good, and at this stage it is impossible to predict which will most correctly conform to reality. If, however, *perestroika* fails to deliver improved living standards and/or technological regeneration, the conservative forces now relatively dormant might again regain the ascendancy. Mr Gorbachev might be removed from office. He might remain but his progressive policies be allowed to wither and die. The different possible political outcomes will in turn impact on the intensity and the morphology of the East–West arms race.

For the USSR, as for the USA, the burden of defence is perceived as being increasingly onerous and at the same time less useful for foreign policy purposes. Power and influence are increasingly functions of economic wealth and technological progress rather than solely military might, such that despite continued expenditure on armaments, the hegemonic power of both superpowers is being eroded[114] slowly and at the edges, but inexorably. The structural organisations which in each country give so much domestic momentum to the arms race remain essentially intact. The political climate within which they exercise power is however changing. Whether the arms race sustains its long post-war morphology or is transformed to a less threatening manifestation of inevitable great power rivalry depends in each country on the balance of conservative and progressive forces.

Notes and References

1 The International Dimension

1. B. Buzan, *An Introduction to Strategic Studies: Military Technology and International Relations* (London: Macmillan, 1987) p. 69.
2. M. Atfield, 'Arms Races and Escalation. A Comment on Wallace', *International Studies Quarterly*, vol. 27, no. 2, 1983, p. 226.
3. H. Mosley, *The Arms Race: Economic and Social Consequences* (Lexington: Lexington Books, 1985) p. 18.
4. J. Vasquez, 'The Steps to War': Toward a Scientific Explanation of Correlates of War Finding, *World Politics*, vol. 40, no. 1, 1987, p. 135.
5. T. Schelling, *The Strategy of Conflict* (Oxford: Oxford University Press, 1963) p. 208.
6. G. Prins (ed), *Defended to Death* (London: Penguin Books, 1983) p. 93.
7. C. Gray, 'The Arms Race Phenomenon', *World Politics*, vol. 24, no. 1, 1971.
8. R. Gilpin, *War and Change in World Politics* (Cambridge: Cambridge University Press, 1981) ch. 5.
9. T. Cusak and M.Ward, 'Military Spending in the United States, Soviet Union and the People's Republic of China', *Journal of Conflict Resolution*, vol. 25, no. 3, 1981, p. 452.
10. S. Majeski and D. Jones, 'Arms Race Modeling, Causality Analysis and Model Specification', *Journal of Conflict Resolution*, vol. 25, no. 2, 1981, p. 273.
11. A. Wohlstetter, 'Is there a Strategic Arms Race?', *Foreign Policy*, no. 15, Summer 1974, no. 16, Fall 1974.
12. M. Ward, 'Differential Paths to Parity: A Study of the Contemporary Arms Race', *American Political Studies Review,* vol. 78, no. 2, 1984, p. 298.
13. I. Bellamy, 'The Richardson Theory of Arms Races: Themes and Variations', *British Journal of International Studies*, vol. 1, no. 2, 1975, p. 129.
14. D. Byers and D. Peel, 'The Determinants of Arms Expenditures of NATO and the Warsaw Pact: Some Further Evidence', *Journal of Peace Research*, vol. 26, no. 1, 1989, p. 76.
15. M. McGuire, 'A Quantitative Study of the Strategic Arms Race in the Missile Age', *Review of Economics and Statistics*, vol. LIX, no. 3, 1977, p. 331.
16. T. Cusak and M. Ward, op. cit., 1981, p. 450.
17. C. Jacobsen, *The Soviet Defence Enigma. Estimating Costs and Burdens* (Oxford: Oxford University Press, 1987) p. 3.
18. M. Leidy and R. Steiger, 'Economic Issues and Methodology in Arms Race Analysis', *Journal of Conflict Resolution,* vol. 29, no. 3, 1985, p. 505.
19. S. Huntington, 'Arms Races: Pre-requisites and Results', in J. Mueller (ed), *Approaches to Measurement in International Relations. A non-evangelical Survey* (New York: Appleton–Century–Crofts, 1969) p. 16.

20. W. Saris and C. Middendorp, 'Arms Races: External Security or Domestic Pressure', *British Journal of Political Science*, vol. 10, part 1, 1980, p. 124.
21. R. Jervis, 'Co-operation Under the Security Dilemma', *World Politics*, vol. 30, no. 2, 1978, p. 187.
22. C. Schmidt, 'Semantic Variations on Richardson's Armaments Dynamics', in C. Schmidt (ed), *The Economics of Military Expenditures* (London: Macmillan, 1987) p. 148.
23. C. Gray, *The Soviet American Arms Race*, (Lexington: Saxon House, 1976) p. 5.
24. C. Schmidt, op. cit., 1987, p. 148.
25. A. Becker, 'The Meaning and Measure of Soviet Military Expenditures', in *The Soviet Economy in a Time of Change Part 1*. A Compendium of Papers submitted to the Joint Economic Committee, Congress of the United States, Washington DC, 1979, p. 352.
26. M. Ward, op. cit., 1983, p. 307.
27. Ibid., p. 298.
28. Ibid., p. 299.
29. Ibid., p. 304.
30. G. Prins, op. cit., 1983, p. 84.
31. M. Ward, op. cit., 1983, p. 311.
32. National Foreign Assessment Center, *Estimating Soviet Defence Spending: Trends and Prospects*, June 1978, SR78–10121, Washington DC, p. 3.
33. M. Acland-Hood, 'Estimating Soviet Military R and D Spending', in C. Jacobsen (ed), *The Soviet Defence Enigma – Estimating Costs and Burden* (Oxford: Oxford University Press, 1987).
34. J. Fallows, *National Defense* (New York: Random House, 1981), p. 70.
35. R. Smith, 'Soviets Drop Further Back in Weapons Technology', *Science*, 16 March 1984, vol. 222, no. 4641. B. Inman, 'Control of Technology Transfer to the Soviet Union', ACDA *World Military Expenditures and Arms Transfers*, 1985, Washington DC.
36. W. Saris and C. Middendorp, op. cit., 1980, p. 122.
37. M. Halperin, 'The Decision to Deploy the ABM. Bureaucratic and Domestic Politics in the Johnson Administration', *World Politics*, vol. 25, no. 1, 1973, p. 64.
38. M. Thee, 'The Dynamics of the Arms Race: Military R and D and Disarmament', *International Social Science Journal,* vol. XXX, no. 4, 1978, p. 915.
39. G. Prins (ed), op. cit., 1983, p. 89.
40. C. Gray, op. cit., 1976, p. 25.
41. J. Fallows, op. cit., 1981, p. 62.
42. M. Thee, *Military Technology, Military Strategy and the Arms Race* (London: Croom Helm, 1986) p. 106.
43. C. Gray, op. cit., 1976, p. 8.
44. S. Rosefielde, 'Economic Foundations of Soviet National Security', *Orbis*, vol. 30, no. 2, 1986, p. 318.
45. C. Schmidt, op. cit., 1987, p. 157.
46. J. Gillespie *et al.* 'An Optimal Control Model of the Arms Race',

American Political Science Review, vol. 71, no. 1, 1977, p. 226.
47. C. Gray, 'The Urge to Compete: Rationales for Arms Racing', *World Politics*, vol. 26, no. 2, 1974, p. 214.
48. C. Gray, op. cit., 1971, p. 43.
49. S. Huntington, op. cit., 1969, p. 28.
50. Ibid., p. 32.
51. C. Joynt, 'Arms Races and the Problem of Equilibrium', *The Yearbook of World Affairs* (London: Stevens and Son, 1964), p. 24.
52. H. York and A. Greb, 'Military R and D. A Post War History', *Bulletin of the Atomic Scientists*, vol. 33, no. 1, 1977, p. 13.
53. B. Russett, *The Prisoners of Insecurity* (San Francisco: W.H. Freeman, 1983) ch. 4.
54. M. Thee, op. cit., 1978, p. 910.
55. R. Gartoff, 'On Estimating and Imputing Intentions', *International Security*', vol. 2, no. 3, 1977–78.
56. S. Smith, 'SDI and the New Cold War', in R. Crockatt and S. Smith, (eds), *The Cold War Past and Present* (London: Allen and Unwin, 1987) p. 161.
57. S. Majeski, 'Technological Innovation and Co-operation in the Arms Race', *International Studies Quarterly*, vol. 30, no. 2, 1986, p. 187.
58. J. Gaddis, 'The Long Peace: Elements of Stability in the Post War International System', *International Security*, vol. 10, no. 4, 1985–86, p. 100.
59. J. Houwelling and J. Siciamo, 'The Arms Race – War Relationship. Why Serious Disputes Matter', *Arms Control*, vol. 2, no. 2, 1981, p. 100.
60. L. Freedman, 'Nuclear Weapons in Europe: Is there an Arms Race?', *Journal of International Studies*, vol. 13, no. 1, 1984, p. 63.
61. C. Gray, op. cit., 1974, p. 209.
62. J. Lambert, 'Arms Races as Good Things', in U. Luterbacher M. Ward (eds), *Dynamic Models of International Conflict*, (Boulder: Lynne Reiner, 1985) p. 162.
63. J. Vasquez, op. cit., 1987, p. 12.
64. S. Huntington, op. cit., 1969, p. 28.
65. M. Intriligator and D. Brito, 'Heuristic Decision Rules, The Dynamics of the Arms Race and War Initiation', in U. Luterbacher and M. Ward, op. cit., 1985, p. 143.
66. T. Mayer, 'Arms Races and War Initiation: Some Alternatives to the Intriligator–Brito Model', *Journal of Conflict Resolution*, vol. 30, no. 1, 1986, p. 11.
67. P. Diehl, 'Arms Races and Escalation – A Closer Look', *Journal of Peace Research*, vol. 20, no. 3, 1983, p. 208.
68. W. Wallace, 'Arms Races and Escalation', *Journal of Conflict Resolution*, vol. 23, no. 1, 1979, p. 6.
69. M. Atfield, 'Arms Races and Escalation. A Comment on Wallace', *International Studies Quarterly*, vol. 27, no. 2, 1983, p. 226.
70. W. Wallace, 'Armaments and Escalation. Two Competing Theories', *International Studies Quarterly*, vol. 26, no. 1, 1982, p. 545.
71. P. Diehl, op. cit., 1983, p. 107.
72. Ibid., p. 209.

73. J. Vasquez, op. cit., 1987, p. 136.
74. W. Wallace, 'Old Nails in New Coffins. Para Bellum Hypothesis Revisited', *Journal of Peace Research*, vol. 18, no. 11, 1981, pp. 92–93.
75. J. Houwelling and J. Siciamo, op. cit., 1981, p. 162.
76. Ibid., 1981, p. 170.
77. T. Smith, 'The Insurance Factor: An Assessment of War Costs', *Journal of Peace Research*, vol. 22, 1985, pp. 101–104.
78. Ibid., p. 109.
79. S. Kull, 'Nuclear Nonsense', *Foreign Policy*, no. 58, Spring 1985, p. 28.
80. K. Tsipis, 'The Arms Race as Posturing' in D. Carlton and C. Schaerf (eds), *The Dynamics of the Arms Race* (London: Croom Helm, 1977).
81. P. Wallerstein, 'Armed Forces are not only for War', *Journal of Peace Research*, vol. X1X, no. 1, 1982, p. 81.
82. R. Constanza, 'Nuclear Arms Races and Theory of Social Traps', *Journal of Peace Research*, vol. 21, no. 1, 1984, p. 7.
    J. Conybeare, 'Public Goods, Prisoner's Dilemma and the International Political Economy', *International Studies Quarterly*, vol. 28, no. 1, 1984, p. 7.
84. R. Axelrod, 'The Emergence of Co-operation Among Egoists', *American Political Science Review*, vol. 75, no. 2, 1981.
85. S. Majeski, op. cit., 1986, p. 187.
86. D. Lee, 'Arms Negotiations, the Soviet Economy and Democratically Induced Illusions', *Contemporary Policy Issues*, Vol. IV, October 1986.
87. C. Rice, 'Defence and Security', in M. McCauley (ed), *The Soviet Union Under Gorbachev* (London: Macmillan, 1987) p. 192.
88. D. Lee, op. cit., 1986.
89. J. Fallows, op. cit., 1981.

2   The American Defence Economy

1. S. Zuckerman, 'Technology for a Cold War', in R. Crockatt and S. Smith, *The Cold War: Past and Present* (London: Allen and Unwin, 1987) p. 24.
2. H. Mosley, *The Arms Race: Economic and Social Consequences* (Lexington: Lexington Books, 1985) p. 5.
3. Ibid., p. 174.
4. J. Wilson, *American Government: Institutions and Policies*, 3rd ed. (Lexington: D.C. Heath, 1986) p. 599.
5. A. Yarmolinsky, *The Military Establishment* (New York: Harper and Row, 1971) p. 11.
6. R. Maidment and A. McGraw, *The American Political Process* (London: Sage, 1986) p. 154.
7. J. Gansler, *The Defense Industry* (Cambridge Mass.: MIT Press, 1980) p. 73.
8. R. Maidment and A. McGraw, op. cit., 1986, p. 154.
9. A. Yarmolinsky, op. cit., 1971, p. 411.
10. M. Weidenbaum, 'Economics and the National Security', *The Washington Quarterly*, vol. 11, no. 4, 1988, p. 39.
11. M. Halperin, 'The Good, The Bad and The Wasteful', *Foreign Policy*,

no. 6, Spring 1972, p. 69.
12. Ibid., p. 72.
13. J. Fallows, *National Defense* (New York: Random House, 1981) p. 34.
14. E. Luttwak, 'Why we need more Waste, Fraud and Mismanagement in the Pentagon, *Survival*, vol. 24, 1982, p. 117.
15. D. Sorensen, 'Declining Defense Budgets and the Future of the US Defense Industry', *Defense Analysis*, vol. 4, no. 2, 1988, p. 170.
16. H. Mosley, op. cit., 1985, p. 33.
17. C. Kegley and E. Wittkopf, *American Foreign Policy: Pattern and Process*, 3rd ed. (London: Macmillan, 1987) p. 272.
18. N. Frohlich *et al*, 'Individual Contribution for Collective Goods', *Journal of Conflict Resolution*, vol. 19, 1975.
19. J. Fallows, op. cit., 1981, p. 31.
20. D. Robertson, 'Defence Policy Options for Britain and the New Cold War', in R. Crockatt and S. Smith, op. cit., 1987, p. 174.
21. J. Gansler, Hearings before the subcommittee on Economic Goals and Intergovernmental Policy of the Joint Economic Committee of the United States, October, December 1982, Washington DC, p. 92.
22. I. McLean, *Public Choice: An Introduction* (Oxford: Blackwell, 1984) p. 20.
23. D. Smith and R. Smith, *The Economics of Militarism* (London: Pluto, 1983) p. 41.
24. I. McLean, op. cit., 1984, p. 86.
25. Ibid., pp. 100–101.
26. P. Jackson, *The Political Economy of Bureaucracy* (Deddington: Philip Allan, 1982) p. 133.
27. R. Cornes and T. Sandler, *The Theory of Externalities, Public Goods and Club Goods* (Cambridge: Cambridge University Press, 1986) p. 237.
28. J. Gansler, op. cit.
29. J. Fallows, 'America's High Tech Weaponry', *The Atlantic*, vol. 247, 5 May 1971, p. 31.
30. R. Maidment and A. McGraw, op. cit., 1986, p. 143.
31. M. Halperin, *Bureaucratic Politics and Foreign Policy* (Washington: Brookings, 1974) pp. 11–12.
32. R. de Grasse, *Military Expansion and Economic Decline: The Impact of Military Spending on US Economic Performance* (Armonk: M.E., Sharpe, 1983) p. 3.
33. A. Yarmolinsky and G. Foster, *Paradoxes of Power: The Military Establishment in the Eighties* (Bloomington: Indiana University Press, 1983) p. 2.
34. Ibid., p. 4.
35. H. Mial, *Nuclear Weapons: Who's in Charge?* (London: Macmillan, 1987) p. 67.
36. W. Adams and W. Adams, 'The Military Industrial Complex: A Market Structure', *American Economic Review*, vol. 62, 1972 (1), p. 281.
37. A. Yarmolinsky and G. Foster, op. cit., 1983, p. 5.
38. L. Freedman, *US Intelligence and The Soviet Strategic Threat* (London: Macmillan, 1986) 2nd ed, p. 2.
39. A. Yarmolinsky, op. cit., 1971, p. 261.

40. L. Aspin, 'Games the Pentagon Plays', *Foreign Policy*, no. 11, Summer 1973.
41. C. Gray, 'The Arms Race Phenomenon', *World Politics*, vol. XXIV, no. 1, 1971, p. 63.
42. A. Yarmolinsky and G. Foster, op. cit., 1983, p. 96.
43. C. Kegley and E. Wittkopf, op. cit., 1987, p. 272.
44. L. Aspin, op. cit., 1973 pp. 89–90.
45. Ibid., p. 90.
46. C. Kegley and E. Wittkopf, op. cit., 1987, p. 272.
47. J. Gansler, 'We Can Afford Security', *Foreign Policy*, no. 1, Summer 1983, p. 80.
48. J. Fallows, op. cit., 1981, pp. 32–33.
49. The President's Blue Ribbon Commission on Defense Management (Packard Commission) *A Quest For Excellence: Final Report to the President*, Washington DC, 1986, p. XVII.
50. S. Cobb, 'Defence Spending and Defence Voting in the House. An Empirical Study of an Aspect of the Military Industrial Complex Thesis', *American Journal of Sociology*, vol. 82, no. 1, 1976, p. 164.
51. J. Fallows, op. cit., 1981, p. 69.
52. J. Wilson, op. cit., 1986, p. 597.
53. H. Mial, op. cit., 1987, p. 45.
54. M. Halperin, op. cit., 1974, p. 41.
55. P. Kennedy, *The Rise and Fall of the Great Powers. Economic Change and Military Conflict* (London: Unwin Hyman, 1988) p. 522.
56. M. Halperin, op. cit., 1972, p. 72.
57. B. Posen and S. Van Evera, 'Defense Policy and the Reagan Administration', *International Security*, vol. 8, no. 1, 1983, pp. 3–4.
58. H. Levine, *Challenge of Controversy: American Political Issues of our Time*, (Englewood Cliffs: Prentice Hall, 1985) p. 134.
59. J. Wilson, op. cit., 1986, p. 601.
60. C. Weinberger, Secretary of Defense, *Annual Report to the Congress*, Fiscal Year 1987 Washington, 1986, p. 17.
61. S. Huntington, The Defense Policy of the Reagan Administration 1981–82, F. Greenstein (ed), *The Reagan Presidency: An Early Assessment* (Baltimore: Johns Hopkins University Press, 1983)
62. D. Calleo, *Beyond American Hegemony: The Future of the Western Alliance* (New York: Basic Books, 1987) p. 116.
63. M. Hunt, *Ideology and US Foreign Policy* (New Haven: Yale University Press, 1987)
64. J. Gaddis, *The United States and the Origins of the Cold War* (New York: Columbia University Press, 1972) p. 352.
65. H. Mclosky and J. Zaller, *The American Ethos: Public Attitudes Towards Capitalism and Democracy* (Cambridge: Harvard University Press, 1984) p. 134.
66. M. Nincic, 'The American Public and the Soviet Union: The Domestic Context of Discontent', *Journal of Peace Research*, vol. 22, no. 4, 1985, p. 347.
67. M. Thee, *Military Technology, Military Strategy and the Arms Race* (London: Croom Helm, 1986) p. 14.

68. *The Dynamics of World Military Expenditures World Armaments and Disarmament*, SIPRI Yearbook 1974 (Cambridge, Mass.,: MIT Press, 1974) p. 127.
69. F. Long, 'Advancing Military Technology: Recipe for an Arms Race', *Current History*, vol. 82, no. 484, 1983, p. 215.
70. D. Yergin, *Shattered Peace: The Origins of the Cold War and the National Security State* (London: Penguin, 1978) p. 267.
71. H. York and A. Greb, 'Military R and D: A Post War History', *Bulletin of the Atomic Scientists*, vol. 33, no. 1, 1977, p. 14.
72. J. Fallows, op. cit., 1981, p. 59.
73. F. Long, 'Federal R and D Budget: Guns v. Butter', *Science*, 16 March 1984, vol. 222, no. 4641, p. 1133.
74. J. Fallows, op. cit., 1981, p. 35.
75. C. Coker, *US Military Power in the 1980s* (London: Macmillan, 1983) p. 87.
76. A. Markusen, 'The Militarised Economy', *World Policy Journal*, vol. 3, Summer 1986, p. 508.
77. Ibid., p. 501.
78. J. Rubel, 'Military R and D: The Most Fruitful Source of Long Term Growth', in J. Clayton (ed), *The Economic Impact of the Cold War: Sources and Readings* (New York: Harcourt, Brace and World, 1970) p. 148.
79. M. Handel, 'Numbers Do Count. The Question of Quality versus Quantity', in S. Huntington (ed), *The Strategic Imperative: New Policies for American Security* (Cambridge, Mass.,: Ballinger, 1982) p. 196.
80. U. Albrecht, 'Military R and D Communities', *International Social Science Journal*, vol. XXXV, no. 1, 1983, pp. 8–9.
81. M. Halperin, 'The Decision to Deploy the ABM. Bureaucratic and Domestic Policy in the Johnson Administration', *World Politics*, vol. 25, no. 1, 1973, p. 70.
82. H. Mial, op. cit., 1987, p. 26.
83. A. Yarmolinsky, op. cit., 1971, p. 56.
84. R. Art, op. cit., 1972, pp. 100–101.
85. M. Kaldor, 'Military R and D: Cause or Consequence of the Arms Race', *International Social Science Journal*, vol. XXV, no. 1, 1983, p. 3.
86. G. Adams, *The Politics of Defense Contracting. The Iron Triangle* (New Brunswick: Transactions Books, 1982) p. 22.
87. J. O'Shea, 'The Real Nuts and Bolts of Pentagon Contracting', *Bulletin of the Atomic Scientists*, vol. 42, no. 8, 1986, pp. 19–20.
88. R. Art, 'Why We Overspend and Underachieve', *Foreign Policy*, no. 6, Spring 1972, p. 96.
89. R. Perry, 'The American Style of Military R and D', in F. Long and J. Reppy (eds), *The Genesis of New Weapons: Decision Making for Military R and D* (New York: Pergamon Press, 1980)
90. M. Halperin, op. cit., 1973, p. 64.
91. G. Prins, *Defended to Death* (London: Penguin, 1983) p. 84.
92. R. DeLauer, 'The FY Department of Defense Program for Research, Development and Acquisition', Washington, 1984, p. 11.
93. D. Holloway, 'Innovation in the Defence Sector', in R. Amann and J.

Cooper (eds), *Innovation in the Soviet Union* (New Haven: Yale University Press, 1982) p. 276.

94. J. Fallows, op. cit., 1981, p. 38.
95. Hearings, op. cit., 1982, p. 35.
96. N. Rosenberg, *Inside the Black Box* (New York: Cambridge University Press, 1982) p. 194.
97. R. Art, op. cit., 1972, p. 98.
98. M. Kaldor, op. cit., 1983, p. 32.
99. J. Fallows, op. cit., 1981, p. 37.
100. C. Coker, op. cit., 1983, pp. 84–85.
101. R. Art, op. cit., 1972, p. 98.
102. R. Perry, op. cit., 1980, p. 123.
103. J. Fallows, op. cit., 1981, p. 38.
104. Ibid., p. 22.
105. J. Merritt and P. Sprey, 'Negative Marginal Returns in Weapons Acquisitions', in R. Head, E. Rokke (eds), *American Defense Policy* 3rd ed. (Baltimore: Johns Hopkins University Press, 1973) p. 491.
106. J. Gansler, op. cit., 1983, p. 81.
107. J. Fallows, op. cit., 1981, p. 27.
108. J. O'Shea, op. cit., 1986, p. 20.
109. *The Guardian*, 12 February 1988.
110. A. Yarmolinsky and G. Foster, op. cit., 1983, p. 173.
111. A. Yarmolinsky, op. cit., 1971, pp. 72–73.
112. J. Merritt and P. Sprey, op. cit., 1973, p. 493.
113. S. Miller, 'Technology and War', *Bulletin of the Atomic Scientists*, vol. 41, no. 1, 1985.
114. J. Kurth, 'Why We Buy The Weapons We Do?', *Foreign Policy*, no. 11, Summer 1972–73.
115. J. Fallows, op. cit., 1981, p. 29.
116. Ibid., p. 26.
117. J. Gansler, op. cit., 1980, p. 90.
118. M. Kaldor, op. cit., 1983, p. 32.
119. U. Albrecht, op. cit., 1983, p. 12.
120. M. Kaldor, op. cit., 1983, p. 30.
121. A. Yarmolinsky and G. Foster, op. cit., 1983, p. 56.
122. M. Thee, op. cit., 1986, p. 31.
123. Ibid., p. 113.
124. G. Adams, op. cit., 1982, p. 98.
125. C. Wolfe, 'Military Industrial Simplicities, Complexities and Realities', R. Head and E. Rokke, op. cit., 1973.
126. S. Lens, *The Military Industrial Complex* (Philadelphia: Pilgrim Press, 1970)
127. G. Adams, op. cit., 1982, p. 22.
128. C. Kegley and E. Wittkopf, op. cit., 1987, p. 272.
129. S. Cobb, op. cit., 1976, p. 178.
130. S. Lens, op. cit., 1970.
131. A. Sampson, *The Arms Bazaar* (London: Hodder and Stoughton, 1977) ch. 12.

132. R. Kaufman, 'MIRVing the Boondoggle: Contracts Subsidy and Welfare in the Aerospace Industry', *American Economic Review*, vol. 67, no. 1, 1972, p. 290.
133. H. Schiller and J. Phillips, 'The Military Industrial Establishment: Complex or System', in H. Schiller and J. Phillips (eds) *Super State: Reading in the Military Industrial Complex* (Urbana: University of Illinois Press, 1970) p. 19.
134. J. O'Shea, op. cit., 1986, pp. 19–20.
135. A. Yarmolinsky and G. Foster, op. cit., 1983, p. 56.
136. Ibid., p. 58.
137. J. Gansler, op. cit., 1980.
138. S. Liebersen, 'An Empirical Study of Military–Industrial Linkages', in S. Rosen (ed.), *Testing the Theory of the Military Industrial Complex* (Lexington: Heath, 1973) p. 67.
139. J. Gansler, op. cit., 1980, ch. 2.
140. J. Gansler, op. cit., 1980.
141. J. Epstein, *The 1988 Defense Budget Studies in Defence Policy* (Washington DC: Brookings, 1987) pp. 55–56.

3 The Soviet Defence Economy

1. D. Holloway, *The Soviet Union and the Arms Race* (New Haven: Yale University Press, 1984) p. 3.
2. Ibid., p. 6.
3. N. Jasny, *Soviet Industrialisation 1928–1952* (Chicago: Chicago University Press, 1960) p. 4.
4. D. Holloway, 'Innovation in the Defence Sector', in R. Amann and J. Copper, *Industrial Innovation in the Soviet Union* (New Haven: Yale University Press; 1982) p. 280.
5. M. Harrison, *Soviet Planning in Peace and War 1938–45*, (Cambridge: CUP, 1985) p. 8.
6. Ibid., p. 6.
7. R. Tullberg and G. Hagmeyer-Gaverns, 'World Military Expenditures', in *World Armaments and Disarmament*, SIPRI Yearbook 1987 (Oxford: Oxford University Press, 1987) p. 131.
8. *Allocation of Resources in the Soviet Union and China 1985*. Hearings Before the subcommittee on Economic Resources, Competitiveness and Security Economics of the Joint Economic Committee, Congress of the United States, Washington DC, 1986, p. 156.
9. *The Soviet Economy Under a New Leader*. A Report presented to the subcommittee on Economic Resources, Competitiveness and Security Economics, of the Joint Economic Committee, by the CIA and the DIA, Washington DC, 1986, p. 3.
10. C. Jacobson, *The Soviet Defence Enigma. Estimating Costs and Burden* (Oxford: Oxford University Press, 1987).
11. M. Checinski, 'The Costs of Armaments Production and the Profitability of Armaments Exports in COMECON Countries', *Osteuropa Wirtschaft*, vol. 20, no. 2, 1975, p. 117.

12. G. Offer, *The Opportunity Cost of the Non-Monetary Advantages of the Soviet Military R and D Effort*, Rand R-1741 DDRE, Santa Monica 1975.
13. D. Holloway, 'Technology and Political Decision in Soviet Armaments Policy', *Journal of Peace Research*, vol. XI, no. 4, 1974, p. 263.
14. C. Rice, 'The Party, The Military and Decision Authority in the Soviet Union', *World Politics*, vol. XL, no. 1, 1987 p. 55.
15. Ibid., p. 66.
16. D. Holloway, op. cit., 1984, p. 111.
17. J. Hough, 'The Historical Legacy in Soviet Weapons Development', J. Valente and W. Potter (eds), *Soviet Decision Making for National Security* (London: Allen and Unwin, 1984) p. 106.
18. D. Holloway, 'Doctrine and Technology in Soviet Armaments Policy', in D. Leebart (ed)., *Soviet Military Thinking* (London: Allen and Unwin, 1981) p. 277.
19. A. Warner, *The Military in Contemporary Soviet Politics* (New York: Praeger, 1977) p. 175.
20. D. Holloway, op. cit., 1984, p. 112.
21. A. Alexander, 'Decision Making in Soviet Weapons Procurement', *Adelphi Papers*, 147/148, Winter, 1978/79.
22. E. Jahn, 'The Role of the Armaments Complex in Soviet Society: Is there a Soviet Military Industrial Complex?', *Journal of Peace Research*, vol. XII, no. 3, 1975.
23. J. Hough, 'Soviet Decision Making in Defence', *Bulletin of the Atomic Scientist*, vol. 41, no. 7, 1985, p. 84.
24. D. Holloway, op. cit., 1982, p. 150.
25. CIA, *Soviet Weapons Industry: An Overview*, PB 86-928107–produced by the US Commerce Department, Washington DC, 1986, p. 15.
26. J. Gansler, 'We Can Afford Security', *Foreign Policy*, no. 51, Summer 1983, p. 80.
27. *Allocation of Resources in the Soviet Union and China 1983*. Hearings before the Subcommittee on International Trade, Finance and Security Economics of the Joint Economic Committee Congress of the United States, Washington DC, 1984, p. 82.
28. D. Holloway, 'Lessons of the Arms Race', *Bulletin of the Atomic Scientist*, vol. 41, no. 7, 1985, p. 83.
29. J. Kiser, 'How the Arms Race Really Helps Moscow', *Foreign Policy*, no. 60, Fall 1985, p. 50.
30. J. Cooper, 'Nuclear Milking Machines and Perestroika', *Detente* no. 14, 1989.
31. Allocation of Resources, 1984, op. cit., p. 82.
32. P. Munkholt, *The Soviet Economy: Protection of the Military Sector in Case of a Protracted Deterioration*, Sonderveroffentlichung des Bundesinstitats fur ostwissenshaftliche und international Studien, Koln, 1985, p. 12.
33. D. Holloway, op. cit., 1974, pp. 266–268.
34. A. Marshall, 'Estimating Soviet Defence Spending', *Survival*, vol. XVIII, no. 2, March–April 1976, p. 73.
35. L. Whetten and J. Waddell, 'Motor Vehicle Standardisations in the

Services Institute for Defence Studies, vol. 124, no. 1, 1979, p. 55.
36. M. Checinski, op. cit., 1975, p. 122.
37. G. Offer, op. cit., 1975, p. 6.
38. C. Rice, op. cit., 1987, p. 65.
39. J. Hough, op. cit., 1985, p. 86.
40. V. Aspaturian, 'The Soviet Military Industrial Complex, Does it Exist?', *Journal of International Affairs*, vol. 26, no. 1, 1972, p. 3.
41. D. Holloway, op. cit., 1981, p. 281.
42. J. Hough, op. cit., 1985, p. 86.
43. E. Jahn, op. cit., 1975, p. 191.
44. V. Aspaturian, op. cit., 1972, p. 1.
45. J. McDonnell, 'The Defence Industry as a Pressure Group', in M. MccGuire, K. Booth and J. McDonnell (eds), *Soviet Naval Policy: Objectives and Constraints* (New York: Praeger, 1975) p. 82.
46. M. Nincic, *The Arms Race: The Political Economy of Military Growth* (New York: Praeger, 1982) p. 67.
47. H. Schaefer, 'Soviet Power and Intentions: Military Economic Choices', *Soviet Economy in a Time of Change*. A Compendium of Papers submitted to the Joint Economic Committee, Congress of the United States, Washington DC, 1979, p. 341.
48. A. Becker, *The Burden of Soviet Defense: A Political Economic Essay*, Rand R–2752–AF Santa Monica, 1981, p. 54.
49. R. Hutchings, *The Soviet Budget* (London: Macmillan, 1985) p. 142.
50. R. Kaufman, 'Causes of the Slowdown in Soviet Defense Spending', *Soviet Economy*, vol. 1, January–March 1985, p. 234.
51. *Allocation of Resources in the Soviet Union and China 1984*. Hearings before the Subcommittee on Economic Resources, Competitiveness and Security Economics of the Joint Economic Committee, Congress of the United States, Washington DC, 1985, p. 234.
52. G. Schroeder, 'The Slowdown in Soviet Industry. 1971–82', *Soviet Economy*, vol. 1, no. 1, 1985.
53. E. Denton, 'Soviet Perception of Economic Prospects', *Soviet Economy in the 1980s Problems and Prospects*. Selected Papers submitted to the Joint Economic Committee, Congress of the United States, Washington DC, 1982.
54. Allocation of Resources, op. cit., 1985, p. 7.
55. C. Checinski, op. cit., 1975, p. 118.
56. 'How to Strengthen Interaction', *Pravda*, 26 April 1982, in *Current Digest of the Soviet Press*, vol. XXXIV, no. 17. 1982, p. 6.
57. G. Schroeder, 'Soviet Economic Reform Decrees: More Steps on the Treadmill', *Soviet Economy in the 1980s Problems or Prospects Part 1*, op. cit., p. 84.
58. T. Buck, *Comparative Industrial Systems* (London: Macmillan, 1982) p. 51.
59. Ibid., ch. 3.
60. P. Jackson, *The Political Economy of Bureaucracy* (Deddington: Philip Allan, 1982) p. 182.
61. N. Nimitz, *The Structure of Soviet Outlays on R and D 1960 and 1968*, Rand R-1207-DDRE, Santa Monica, 1974, p. 43.
62. J. Kiser, op. cit., 1985, p. 43.

63. H. Scott and W. Scott, *The Armed Forces of the USSR* (Boulder: Westview Press, 1979) p. 297.
64. E. Jones, 'Defense R. and D.: Policy Making in the USSR' in J. Valente and W. Potter, op. cit., 1984, p. 126.
65. N. Nimitz, op. cit., 1974, p. 55.
66. G. Offer, op. cit., 1975, p. 34.
67. D. Miller, 'The Development of the Russian Main Battle Tank 1946–77', *Journal of the Royal United Services Institute for Defence Studies*, vol. CXXIII, no. 1, 1978, p. 35.
68. K. Hartley, *NATO Arms Co-operation: A Study in Economics and Politics* (London: Allen and Unwin, 1983) p. 67.
69. J. Kiser, op. cit., 1985, p. 42.
70. L. Nolting and M. Feshback, 'R. and D. Employment in the USSR: Definitions, Statistics and Comparisons' in *Soviet Economy in a Time of Change*. A Compendium of Papers submitted to the Joint Economic Committee, Congress of the United States Washington DC, 1979.
71. *Soviet and US Defense Activities. A Dollar Cost Comparison* SR80-10005 Washington DC, 1980, p. 3.
72. M. Acland-Hood, 'Estimating Soviet Military R and D Spending', in C. Jacobsen (ed), *The Soviet Defense Enigma: Estimating Costs and Burdens* (Oxford: Oxford University Press, 1987) pp. 144–145.
73. M. Leitenberg, 'The Counterpart of Defense Industry Conversion in the United States in the USSR Economy. Defense Industry and Military Expenditures', *Journal of Peace Research*, vol. XVI, no. 3, 1979. p. 266.
74. R. Amann, 'Industrial Innovation in the Soviet Union: Methodological Perspectives and Conclusion', in R. Amann and J. Cooper (eds), 1982, op. cit., ch. 1.
75. D. Holloway, op. cit., 1984, p. 137.
76. Ibid., pp. 135–137.
77. J. Kiser, op. cit., 1985, p. 46.
78. P. De Lauer, 'The FY 1985 Department of Defense Program for Research Development and Acquisitions', Washington DC, 1984, pp. 11, 32–33.
79. B. Inman, 'Control of Technology Transfer to the Soviet Union', US Arms Control and Disarmament Agency, *World Military Expenditure and Arms Transfer*, Washington DC, 1985, p. 26.
80. R. De Lauer, op. cit., 1984, pp. 11–32.
81. D. Holloway, op. cit., 1981.
82. R. De Lauer, op. cit., 1984, pp. 11–15.
83. 'Around the Machine Tool. Ekonomika i organizatsia', *Promyshlennovo proizvodstra*, no. 1, January 1982, *Current Digest of the Soviet Press*, vol. XXXIV, no. 18, p. 7.
84. A. Alexander, op. cit., 1978–9, p. 25.
85. R. Perry, 'The American Style of R and D', in F. Long and J. Reppy (eds), *The Genesis of New Weapons: Decision Making for Military R and D* (New York: Pergamon, 1980)
86. Allocation of Resources, op. cit., 1985, p. 180.
87. M. Agursky and H. Adomeit, 'The Soviet Military Complex', *Survey*, vol. 24, no. 2, 1979, p. 110.

88. D. Miller, op cit., 1978, p. 36.
89. A. Alexander, op. cit., 1978–9, p. 25.
90. G. Offer, op. cit., 1975, p. 39.
91. S. Sestanovich, 'Gorbachev's Foreign Policy: A Diplomacy of Decline', *Problems of Communism*, January-February 1988.
92. J. McConnell, 'SDI, The Soviet Investment Debate and Soviet Military Policy', *Strategic Review*, vol. 16, 1988.

4 The NATO Alliance

1. E. Fedder, 'Transformations in the Alliance', in E. Fedder (ed), *Defence Politics of the Atlantic Alliance* (New York: Praeger, 1980) p. 5.
 2. Ibid., p. 7.
 3. E. Cohen, 'The Long Term Crisis of the Alliance', *Foreign Affairs*, vol. 61, no. 2, 1982–83, p. 328.
 4. K. Hartley, *NATO Arms Cooperation: A Study in Economics and Politics* (London: Allen and Unwin, 1983) ch. 6.
 5. T. Sandler and J. Cauley, 'On the Economic Theory of Alliances', *Journal of Conflict Resolution*, vol. 19, no. 2, 1975, p. 333.
 6. T. Sandler, 'Impurity of Defence', An Application To The Economics of Alliances', *Kyklos*, vol. 30, fasc. 3, 1977, p. 449.
 7. R. Osgood, *NATO: The Entangling Alliance* (Chicago: Chicago University Press, 1962) p. 373.
 8. N. Petersen, 'The Alliance Policies of the Smaller NATO Countries', L. Kaplan and R. Clawson (eds), *NATO After Thirty Years* (Wilmington: Scholarly Resources 1981) p. 85.
 9. P. Taylor, Weapons Standardisation in NATO, *International Organization*, vol. 36, no. 1, 1982, p. 96.
10. D. Calleo, *Beyond American Hegemony: The Future of the Western Alliance* (New York: Basic Books, 1987) p. 9.
11. A. De Porte, 'The United States and Europe. A Perspective', E. Fedder, op. cit., 1980, p. 23.
12. C. Gordon, 'NATO and the Larger European States', L. Kaplan and R. Clawson (eds), op. cit., 1981, p. 61.
13. T. Geiger, *The Future of the International System: The United States and the World Political Economy* (Boston: Unwin Hyman, 1988) pp. 15-16.
14. J. Raymond, 'Growing Threat of our Military–Industrial Complex', M. Hickman (ed), *The Military and American Society* (Beverly Hills: Glencoe, 1971) p. 68.
15. R. Bartlett, *The Long Retreat: A Short History of British Defence Policy 1945–1970* (London: Macmillan, 1972) p. 53.
16. J. Carlton, 'NATO Standardisation: An Organizational Analysis', R. Clawson and L. Kaplan, op. cit., 1981, p. 200.
17. L. Radi, 'A European Initiative for Cooperation in the Armaments Field', *NATO Review*, no. 3, June 1977, p. 8.
18. K. Hartley, op. cit., 1983, p. 21.
19. C. Gordon, op. cit., 1981, p. 81.
20. S. Kirby, 'The Independent European Programme Group. The Failure of Low Profile High Politics', *Journal of Common Market Studies*, vol.

18, no. 2, 1979–80, p. 178.
21. C. Trebilcock, 'Spin-offs in British Economic History: Armaments and Industry, *The Economic History Review*, vol. XXII, no. 3, 1969.
22. C. Catrina, *Arms Transfers and Dependence* (New York: Taylor and Francis: UNIDR, 1988) ch. 13.
23. K. McDonald, 'Collaboration in Procurement versus the National Interest', *RUSI–Brassey's Defence Yearbook*, 1986, p. 168.
24. A. Cornell, 'Collaboration in Weapons and Equipment', *NATO Review*, vol. 28, 1980, part 2, p. 15.
25. T. Taylor, *Defence Technology and International Integration* (London: Pinter) 1982, p. 78.
26. K. Hartley, op. cit., 1983, p. 63.
27. M. Kaldor, *European Defence Industries: National and International Implications*, ISIO Monographs no. 8, Brighton: University of Sussex, 1972, pp. 33-36.
28. T. Callaghan, 'A Common Market for Atlantic Defence', *Survival*, vol. XVII, May–June 1975, p. 129, p. 136.
29. *Report of the Committee of Inquiry into the Aircraft Industry*. Cmnd 2853, HMSO, London, 1965, p. 9.
30. Ibid., p. 9.
31. K. Hartley, op. cit., 1983, p. 9.
32. Ibid., p. 67.
33. J. Viner, *The Customs Union Issue* (Washington: Carnegie Endowment for International Peace, 1950) pp. 41–45.
34. T. Callaghan, op. cit., 1975, p. 129, p. 138.
35. R. Dean, 'Future of Collaborative Weapons Acquisition', *Survival*, vol. XXI, no. 4, 1979, p. 155.
36. S. Kirby, op. cit., 1979–80, p. 178.
37. R. Dean, op. cit., 1979, p. 160.
38. *UK Military R and D*, Report of a Working Party of the Council of Science and Society (Oxford: Oxford University Press, 1986) pp. 40–42.
39. M. Kaldor, 'Military R and D: Cause or Consequence of the Arms Race', *International Social Science Journal*, vol. 35, no. 96, 1983, p. 37.
40. E. Koldziej, 'French Arms Trade: The Economic Determinants', *World Armaments and Disarmament*, SIPRI Yearbook 1983 (London: Taylor and Francis, 1983) p. 372.
41. J. Reppy, 'Military R and D, and International Trade Performance'. Paper prepared for the Annual Meeting of the International Studies Association. 14–18 April 1987, Washington DC.
42. Committee of Inquiry into the Aircraft Industry, op. cit., 1965, p. 9.
43. M. Kaldor, op. cit., 1972, p. 53.
44. D. Greenwood, 'Defence and National Priorities Since 1945', in J. Baylis (ed), *British Defence Policy in a Changing World* (London: Croom Helm, 1977).
45. J. Carlton, op. cit., 1981, p. 201.
46. Ibid.
47. K. McDonald, op. cit., 1986, p. 169.
48. W. Walker, 'The Multi-Role Combat Aircraft (MRCA) A Case Study in European Collaboration', *Research Policy*, vol. 2, January 1974, p. 289.

49. A. Cornell, op. cit., part 1, p. 15.
50. W. Walker, op. cit., 1974, pp. 284-5.
51. T. McNaugher, 'Problems of Collaborative Weapons Development; The MBT-70', *Armed Forces and Society*, vol. 10, no. 1, 1983–84.
52. Janes Defence Weekly, vol. 7, no. 3, 24 January 1987, p. 95.
53. F. Thomson, 'Martel: International Industrial Collaboration Between HSD of UK and Matra of France', *Journal of the Royal United Services Institute for Defence Studies*, vol. 123, no. 2, June 1978, p. 75.
54. *European Cooperation in Armaments Research and Development*, Assembly of European Union, Committee on Scientific, Technological and Aerospace Questions, Paris 1988, p. 57.
55. T. Taylor, op. cit., 1982, p. 173.
56. Ibid., p. 129.
57. S. Lunn, *Burden Sharing in NATO* (London: Routledge and Kegan Paul, 1983) p. 14.
58. J. Carlton, op. cit., 1981, p. 207.
59. L. Kaplan, 'NATO: The Second Generation', in L. Kaplan and R. Clawson, op. cit., 1981, p. 12.
60. L. Radi, op. cit., 1977, p. 8.
61. R. Komer, 'Treating NATO's Self-Inflicted Wounds', *Foreign Policy*, no. 13, Winter 1973–74, p. 34.
62. S. Canby, 'NATO Muscle: More Shadow than Substance', *Foreign Policy*, no. 8, Fall 1972, p. 38.
63. T. Taylor, op. cit., 1982, p. 155.
64. T. Taylor, op. cit., 1986, p. 186.
65. S. Kirby, op. cit., 1979–80, p. 191.
66. T. Taylor, op. cit., 1986, p. 191.
67. C. Wolfe and D. Leebart, 'Trade Liberalisation as a Path to Weapons Standardisation in NATO', *International Security*, vol. 2, no. 3, 1978, p. 136.
68. M. Poutillion, *Cooperation between Europe and the USA and Canada in Security Matters*, Assembly of Western European Union, Document 1137, May 1988, p. 8.
69. K. Knorr, 'Burden Sharing in NATO: Aspects of US Policy', *Orbis*, vol. 29, no. 3, 1985, p. 517.
70. D. Calleo, op. cit., 1987, p. 15.
71. K. Knorr, op. cit., 1985–86, p. 530.
72. S. Luns, op. cit., 1983, pp. 58–9.
73. M. Poutillon, op. cit., 1988, p. 8.
74. 'Sharing NATO's Burden', *National Journal*, vol. 19, May 1987.
75. J. Palmer, *Europe Without America* (Oxford: Oxford University Press, 1988) p. 1.

5 The Warsaw Pact

1. D. Nelson, *Alliance Behaviour in the Warsaw Pact* (Boulder: Westview Press, 1986) p. 5.
2. A. Johnson, 'The Warsaw Pact: Soviet Military policy in Eastern Europe', in S. Terry (ed), *Soviet Policy in Eastern Europe* (London: Yale University Press, 1984) p. 259.

3. J. Ericson, 'Military Management: Modernizations within the Warsaw Pact', in R. Clawson and L. Kaplan (eds), *The Warsaw Pact: Political Purpose and Military Means* (Washington: Scholarly Resources, 1984) p. 217.

4. T. Alton *et al*, 'East European Defence Expenditures 1965–82', in *East European Economics: Slow Growth in the 1980s vol. 1, Economic Performance and Policy.* Selected Papers submitted to the Joint Economic Committee, Congress of the United States, Washington DC, 1985, p. 480.

5. T. Alton *et al*, 'Defense Expenditures in Eastern Europe 1965–76', in *East European Economies Post Helsinki*, A Compendium of Papers submitted to the Joint Economic Committee, Congress of the United States, Washington DC, 1977, p. 284.

6. M. Checinski, 'Warsaw Pact–CMEA Military Economic Trends', *Problems of Communism*, vol. XXXV, March–April 1987, p. 16.

7. T. Clements, 'The Cost of Defense in the Non-Soviet Warsaw Pact: A Historical Perspective', *East European Economies: Slow Growth 1985*, op. cit., p. 452.

8. V. Bunce, 'The Empire Strikes Back. The Evolution of the Eastern Block from a Soviet Asset to a Soviet Liability', *International Organization*, vol. 39, 1985, p. 26.

9. W. Reisinger, 'East European Military Expenditure in the 1970s', *International Organization*, vol. 37, no. 1, 1983, p. 143.

10. D. Nelson, op. cit., 1986, pp. 74–79.

11. M. Checinski, op. cit., 1987, p. 15.

12. I. Volgyes, 'Troubled Friendship or Mutual Dependence. Eastern Europe and the USSR in the Gorbachev Era', *Orbis*, vol. 30, 1986, p. 350.

13. T. Alton, op.cit., 1985, p. 492.

14. T. Clement, op. cit., 1985, p. 474.

15. S. Bialer, 'Soviet Foreign Policy: Sources, Perception, Trends', in S Bialer (ed), *The Domestic Context of Soviet Foreign Policy*, (Boulder: Westview Press, 1981) p. 432.

16. S. Bialer and J. Afferica, 'Andropov's Burden: Socialist Stagnation and Communist Encirclement', *Adelphi Papers*, no. 189, 1984, p. 18.

17. M. Mackintosh, 'Military Considerations in Soviet–East-European Relations', in K. Dawisha and P. Hanson (eds), *Soviet-East European Dilemmas: Coercion, Competition and Consent* (London: Heinemann, 1981) p. 147.

18. R. Cutler *et al*, 'The Political Economy of East South Military Transfers', *International Studies Quarterly*, vol. 31, no. 3, 1987, p. 283.

19. Ibid., p. 290.

20. T. Snitch, 'East European Involvement in Worlds Arms Market: US Arms Control and Disarmament Agency', *World Military Expenditures and Arms Transfers*, Washington DC, 1983.

21. C. Rice, 'Defence Burden Sharing', in D. Holloway and J. Sharpe (eds), *The Warsaw Pact: Alliance in Transition* (London: Macmillan, 1984) p. 70.

22. M. Checinski, op. cit., 1987, p. 16.

23. R. Campbell, 'Management Spillovers from Soviet Space and Military Programmes', *Soviet Studies*, vol. 23, no. 4, 1971–72.
24. L. Whetton and J. Waddel, 'Motor vehicle standardisation in the Warsaw Pact. Problems and Limitations', *RUSI: The Journal of the Royal United Services Institute for Defence Studies*, vol. 124, no. 1, 1979, p. 55.
25. K. Hartley, *NATO Arms Cooperation: A Study in Economics and Politics*, (London: Allen and Unwin, 1983) p. 67.
26. T. Callaghan, 'A Common Market for Atlantic Defence', *Survival*, vol. XVII, no. 3, March–June 1975, p. 130.
27. J. Ericson, op. cit., 1984, p. 222.
28. L. Whetton and J. Waddell, op. cit., 1979, p. 58.
29. M. Checinski, op. cit., 1987, p. 16.
30. M. Thee, *Military Technology, Military Strategy and the Arms Race* (London: Croom Helm, 1986) p. 73.
31. J. Ericson, 'The Warsaw Pact – The Shape of Things To Come?' in K. Dawisha and P. Hanson (ed), op. cit., 1981, p. 167.
32. M. Checinski, op. cit., 1987, p. 28.
33. The following section draws on M. Checinski op. cit., 1987.
34. R. Cutler *et al*, op. cit., 1987, p. 294.
35. F. Holzman, *International Trade Under Communism: Politics and Economics*, (London: Macmillan, 1976) p. 74.
36. P. Marer. 'Has Eastern Europe Become a Liability to the Soviet Union: The Economic Aspect', in C. Gati (ed), *The International Politics of Eastern Europe* (New York: Praeger, 1977) p. 64.
37. F. Holzman, op. cit., 1976, p. 64.
38. V. Bunce, op. cit., 1985, p. 5.
39. J. Campbell, 'Soviet Policy in Eastern Europe: An Overview', in S. Terry, op. cit., 1984, p. 18.
40. Ibid., p. 13.
41. V. Bunce, op. cit., 1985, p. 12.
42. P. Marer, op. cit., 1977, pp. 65–69.
43. E. Hewett, 'Soviet Economic Relations with CMEA Countries', *The Soviet Economy After Brezhnev*, NATO Colloquium, Brussels 1984, p. 241.
44. P. Summerscale, 'Is Eastern Europe a Liability to the USSR', *International Affairs*, vol. 57, no. 4, 1981, p. 588.
45. J. Kramer, 'Soviet–CMEA Energy Ties', *Problems of Communism*, July–August, vol. XXXIV, no. 4, 1985, p. 34.
46. M. Lavigne, 'The Soviet Union outside COMECON', *Soviet Studies*, vol. XXV, no. 2, 1983, p. 140.
47. Ibid., p. 139.
48. J. Vanous, 'East European Economic Slowdown', *Problems of Communism*, July–August, vol. XXXI, no. 4, 1982, p. 8.
49. J. Zoeter, 'USSR Hard Currency Trade and Payments', Joint Economic Committee, op. cit., 1982, p. 490.
50. E. Hewett, op. cit., 1984, p. 247.
51. P. Marer, op. cit., 1977, p. 23.
52. V. Bunce, op. cit., 1985, p. 20.
53. J. Brabant, 'The USSR and Socialist Economic Integration', *Soviet*

Studies, vol. XXXVI, no. 1, 1984, p. 130.
54. F. Pitzner-Jorgensen. 'Soviet Economic Cooperation with CMEA Countries – A Breakthrough for Industrial Cooperation?' *The Soviet Economy: A New Course*? NATO Colloquium, Brussels, 1987, p. 263.
55. M. Marrese and J. Vanous, 'Unconventional Gains from Trade', *Journal of Comparative Economics*, vol. 7, 1983, p. 385.
56. I. Neumann, 'Soviet Foreign Policy Towards Her European Allies: Interest and Instruments', *Cooperation and Conflict*, vol. XXIII, no. 4, 1988, p. 217.
57. D. Jones. 'The Soviet Defence Burden Through the Prism of History', in C. Jacobsen (ed), *The Soviet Defence Enigma: Estimating Costs and Burdens* (Oxford: Oxford University Press, 1987)
58. M. Brzezinski, 'The Soviet Union: Her Aims, Problems and Challenges to the West', *Adelphi Papers*, no. 189, 1984, p. 3.
59. I. Neumann, op. cit., 1988, p. 227.
60. E. Goldstein, 'Soviet Economic Assistance to Poland', Joint Economic Committee, op. cit., 1985, part 2, p. 567.
61. D. Nelson, op. cit., 1987, p. 109.
62. M. Checinski, op. cit., 1987, p. 28.

6 The Defence Burden

1. E. Benoit, 'Growth and Defense in Developing Countries'. *Economic Development and Cultural Change*, vol. 26, 1977–78.
2. *North-South: A Programme for Survival*. Report of the Independent Commission on International Development Issues under the Chairmanship of Willy Brandt (London: Pan, 1980) ch. 7.
3. H. Mosley, *The Arms Race: Economic and Social Consequences* (Lexington: Lexington Books, 1985) p. 35.
4. W. Domke, R. Eichenberg and C. Kelleher, 'The Illusion of Choice: Defence and Welfare in Advanced Industrial Democracies', *The American Political Science Review*, vol. 77, no. 1, 1983, p. 21.
5. D. Smith and R. Smith, *The Economics of Militarism* (London: Pluto, 1983) pp. 96–99.
6. R. Smith, 'The Resource Cost of Military Expenditures', in M. Kaldor *et al* (eds), *Democratic Socialism and the Cost of Defense*, (London: Croom Helm, 1979), p. 264.
7. S. Chan, 'The Impact of Defence Spending on Economic Performance: A Survey of Evidence and Problems', *Orbis*, vol. 29, no. 2, 1985, p. 431.
8. M. Checinski, 'The Costs of Armaments Production and the Profitability of Armaments Exports in COMECON Countries', *Ost-Europa Wirtschaft*, vol. 20, no. 2, 1975.
9. D. Dabelko and J. McCormick, 'The Opportunity Cost of Defense: Some Cross-national evidence', *Journal of Peace Research*, vol. XIV, no. 2 , 1977, p. 147.
10. H. Mosley, op. cit., 1987, p. 56.
11. D. Smith and R. Smith, op. cit., 1983, pp. 84–7.
12. S. Chan, op. cit., 1985, p. 407.

13. R. De Grasse, *Military Expansion and Economic Decline. The Impact of Military Spending on US Economic Performance* (Armonk: M. E. Sharpe, 1983) p. 2.
14. H. Mosley, op. cit., 1987, pp. 7–10.
15. Congressional Budget Office, *Defence Spending and the Economy*, Washington DC, 1983, p. 27.
16. M. Nincic and T. Cusak, 'The Political Economy of US Military Spending', *Journal of Peace Research*, vol. XVI, no. 2, 1979, p. 108.
17. A. Markusen, 'The Militarized Economy', *World Policy Journal*, vol. 3, no. 4, 1986, p. 497-8.
18. *Report of the Committee of Inquiry into the Aircraft Industry*, HMSO, London, 1965, Cmnd 2853, p. 29.
19. Ibid., p. 29.
20. *UK Military R and D*. Report of a Working Party, Council for Science and Society, (London: OUP, 1986) p. 41.
21. E. Koldziej, 'French Arms Trade: The Economic Determinants', *World Armaments and Disarmament*, SIPRI Yearbook 1983 (London: Taylor and Francis, 1983) p. 379.
22. C. Trebilcock, 'Spin-offs in British Economic History; Armaments and Industry 1760–1914', *Economic History Review*, vol. XXII, no. 3, December 1969, p. 480.
23. R. de Grasse, op. cit., 1983, p. 77.
24. Ibid., p. 77.
25. Ibid., p. 108.
26. Ibid., p. 85.
27. H. de Haan, 'Military Expenditure and Economic Growth: Some Theoretical Remarks', in C. Schmidt (ed), *The Economics of Military Expenditures* (London: Macmillan, 1987) p. 94.
28. C. Rice, 'Defence and Security', in M. McCauley (ed), *The Soviet Union Under Gorbachev*, (London: Macmillan, 1987) p. 192.
29. B. Russett, 'Who Pays for Defense?', *American Political Science Review*, vol. 63, no. 2, 1969, p. 420.
30. K. Peroff and M. Podolak-Warren, 'Does Spending on Defence Cut Spending on Health? A Time Series Analysis of the US Economy', *British Journal of Political Science*, vol. 9, part 1, 1979, p. 37.
31. The President's Blue Ribbon Commmission on Defense Management (Packard Commission), *A Quest for Excellence: Final Report to the President*, Washington DC, 1986, p. XVII.
32. K. Peroff and M. Podolak-Warren, op. cit., 1979, p. 37.
33. B. Russett, 'Defence Expenditures and National Well-Being', *American Political Science Review*, vol. 76, no. 4, 1982, p. 774.
34. Ibid., p. 774.
35. K. Peroff and M. Podolak-Warren, op. cit., 1979, p. 39.
36. P. Hartland-Thunberg, 'From Guns and Butter to Guns versus Butter: The Relationship Between Economics and Security in the United States', *The Washington Quarterly*, vol. 11, no. 4, 1988.
37. M. Chalmers, *Paying for Defence. Military Spending and British Decline* (London: Pluto, 1985) p. 117.
38. R. Smith, 'Military Expenditures and Investment in OECD Countries',

Journal of Comparative Economics, vol. 4, no. 1, 1980, p. 31.

39. Hearings before the Subcommittee on Economic Goals and Intergovernmental Policies of the Joint Economic Committee, Congress of the USA, Washington DC, October–December 1982, p. 296.

40. C. Nardielli and G. Ackerman, 'Defence Expenditures and the Survival of American Capitalism', *Armed Forces and Society*, vol. 3, no. 1, 1976, p. 15.

41. G. Stafford, *An End to Economic Growth: Growth and Decline in the UK Since 1945* (Oxford: Martin Robertson, 1981) ch. 6.

42. D. Calleo, *The Imperious Economy* (Cambridge, Mass.,: Harvard University Press 1982).

43. S. Huntington, 'The US: Decline or Renewal', *Foreign Affairs*, vol. 67, no. 2, 1988–89, p. 79.

44. K. Rothschild, 'Military Expenditures, Exports and Growth', *Kyklos*, vol. 26, fasc. 4, 1973, p. 809.

45. P. Kennedy, *The Rise and Fall of the Great Powers. Economic Change and Military Conflict* (London: Unwin Hyman, 1988) pp. 515–521.

46. C. Catrina, *Arms Transfers and Dependence*, (New York: Taylor and Francis, 1988) ch. 13.

47. D. Smith and R. Smith, op. cit., 1983, p. 90.

48. R. Smith *et al*, 'The Economics of Exporting Arms', *Journal of Peace Research*, vol. 2, no. 2, 1985, pp. 241–2.

49. S. Neuman, 'Offsets in the International Arms Market. US Arms Control and Disarmament Agency', *World Military Expenditures and Arms Transfers 1985*, Washington DC, 1985, p. 37.

50. J. Reppy, Military Research and Development and International Trade Performance. Paper presented for the Annual Meeting of the International Studies Association 14–18, April 1987, Washington DC, Table 3.

51. UK Military R and D, op. cit., 1986, p. 42.

52. M. Kaldor *et al*, 'Industrial Competitiveness and Britain's Defence', *Lloyd's Bank Review*, October 1986, no. 162, p. 41.

53. J. Reppy, op. cit., 1987, Table 3.

54. F. Long, 'Federal Defence Budget. Guns versus Butter', *Science*, 16 March 1984, vol. 223, no. 4641, p. 1133.

55. J. Stowsky, 'Competing with the Pentagon', *World Policy Journal*, Fall 1986, pp. 697–8.

56. R. Nimrody *et al*, *Star Wars: The Economic Fall Out*, Council on Economic Priorities (Cambridge, Mass.: Ballinger, 1988) p. 138.

57. A. Markusen, op. cit., 1986, p. 504.

58. UK Military R and D, op. cit., 1986, p. 35.

59. K. Oye, 'Constrained Confidence and the Evolution of Reagan Foreign Policy', in K. Oye *et al* (eds), *Eagle Resurgent? The Reagan Era in American Foreign Policy* (Boston: Little, Brown, 1983) p. 20.

60. UK Military R and D, op. cit., 1986, p. 32.

61. J. Reepy, 'Military R and D and the Civilian Economy', *Bulletin of the Atomic Scientist*, vol. 41, no. 9, 1985, p. 13.

62. R. Nimrody *et al*, op. cit., 1988, p. 138.

63. R. De Grasse, op. cit., 1983, p. 86.

64. UK Military R and D, op. cit., 1986, p. 44.

65. J. Stowsky, op. cit., 1986, p. 709.
66. H. Mosley, op. cit., 1987, p. 78.
67. I. Maddock, *Civilian Exploitation of Defence Technology*, Report to the Electronics EDC, National Economic Development Office, London 1983.
68. UK Military R and D, op. cit., 1986, p. 40.
69. J. Stowsky, op. cit., 1986, p. 701.
70. Ibid., p. 701.
71. M. Kaldor, op. cit., 1986, p. 41.
72. *The Independent*, 20 July 1988.
73. J. Reppy, op. cit., Table 3.
74. G. Adams, 'Recasting the Military Spending Debate', *Bulletin of the Atomic Scientist*, October 1986, p. 27.
75. A. Cappelan *et al*, Military Spending and Economic Growth in OECD Countries, *Journal of Peace Research*, vol. 24, no. 4, 1984, p. 371.
76. C. Kegley and E. Wittkopf, *American Foreign Policy: Pattern and Process*, 3rd ed. (London: Macmillan, 1987) p. 271.
77. R. De Grasse, op. cit., 1983, p. 12.
78. Congressional Budget Office, op. cit., 1983, p. 27.
79. M. Kaldor, op. cit., 1986, p. 39.
80. Congressional Budget Office, op. cit., 1983, p. 43.
81. D. Calleo, op. cit., p. 36.
82. H. Starr *et al*, 'The Relationship Between Defense Spending and Inflation', *Journal of Conflict Resolution*, vol. 28, no. 1, 1984, p. 111.
83. G. Adams, op. cit., 1986, p. 28.
84. Ibid., p. 28.
85. H. Mosley, op. cit., 1987, p. 127.
86. G. Adams, op. cit., 1986, p. 28.
87. H. Starr *et al*, op. cit., 1984, pp. 116–117.
88. W. Domke, op. cit., 1983, p. 33.

7 The Defence Burden in the Socialist States

1. J. Cooper, 'Nuclear Milking Machines and Perestroika', *Detente*, no. 14, 1989, p. 11.
2. M. Checinski, 'An Estimate of Current Soviet Military Industrial Output and the Development of the Soviet Arms Industry in the Eighties', *Osteuropa Wirtschaft*, vol. 29, no. 2, 1984, p. 148.
3. P. Munkholt, *The Soviet Economy: Protection of the Military Sector in Case of a Protracted Deterioration*. Sonderffentlichung des Bundesinstituts fur ostwissenschaftliche und internationale Studien, Koln 1985, p. 12.
4. Ibid., p. 35.
5. R. Hutchings, *The Soviet Budget*, (London: Macmillan, 1983) p. 126.
6. G. Offer, *The Opportunity Cost of the Non-monetary Advantages of the Soviet Military R and D Effort*, Rand R. 1741–DDRE Santa Monica, 1975, p. 3.
7. N. Nimitz, *The Structure of Soviet Outlays on R and D 1960 and 1968*, Rand R-1207–DDRE Santa Monica, 1974, p. 43.

8. S. Cohn, 'Declining Soviet Capital Productivity and the Soviet Military–Industrial Complex. US Arms Control and Disarmament Agency', *World Military Expenditures and Arms Transfers 1972–82*, Washington DC, 1982, p. 111.
9. N. Jasny, *Soviet Industrialization 1928–52* (Chicago: Chicago University Press, 1960) p. 4.
10. R. Amann, 'Industrial Innovation in the Soviet Union', in R. Amann and J. Cooper (eds), *Industrial Innovation in the Soviet Union* (New Haven: Yale University Press, 1982) ch. 1.
11. H. Schaefer, 'Soviet Power and Intentions: Military Economic choices', *Soviet Economy in a Time of change*, a compendium of Papers submitted to the Joint Economic Committee, Congress of the United States, Washington, DC, 1979.
12. S. Bialer. 'Soviet Foreign Policy: Sources, Perceptions, Trends', in S. Bialer (ed), *The Domestic Context of Soviet Foreign Policy* (Boulder: Westview Press, 1981) p. 426.
13. S. Bialer, 'New Thinking and Soviet Foreign Policy', *Survival*, vol. XXX, no. 4, July–August 1988, p. 309.
14. T. Colton, 'The Impact of the Military on Soviet Society', in S. Bialer (ed), op. cit., 1981, p. 119.
15. E. Jones, 'Manning the Soviet Military', *International Security*, vol. 7, no. 1, 1982.
16. W. Odeen, 'How Far Can Soviet Reform Go?' *Problems of Communism*, November–December, vol. XXXV, no. 6, 1987, p. 27.
17. R. Campbell, 'Management Spill Overs From Space and Military Programmes', *Soviet Studies*, vol. 23, no. 4, 1971–72.
18. T. Colton, op. cit., 1981, p. 124.
19. F. Rubin, 'The Theory and Concept of National Security in the Warsaw Pact Countries', *International Affairs*, vol. 58, no. 4, 1982, p. 655.
20. F. Griffiths, 'Ideological Development and Foreign Policy', S. Bialer (ed), op. cit., 1981, p. 24.
21. S. Bialer, op. cit., 1988, p. 299.
22. *Allocation of Resources in the Soviet Union and China 1983*. Hearings before the subcommittee on International Trade, Finance and Security Economics of the Joint Economic Committee, Congress of the United States, Washington DC, 1984, p. 76.
23. M. Checinski, op. cit., 1984, p. 117.
24. J. Cooper, *Defence Production and the Soviet Economy 1929–1941*, CREES Discussion Paper, Soviet Industrialization Project Series No. 3, University of Brimingham, 1976, p. 3.
25. D. Holloway, *The Soviet Union and the Arms Race* (New Haven: Yale University Press, 1985) p. 280–1.
26. J. Cooper, op. cit., 1976, p. 4.
27. E. Carr and R. Davies, *Foundations of a Planned Economy 1926–29*, vol. 1, no. 1, (London: Macmillan, 1969) p. 426.
28. N. Jasny, op. cit., 1960, p. 4.
29. A. Erlich, *The Soviet Industrialization Debate 1924–28* (Cambridge Mass.,: Harvard University Press, 1960).
30. N. Spulber, *Soviet Strategy for Economic Growth* (Bloomington: Indiana

University Press, 1964) p. 20.
31. E. Zaleski, *Stalinist Planning for Economic Growth 1933–52* (London: Macmillan, 1980) p. 482.
32. D. Holloway, op. cit., 1985, p. 280.
33. J. Thomas, 'Political Strategic Factors in Soviet Modernization. Continuity and Change', JEC, op. cit., 1979, p. 90.
34. G. Grossman, 'Scarce Capital and Soviet Doctrine', *Quarterly Journal of Economics*, vol. LXVII, no. 3, 1953, p. 313.
35. M. Harrison, *Soviet Planning in Peace and War* (Cambridge: Cambridge University Press, 1985) p. 3.
36. N. Spulber, op. cit., 1964, p. 116.
37. D. Green and C. Higgins, *SOVMOD 1: Macroeconomic Model of the Soviet Union* (New York: Academic Press, 1977) p. 71.
38. *Allocation of Resources in the Soviet Union and China*, op. cit., 1984, p. 13.
39. *Allocation of Resources in the Soviet Union and China 1984*, Hearings before the Subcommittee on International Trade, Finance and Security Economics of the joint Economic Committee, Congress of the United States, Washington DC, 1985, p. 65.
40. S. Cohn, op. cit., 1982, p. 114.
41. *Allocation of Resources in the Soviet Union and China*, op. cit., 1985, p. 77.
42. J. Cooper, 'Western technology and the Soviet Defence Industry', in B. Parrot (ed), *Trade, Technology and Soviet American Relations* (Bloomington: Indiana University Press, 1985) p. 180.
43. S. Cohn, op. cit., 1982, p. 114.
44. M. Gorbachev, 'Initiative, Organization and Efficiency', *Pravda*, 12 April 1985, *Current Digest of the Soviet Press* vol. XXXVII, no. 15, 1985.
45. *The Guardian*, 28 November 1987.
46. Draft Basic Guidelines for The Economic and Social Development of the USSR 1986–1990 and the Period up to the Year 2000, *Pravda* 9 November 1985, *Current Digest of the Soviet Press*, vol. XXXVII, no. 45, 1985, p. 21.
47. B. Rummer, 'Structural Imbalance in the Soviet Economy', *Problems of Communism*, vol. XXXIII July–August 1984, p. 28.
48. 'Around the Machine Tool. Economika i organizatsia', *Promyshlennovo proizvodstra*, 1 January 1982, *Current Digest of the Soviet Press*, vol. XXXIV, no. 18, p. 7.
49. J. Grant, 'Soviet Machine Tools. Lagging Technology and Rising Imports', *Soviet Economy in a time of change*, op. cit., 1979, p. 555.
50. 'On the work of the Ministry of the Machine Tool and Tool Industry', *Pravda*, 13 December 1986, *Current Digest of the Soviet Press*, vol. XXXVII, no. 50, 8 January 1986, p. 10.
51. M. Leitenberg. 'The Counterpart of Defence Industry Conversion in the United States. The USSR Economy, Defence Industry and Military Expenditure', *Journal of Peace Research*, vol. XVI, no. 3, 1979, p. 266.
52. H. Levine, 'Possible causes of the deterioration of Soviet productivity growth in the period 1976–1980', *Soviet Economy in the 1980s: Problems and Prospects*, Selected papers submitted to the Joint Economic Com-

mittee, Congress of the United States, Washington DC, 1982, p. 158.

53. D. Bond and H. Levine, 'An Overview', in A. Bergson and H. Levine (eds), *The Soviet Economy: Towards the Year 2000* (London: Allen and Unwin, 1983) pp. 18–19.

54. G. Hildebrandt, 'The Dynamic Burden of Soviet Defence Spending', *Soviet Economy in the 1980s*, op. cit., 1982, pp. 336–41.

55. M. Hopkin and M. Kennedy, *Comparisons and Implications of Alternative Views of the Soviet Economy*, Rand R-3075–NA, Santa Monica 1984.

56. L. Calmfors and J. Rylander, 'Economic Restrictions on Soviet Defence Expenditures', *Soviet Economy in a New Perspective*, a compendium of papers submitted to the Joint Economic Committee, Congress of the United States, Washington DC, 1976.

57. G. Offer, op. cit., 1974, p. 14.

58. L. Nolting and M. Feshback, 'R & D. Employment in the USSR Definitions Statistics and Comparisons', *Soviet Economy in a Time of Change*, op. cit, 1979, p. 731.

59. J. Martens and J. Young, 'Soviet Implementation of Domestic Inventions. First Results', Ibid., p. 488.

60. R. Campbell, op. cit., 1971–2.

61. E. Zaleski, op. cit., 1980, p. xxx.

62. D. Dyker, *The Future of the Soviet Economic Planning System* (London. Croom Helm, 1985) p. 15, p. 30.

63. M. Ellman, 'The Macroeconomic Situation in the Soviet Union. Retrospect and Prospect', *Soviet Studies*, vol. 38, no. 4, 1986, pp. 531, 535.

64. P. Hanson, 'The Soviet Economy at the End of Year IV', *Detente*, no. 14, 1989, p. 9.

65. R. Leggett, 'Soviet Investment Policy in the 11th Five Year Plan', *Soviet Economy in the 1980s: Problems and Prospects*, op. cit., 1982, p. 139.

8 International Arms Trade

1. A. Pierre, *The Global Politics of Arms Sales* (Princeton: Princeton University Press, 1982) p. 4.

2. J. Sutton and G. Kemp, 'Arms to Developing Countries 1945–65', *Adelphi Papers*, no. 28, 1966, p. 31.

3. R. Harkavy, *The Arms Trade and International Systems*, (Cambridge, Mass.,: Ballinger, 1975) p. 11.

4. A. Ross, 'The Political Economy of the International Arms Trade: A Supply Side, Market Analysis'. Paper prepared for presentation at the Annual Meeting of the International Studies Association, 14–18 April 1987, Washington DC, p. 9.

5. R. Smith *et al*, 'The Economics of Exporting Arms', *Journal of Peace Research*, vol. 2, no. 3, 1985, p. 239.

6. P. Wiles, 'Whatever Happened to the Merchants of Death? Normal Supply versus Catastrophic Demands', *Journal of International Studies*, vol. 15, no. 3, 1983, p. 296.

7. R. Lugar, 'US Arms Sales and the Middle East', *Journal of International Affairs*, vol. 40, no. 1, 1986, p. 26.

8. S. Sen and R. Smith, *The Economics of International Arms Transfers*, Birkbeck College Discussion Paper No. 135, Department of Economics, Birkbeck College, London 1983, p. 3.

9. P. Wiles, op. cit., 1983, p. 297.

10. M. Klare, 'Deadly Convergence: The Perils of the Arms Trade', *World Policy Journal*, vol. VI, no. 1, 1988–89.

11. M. Nincic, *The Arms Race. The Political Economy of Military Growth*, (New York: Praeger, 1982) pp. 120-121.

12. C. Pell, 'Problems in Security Assistance', *Journal of International Affairs*, vol. 40, no. 1, 1986, p. 34.

13. A. Cahn and J. Kruzel, 'Arms Trade in the 1980s', in A. Cahn *et al* (eds), *Controlling Future Arms Trade*, (New York: McGraw Hill, 1977) p. 35.

14. D. Smith, 'The Arms Trade and Arms Control', *RUSI–Brassey's Defence Yearbook* (London: Brassey's, 1982) p. 127.

15. W. Koch, 'Security Assistance to the Third World', *Journal of International Affairs*, vol. 40, no. 1, 1986, p. 43.

16. A. Cahn and J. Kruzel, op. cit., 1977, p. 35.

17. M. Nincic, op. cit., 1982, p. 121.

18. A. Cahn and J. Kruzel, op. cit., 1977, p. 35.

19. N. Koch, op. cit., 1986, p. 44.

20. D. Bowls, 'Soviet Russia as a Model for Under Developed Areas', *World Politics*, vol. 14, no. 3, 1962.

21. W. Lewis, 'Emerging Choices for the Soviets in Third World Arms Transfer Policy. Arms Control and Disarmament Agency', *World Military Expenditure and Arms Transfer*, Washington DC, 1985, p. 30.

22. R. Pajak, 'Soviet Arms Transfer as an Instrument of Influence', *Survival*, vol. XXIII, no. 4, 1981, p. 167.

23. T. Ohlson and E. Loose-Weintraub, 'Trade in Major Conventional Weapons', *World Armaments and Disarmament*, SIPRI Yearbook 1983 (London: Taylor and Francis, 1983), p. 267.

24. J. Krause, 'Soviet Military Aid to the Third World', *Aussen Politik*, vol. 24, no. 4, 1983, p. 397.

25. S. Deger, *Soviet Arms Sales to LDCs, The Economic Forces*, Birkbeck Discussion Paper No. 152, Birkbeck College, London 1984, p. 18.

26. M. Klare, 'The Global Reach of the Superpowers', *South*, August 1983, p. 17.

27. A. Cahn, op. cit., 1977, p. 35.

28. Ibid., p. 31.

29. C. Catrina, *Arms Transfers and Dependence*, UNIDIR (New York: Taylor and Francis, 1988) p. 93.

30. T. Ohlson and M. Brzoska, 'The Trade in Major Conventional Weapons', SIPRI *World Armaments and Disarmament* (London: Taylor and Francis, 1984) p. 187.

31. E. Kolodziej, 'French Arms Trade: The Economic Dimension', *World Armaments and Disarmament* SIPRI Yearbook 1983 (London: Taylor and Francis, 1983) p. 387.

32. A. Cahn, 'The Economics of Arms Transfers', in S. Neuman and R. Harkavy (eds), *Arms Transfers in the Modern World* (New York: Praeger, 1980) pp. 180–1.

33. U. Albrecht, 'New Strategies of Mid Sized Weapons Exporters: The Federal Republic of Germany and Italy', *Journal of International Affairs*, vol. 40, no. 1, 1986, p. 130.
34. R. Cutler, *et al*, 'The Political Economy of East-South Military Transfers', *International Studies Quarterly*, vol. 31, no. 3, 1987, p. 279.
35. R. Smith, *et al*, op. cit., 1985, p. 239.
36. U. Albrecht, Soviet Arms Exports, SIPRI, op. cit., 1983, p. 366.
37. N. Koch, op. cit., 1986, p. 54.
38. M. Brzoska and T. Ohlson, 'The Trade in Major Conventional Weapons', SIPRI *World Armaments and Disarmament 1985* (London: Taylor and Francis, 1985) pp. 350–51.
39. Ibid., p. 345.
40. M. Brzoska, 'The Military Related External Debt of Third World Countries', *Journal of Peace Research*, vol. 2, no. 3, 1983.
41. M. Klare, 'The State of the Trade', *Journal of International Affairs*, vol. 40, no. 1, 1986, p. 14.
42. M. Brzoska and T. Ohlson, op. cit., 1985, p. 347.
43. S. Neuman, 'Offsets in International Arms Market. Arms Control and Disarmament Agency', *World Military Expenditures and Arms Transfers*, Washington DC, 1985, p. 35.
44. S. Woolcock, *Western Policies on East-West Trade* RIIA (London: Routledge and Kegan Paul, 1982) pp. 2–3.
45. T. Gustafson, *Selling the Russians the Rope? Soviet Technology Policy and US Export Controls*, Rand R-2649-ARPA, Santa Monica, 1981, p. 5.
46. J. Cooper, 'Western Technology and the Soviet Defense Industry', in B. Parrot (ed) *Trade, Technology and Soviet American Relations* (Bloomington: Indiana University Press, 1985) p. 174.
47. Ibid., p. 191.
48. G. Bertsch, 'Technology Transfers and Technology Controls: A Synthesis of the Western Soviet Relationship', in G. Bertsch (ed.), *Controlling East–West Trade and Technology Transfer: Power, Politics and Policies* (Durham, NC: Duke University Press, 1988), p. 127.
49. F. Holzman, *International Trade Under Communism: Politics and Economics*, (London: Macmillan, 1976) p. 134.
50. S. Woolcock, op. cit., 1982, p. 49.
51. G. Bertsch, op. cit., 1988, p. 131.
52. S. Huntington, 'Trade, Technology and Leverage', *Foreign Policy*, no. 32, Fall 1978, p. 64.
53. M. Miller, 'Foreign Technology in Soviet Strategy', *Orbis*, vol. 22, no. 3, 1978, p. 539.
54. L. Walinsky, 'Current Defense Strategy: The Case for Economic Denial', *Foreign Affairs*, vol. 61, no. 2, 1982, p. 272.
55. B. Inman, 'Control of Technology Transfer to the Soviet Union. Arms Control and Disarmament Agency', *World Military Expenditure and Arms Transfers*, Washington DC, 1985, p. 26.
56. G. Bertsch, op. cit., 1988, p. 115.
57. *East-West Technology Transfer: A Congressional Dialogue with the Reagan Administration*. A dialogue prepared for the use of the Joint Econ-

omic Committee Congress of the United States, December 1984, Washington DC, p. 92.

58. CIA, Soviet Acquisition of Western Technology', G. Bertsch and J. McIntyre (eds), *National Security and Technology Transfers; The Strategic Dimensions of East–West Trade* (Boulder: Westview Press, 1983) p. 92.

59. The Extent of Technology Transfers from the West to the Soviet Union During the Past Decade and the Contribution such Transfers have made to Strengthen the Soviet Military Industrial Base. Hearings before the Subcommittee on International Finance and Monetary Policy of the Committee on Banking, Housing and Urban Affairs, Washington DC, April 1982, p. 2.

60. B. Inman, op. cit., 1985, p. 28.

61. G. Offer, op. cit., 1981, p. 10.

62. G. Bertsch, op. cit., 1988, p. 122.

63. J. Cooper, op. cit., 1985, p. 189.

64. J. Bucy, 'Technology Transfer and East–West Trade', *International Security*, vol. 50, no. 3, 1980–81.

65. P. Hanson, *Western Economic Statecraft in East-West Relations: Embargo, Sanctions, Linkages, Economic Warfare and Detente* (London: Routledge, Kegan Paul, 1988) p. 26.

66. East-West Technology Transfer, op. cit., 1984, p. 93.

67. M. Miller, op. cit., 1978, p. 557.

68. M. Weitzman, 'Technology Transfers to the USSR. An Econometric Analysis', *Journal of Comparative Economics*, vol. 3, no. 2, 1979, p. 175.

69. J. Cooper, op. cit., 1985, p. 169.

70. M. Miller, op. cit., 1978, p. 562.

9 The Arms Race in the 1980s

1. A. Dallin and G. Lapidus, 'Reagan and the Russians: American Policy Towards the Soviet Union', in K. Oye, R. Lieber and D. Rothschild (eds), *Eagle Resurgent? The Reagan Era in American Foreign Policy* (Boston: Little, Brown, 1987) p. 207.

2. *Allocation of Resources in the Soviet Union and China 1985*. Hearings before the Subcommittee on Economic Resources, Competitiveness and Security Economics, of the Joint Economic Committee, Congress of the United States, Washington DC, 1986, p. 36.

3. S. Huntington, 'The Defence Policy of the Reagan Administration 1981–82', in F. Greenstein (ed), *The Reagan Presidency: An Early Assessment* (Baltimore: Johns Hopkins University Press, 1983)

4. D. Calleo, *Beyond American Hegemony: The Future of the Western Alliance* (New York: Basic Books, 1987) p. 116.

5. R. Stubbing, 'The Defense Program. Build-up or Binge!', *Foreign Affairs*, vol. 63, no. 4, 1985, p. 848.

6. E. Beukel, 'The Reagan Administration, the Soviet Union and Nuclear Arms. Hopes and Fears', *Cooperation and Conflict*, vol. XIX, no. 1, 1984, p. 17.

7. M. Tatu, 'US Soviet Relations: A Turning Point', *Foreign Affairs*, vol.

61, no. 3, 1983, p. 594.
8. E. Beukel, op. cit., 1984, p. 17.
9. C. Kegley and E. Wittkopf, 'The Reagan Administration's World View', *Orbis*, vol. 26, no. 1, 1982, p. 230.
10. K. Oye, 'Constrained Confidence and the Evolution of Reagan Foreign Policy', K. Oye *et al.*, op. cit., 1987, p. 27.
11. S. Bialer and J. Afferica, 'Reagan and Russia', *Foreign Affairs*, vol. 61, no. 2, 1982, p. 249.
12. R. Krikus, *The Superpowers in Crisis: Implications of Domestic Discord* (Washington DC: Pergamon-Brassey, 1987) p. 130.
13. Ibid., p. 132.
14. S. Talbot, *Deadly Gambits* (London: Picador, 1984) p. 227.
15. K. Oye, op. cit., 1987, p. 4.
16. A. Dallin and G. Lapidus, op. cit., 1987, p. 205.
17. R. Stubbing, op. cit., 1985, p. 852.
18. L. Walinsky, 'Current Defense Strategy: The Case for Economic Denial', *Foreign Affairs*, vol. 61, no. 2, 1982, p. 272.
19. M. Thee, *Military Technology, Military Strategy and the Arms Race* (London: Croom Helm, 1986) p. 73.
20. R. Krikus, op. cit., 1987, p. 3.
21. K. Oye, op. cit., 1987, p. 7.
22. D. Calleo, op. cit., 1987, p. 15.
23. F. Halliday, *The Making of the Second Cold War* (London: Verso, 1983) p. 235.
24. K. Oye, op. cit., 1987, p. 14.
25. C. Kegley and E. Wittkopf, op. cit., 1982, p. 232.
26. S. Huntington, op. cit., 1983, p. 88.
27. J. Epstein, *The 1988 Defense Budget: Studies in Defence Policy* (Washington DC: Brookings, 1987) p. 9.
28. R. Nimrody *et al*, *Star Wars: The Economic Fall Out* (Cambridge, Mass.: Ballinger, 1988) p. 138.
29. Ibid., p. 26.
30. J. Epstein, op. cit., 1987, p. 16.
31. R. Nimrody, op. cit., 1988, p. 25.
32. Ibid., p. 2.
33. E. Stubbs and R. Nimrody, 'The Soviet Response to Star Wars', *Challenge*, March–April 1987.
34. A. Smith, 'SDI and the New Cold War', in R. Crockatt and S. Smith, *The Cold War: Past and Present* (London: Allen and Unwin, 1981) p. 159.
35. R. Nimrody *et al.*, op. cit., 1988, p. 152.
36. J. Epstein, op. cit., 1987, p. 23.
37. G. Adler-Karisson, 'Star Wars – Another Form of Economic Warfare', *Scandinavian Journal of Development Alternatives*, vol. VI, nos. 2 and 3, 1987.
38. R. Krikus, op. cit., 1987, p. 132.
39. B. Posen and S. Van Evera, 'Reagan Administration Defense Policy: Departure from Containment', K. Oye *et al.*, op. cit., 1983, p. 91.
40. D. Calleo, op. cit., 1987, p. 115.

41. K. Booth and P. Williams, 'Reagan's Myths About Detente', *World Policy Journal*, vol. 2, no. 3, 1985.
42. S. Talbot, op. cit., 1984, p. 304.
43. R. Stubbing, op. cit., 1985, p. 858.
44. J. Epstein, op. cit., 1987, p. 4.
45. D. Calleo, op. cit., 1987, p. 116.
46. *The Guardian*, 6 January 1987.
47. D. Calleo, op. cit., 1987. p. 71.
48. R. Stubbing, op. cit., 1985, p. 850.
49. Hearings before the Subcommittee on Economic Goals and Intergovernmental Policy of the Joint Economic Committee, Congress of the United States, Washington DC, October–December 1982, p. 303.
50. J. Epstein, op. cit., 1987, pp. 55–56.
51. J. Gansler. Hearings before the Subcommittee on Economic Goals, op. cit., 1982, p. 92.
52. P. Savigear, *Cold War or Detente: The International Politics of American Soviet Relations* (Brighton: Wheatsheaf, 1987) p. 32.
53. P. Hartland-Thunberg, 'From Guns and Butter to Guns or Butter: The Relationship Between Economics and Security in the United States', *The Washington Quarterly*, vol. 11, no. 4, 1988.
54. J. Steinberg, 'Defense, Debt, Dollars and Deficits', *Defense Analysis*, vol. 1, no. 1, 1985. p. 72.
55. E. Rothschild, 'The Reagan Economic Legacy', *New York Review of Books*, 21 July 1988, pp. 33–5.
56. T. Congdon, *The Debt Threat* (Oxford: Blackwell, 1988) p. 15.
57. H. Mosley, *The Economic and Social Consequences of the Arms Race*, (Lexington: Lexington Books, 1985) p. 150.
58. S. Huntington, 'The US–Decline or Renewal', *Foreign Affairs*, vol. 67, no. 2, 1988–89, p. 79.
59. J. Gansler, 'We Can Afford Security', *Foreign Policy*, Summer 1983, p. 64.
60. Hearings before the Subcommittee on Economic Goals, op. cit., 1982, p. 314.
61. K. Oye, op. cit., 1987, p. 20.
62. L. Sullivan, 'A New Approach to Burden Sharing', *Foreign Policy*, no. 60, Fall 1985, p. 97.
63. P. Kennedy, *The Rise and Fall of the Great Powers: Economic Change and Military Conflict* (London: Unwin Hyman, 1988) p. 514.
64. R. Kaufman, 'Causes of the Slowdown in Soviet Defense', *Soviet Economy*, vol. 1, no. 1, 1985.
65. Ibid.
66. *Allocation of Resources in the Soviet Union and China 1985*. Hearings before the subcommittee on Economic Resources, Competitiveness and Security Economics of the Joint Economic Committee, Congress of the United States, Washington DC, 1986, p. 36.
67. Ibid., p. 36.
68. *The Soviet Economy Under a New Leader*. A Report presented to the Subcommittee on Economic Resources, Competitiveness and Security Economics of the Joint Economic Committee by the CIA and the DIA,

Washington DC, March 1986, p. 14.

69. *The Guardian*, 28 July 1988.
70. *Allocation of Resources in the Soviet Union and China 1984*. Hearings before the Subcommittee on Economic Resources, Competitiveness and Security Economics of the Joint Economic Committee, Congress of the United States, Washington DC, 1985, p. 180.
71. CIA, *The Soviet Weapons Industry: An Overview*, PB 86–928107. Produced by the United States Department of Commerce, Washington DC, September 1986, pp. 5–6.
72. *Allocation of Resources in the Soviet Union and China 1984*. op. cit., 1985, p. 77.
73. Ibid., p. 7.
74. R. Strode, 'The Soviet Armed Forces Adaption to Resource Scarcity', *The Washington Quarterly*, vol. 9, no. 2, 1986, p. 60.
75. Ibid., p. 60.
76. J. McConnell, 'The Soviet Investment Debate and Soviet Military Policy', *Strategic Review*, vol. 16, 1988, p. 52.
77. R. Strode, op. cit., 1986, p. 58.
78. T. Hasegawa, 'The Soviets on War Fighting', *Problems of Communism*, vol. XXXV, no. 4, 1986, p. 71.
79. B. Parrot, 'National Security Under Gorbachev', *Problems of Communism*, vol. XXXVII, no. 6, 1988, p. 2.
80. G. Weikhardt, 'Ustinov v. Ogarkov', *Problems of Communism*, vol. XXXIV, no. 1, 1985, p. 78.
81. S. Shenfield, *The Nuclear Predicament: Explorations in Soviet Ideology* (London: Routledge, Kegan Paul 1987) Chatham House Paper No. 37.
82. W. Odeen, 'Soviet Force Posture: Dilemmas and Directions', *Problems of Communism*, vol. XXXIV, no. 4, 1985, p. 8.
83. C. Rice, op. cit., 1987, p. 198.
84. D. Strode and R. Strode, 'Diplomacy and Defense in Soviet National Security Policy', *International Security*, vol. 6, no. 4, 1983, pp. 107–8.
85. M. Ellman, 'The Macroeconomic Situation in the Soviet Union. Retrospect and Prospect', *Soviet Studies*, vol. 38, no. 4, 1986, p. 531 and p. 535.
86. G. Schroeder, 'The Soviet Economy Under Gorbachev', *Current History*, vol. 86, October 1987, p. 317.
87. V. Kantorovich, 'Discipline and Growth in the Soviet Economy', *Problems of Communism*, vol. XXXIV, no. 6, 1985.
88. The Soviet Economy Under a New Leader, op. cit., 1986, p. 11.
89. R. Kaufman, 'Economic Reform and the Soviet Military', *The Washington Quarterly*, vol. 11, no. 3, 1988, p. 205.
90. J. Greenwood and W. Slocombe, 'Economic Constraints on Military Power', *The Washington Quarterly*, vol. 10, no. 3, 1987.
91. The Soviet Economy Under a New Leader, op. cit., 1986, p. 18.
92. J. Hough, 'Gorbachev's Strategy', *Foreign Affairs*, vol. 64, no. 1, 1985–86, p. 39.
93. D. Herspring, 'On *Perestroika*: Gorbachev, Yazov and The Military', *Problems of Communism*, vol. XXXVI, no. 4, 1987, p. 107.
94. W. Odom, 'How Far Can Soviet Reform Go?', *Problems of Communism*, vol. XXXVI, No. 6, 1987, p. 27.

95. J. Hough, op. cit., 1985–86, p. 39.
96. J. McConnell, op. cit., 1988, p. 50.
97. P. Kennedy, op. cit., 1988, p. 500.
98. S. Bialer, 'New Thinking and Soviet Foreign Policy', *Survival*, vol. XXX, no. 4, 1988, p. 309.
99. *Allocation of Resources in the Soviet Union and China 1985*. op. cit., 1986, p. 48.
100. Ibid., pp. 108–9.
101. M. Acland-Hood, 'Estimating Soviet Military R and D Spending', in C. Jacobsen (ed), *The Soviet Defence Enigma: Estimating Costs and Burden* (Oxford: Oxford University Press, 1987) p. 144.
102. D. Herspring, op. cit., 1987, p. 101.
103. M. Checinski, 'An Estimate of Current Soviet Military Industrial Output and of the Development of the Soviet Arms Industry in the Eighties', *Osteuropa Wirtschaft*, vol. 29, no. 2, 1984, p. 147.
104. J. Snyder, 'The Gorbachev Revolution: A Waning of Soviet Expansionism', *International Security*, vol. 12, no. 2, 1987–88, p. 98.
105. S. Bialer, op. cit., 1988, p. 299.
106. G. Wettig, 'Gorbachev and "New Thinking" in the Kremlin's Foreign Policy', *Aussen Politik*, vol. 38, no. 2, 1987, pp. 146–150.
107. R. Kaufman, op. cit., 1983, p. 207.
108. S. Sestanovich, 'Gorbachev's Foreign Policy: A Diplomacy of Decline', *Problems of Communism*, vol. XXXVII, no. 1, 1988.
109. R. Allison, 'Mr. Gorbachev's Xmas Present: What Does It Mean?' *Detente*, no. 14, 1989, p. 22.
110. S. Sestanovich, op. cit., 1988, p. 5.
111. S. Bialer, op. cit., 1988, p. 303.
112. J. Snyder, op. cit., 1987–88, p. 114.
113. P. Hanson, 'The Soviet Economy at the End of Year IV', *Detente*, no. 14, 1989, p. 9.
114. P. Savigear, op. cit., 1987, p. 5.

Index